NO PLACE LIKE HOME

Coping with the Decline and Death of Toxic* Parents

Wounding/Absent/Narcissistic/Traumatic

I hope you enjoy the story!,
Nick Nol...

NICK NOLAN

For Jaime, who's listened, loved, and made me laugh
for thirty-two years.

In Memory of Dave Rogers 1955 - 2019

INTRODUCTION

It seems like horrific parenting is all over the news lately.

Those thirteen Turpin children, who were tortured and chained by their Evangelical Christian homeschooling parents.

Sarah Hart, who intentionally drove her wife and six children off a cliff.

Kevin Spacey's father, who—according to an article in the UK newspaper the *Daily Mail*—was a child rapist and neo-Nazi, and whose wife turned a blind eye to her husband's sexual abuse of their adolescent son Randall, Kevin's elder brother.

Each of these situations is so heinous, so objectionable, that everyone's reaction is the same: *How could they?*

But what about those cases that linger in the gray areas for years or even decades, where the abuse is not quite as egregious but nonetheless inflicts unforgettable damage? Years later, how does that adult survivor weigh his or her anger against a sense of duty when that offending parent—or the parent who stood by—is aged and in failing health?

That's what this book is all about.

I've heard people say, "I had a good childhood," or, "My childhood was horrible," because rare is the adult who's ambivalent about how things were when they were short and vulnerable.

But what if you were like me, and growing up felt like a long highway of soul-grinding years interspersed with occasional happy rest stops...so the idea of completely disowning your parents just wasn't—and still isn't—a reasonable option?

I'm guessing it's been tolerable for you up until now, because as soon as you were old enough, you moved out to begin your *real* life:

You stumbled upon some good friends and began collecting furniture. You steadied the tiller of your career. You learned the necessity of paying those Visa and phone bills on time, and you joined a gym or began jogging or biking as your metabolism waved goodbye to your twenties.

Maybe you got married and had a kid or three.

One year melted into the next, your children grew up and moved out, and you started pondering where it might be nice to retire....

In the meantime, you steeled your patience enough to be civil to Mom or Dad around the holidays or when a relative blew into town; you huffed and sighed when selecting a Father's Day or Mother's Day or anniversary card; and you sat dutifully at yet another family gathering, throwing knowing sideways glances to your siblings every time Dad launched another caustic zinger or Mom let her disapproval be known through a dismissive comment or that pinch of her face and roll of her eyes that green-lighted another bickering match.

It's only a few hours, you told yourself, while refilling your glass of merlot or cracking open another Budweiser or slicing yourself another wedge of pecan pie. *I can do this.*

Then one day you got *the call*:

"Mom's had a heart attack." Or "Pop took a really bad fall."

For me it was, "Dad's had a *major* stroke, and...uh, things don't look good."

That's when all of my childhood demons slid down the banister from my emotional attic.

"Look at the bright side," I told myself nineteen years later, on what seemed like my thousandth trip to visit my father—and occasionally my mother—in the hospital. "At least they didn't *fill in the blank* me."

Because even though my childhood was more *Twilight Zone* than *Father Knows Best*, I always told myself my parents did the best they could.

But maybe they didn't. And maybe there were some commonsense options they should've explored.

Like counseling. Divorce. Antidepressants.

Or maybe just a little genuine introspection and consideration.

And now this father who routinely told me, *If I didn't know your mother better, I would swear you were someone else's son,* has been on the ledge of death so many times over the past two decades, I've lost count. And each time, I've suitcased my anger, postponed whatever I was engaged in, and driven across town to be face-to-face with a man who has nothing to say to me.

Why do I bother?

For the same reason you do:

Honor thy father and mother was branded onto our psyches to the same degree we were potty-trained.

So you took responsibility for almost anything that was wrong.

Perhaps you became the best son or daughter in the family.

Maybe you rebelled and wound up in rehab. Or jail.

Maybe you moved to the other side of the country.

Maybe you did OK, but like someone who'd been wounded during wartime, you were a person for whom things never felt right.

I know those feelings.

No Place Like Home isn't only my story about being raised by a father suffering from probable chronic traumatic encephalopathy, or CTE (which can only be diagnosed postmortem, and as of this writing he's still alive); *No Place Like Home* also shines a light on the clinicians who help people who continue to be poked and nagged by their childhood demons, especially as they're confronting their WANT or LOW parent's age-related decline.

As this book's cover indicates, WANT stands for Wounding/Absent/Narcissistic/Traumatic. These were the singular terms that each of the clinicians I interviewed used…so I pieced them into an easy acronym that's synonymous with *hunger, neediness, dearth, lack,* and *absence,* just as LOW, my other acronym, describes the Look the Other Way parent, who fails to shield his or her child from emotional and/or physical harm.

For example, my mother—who allowed her children to be abused—adamantly refuses to use antidepressants or to seek counseling, and even though she's been married to an emotionally unavailable bully for more than sixty years, her only refuge seems to be wrapping her depression around herself like a cozy blanket.

I ask myself, *Why didn't she leave him?* One might argue that "women didn't do that back then," but "back then" was in the 1960s and 1970s and 1980s, not the 1940s.

She could have. She should have.

But she didn't.

So a little about me:

Not being a licensed clinician, I'm probably not qualified to write a self-help book, if that's what this is: My highest academic accomplishments—and I'm proud of these—are a BA in psychology, two years of postgraduate study that earned me a California Clear Teaching Credential, twelve graduate units in an unfinished MFT program, and five Book of the Year awards along with some critical accolades for my four published novels. Professionally, I worked in retail furniture sales for fifteen years while slowly assembling my aforementioned BA; then, after graduating, I worked for about four years with homeless LGBTQ youth in residential treatment. And for the twenty-plus years since, I've taught grades four through seven in California public schools while writing books in my spare time.

While I was deliberating with my former therapist over whether or not I was competent to write *No Place Like Home*, he said, "You're competent because you've ridden the pony." I asked what he meant, and he told me, "You've witnessed and survived significant abuse and trauma but come through it all—*with the assistance of both therapy and a loving partner*—as a stable, productive, and happily married man."

And so I began writing this book.

First, I chronicled my recollections of growing up in a household headed by a patriarch with probable CTE.

Next, I interviewed practicing doctors and licensed therapists to learn how they might help a patient/client come to terms with her or his own WANT or LOW parent who's in failing health. (In case you're wondering what the differences are between the doctors, psychiatrists, psychologists, clergy, and others who help folks feel better emotionally, a quick visit to *NAMI.org*—the National Alliance on Mental Illness—will probably help to clear up some confusion you might have; NAMI's explanations are user-friendly and succinct.)

After that, I recorded the remembrances of two women and a man who've also *ridden the pony*—or rather *the rodeo bull* in certain cases—been bucked off and trampled, and then climbed back up into their saddles thanks to their courage, stamina, and the professionals who taught them how to better utilize their reins and spurs.

Finally, I compared stories and looked for commonalities and compiled everything into what you'll be reading.

I hope *No Place Like Home* helps you to find peace and to heal… but if nothing else, it'll reassure you that you're not alone.

Best wishes, and thank you for taking a chance on my work.

Sincerely,
Nick Nolan
Los Angeles, California
June 2019

ACKNOWLEDGMENTS

◆

I'd like to thank those who made this book possible: Edward Reed EdD, who so immensely supported this project from the first moment I proposed the idea; Teresa DeCrescenzo LCSW, LMFT and Carol Cushman LCSW, who offered their support, expertise, and undying friendship; Dr. Lawrence J. Martin, who gave so generously of his time and revelatory point-of-view; Dr. Aaron Aronow, who provided me with a much, much-needed missing puzzle piece; Cissy Brady-Rogers LMFT, who's given me a lifetime of friendship, patience, and wisdom; Dr. Adrian Aguilera, for sharing his keen perspectives on PTSD, assimilation, and contrast; Allen Ruyle LCSW, for convincing me that there is always hope; and Eileen Chetti, my brilliant and exacting editor. I'd also like to thank "Jake" and "Brandy" and "Natalie" for baring their souls during our interviews, and my two sisters "Miriam" and "Gwen" who've seen it all and helped me cope. But most of all this book (and book cover!) would not exist without the steadfast love, support, laughter, courage, patience, of my husband J. Where would I be without you?

CONTENTS

CHAPTER 1

◆

Death and Texas

"I'm gonna run ahead to the park!" Jay shouted over his shoulder, as Romeo strained at his leash and harness like an Iditarod husky after the *bang!* of a starting gun.

I waved. "Absolutely, go!"

I glanced down at Princeton sniffing the base of a crepe myrtle tree, its bark as smooth as polished stone. Princey—at ten—was as ponderous and gentle as Romeo was brash and bold; we always laughed about our dogs being complete opposites: a hunter who needed to chase anything that moved and a retriever who needed to scrutinize everything that was nailed down.

"Come on, boy," I urged Prince as Jay rounded the street corner's hedge and disappeared…but Mr. P once again demonstrated his determination to solve this newest olfactory dazzler by bracing his legs and pushing his nose deeper into the tree's base.

I tugged at his leash again and sighed as my phone buzzed inside my pocket, alerting me to a new text:

Hi I know this is weird but I thought you would want to know that my mom passed away yesterday.

Oh my God. Brandy's mom. *Finally.* Knowing that Jay was probably a quarter mile away by now, I tapped a reply:

Are you OK? How's your dad? I can't talk now but tomorrow? I want to talk to you.

It was pretty gnarly at the end call me whenever you can but we're both good I opted to call her just as Prince finally decided to move along.

"Hey," she said.

Princeton sauntered a few feet and then stopped again. "Brandy...are you really OK?"

"Yeaahh," she replied in that Peppermint Patty–ish voice I'd first heard in high school Latin class; hearing it now was as comforting as pulling on a well-worn sweatshirt.

"Can I call you tomorrow...like around nine or ten?"

She coughed. "Um, yeah. That'll work."

"Great. I'm on a walk with Jay and the dogs and we've got a full day planned. *But I want to talk to you.* Sure you're OK?"

"I'm OK—good, actually." And she was; I heard the *good* in her voice just as clearly as I could usually hear the *stressed and angry and really sad.* "We'll talk then."

"OK. Love you."

I ended the call and began trotting toward the distant, diminutive figures of man and dog waiting for us by the park's entrance.

At last, we caught up.

"Were you on the phone?" Jay asked.

"For just a sec." I paused, catching my breath before climbing the dusty trail before us. "Brandy just texted me. Her mom died. I wanted to see if she was OK."

Jay side-eyed me as the dogs picked up speed. "So...it *is* true what they say about death and taxes...or is it *Death and Texas*?"

"*Death and Texas*, that old Charles Durning film where the football superstar is convicted of murder?" I asked. "How do you remember that?"

"Because it reminds me of your father," Jay mumbled. "Especially now that we know about—"

"Don't remind me," I said. "But in this case, it's *taxes*. As in *inevitable*. Nobody believed Brandy's mom would ever die."

"Just like your dad!" Jay shouted, as Romeo began barking at a distant jackrabbit.

"But *my* dad's still alive!"

The rabbit vanished under a bush, so Romeo quieted.

"Exactly." Strolling peacefully once more, Jay looked over at me. "Do you know much about Gore Vidal?"

"I read a collection of his works—and I noticed he doesn't like commas. Why?"

"I just watched this documentary about him," Jay began. "He lived such a lavish and exceptional life, and he said something that made me think of you: One interviewer asked him, 'If there were one thing you could've changed about your life, what might that have been?' And Vidal answered without hesitation, 'My mother. She was awful, and she was a terrible drunk. She and I did battle for years because I was the only person who ever stood up to her. But there came a time when after the worst of our fights I told her, "This is it. I'm done." I left and never saw or spoke with her again, and she died twenty years later.'"

"I can't imagine why that reminded you of me." I laughed, thinking that Mr. Vidal never felt his mother loved him—probably because she didn't.

Just like Brandy's mom probably never loved her.

In my first novel, *Strings Attached*, there's a moment when teenage Jeremy and middle-aged Arthur chat, and eventually the subject of love comes up. Jeremy asks how one knows when one is in love, and Arthur answers, "Just like you know when you're hungry and then you know when you're full…you can't make yourself hungry when you've stuffed yourself, or convince yourself you're not hungry when you're starving. Unless of course you have an eating disorder."

And that's what having a wounding or absent or narcissistic or traumatic parent is like: telling yourself you were loved when you seldom—or ever—felt you were. Your parent might have gone through the motions: house or apartment, food, clothes, medical care, rules and regulations, Little League games, and so on…but there was that dead-eyed look in their eyes that met yours when you walked into the room.

The look that was always on my father's face.

When he looked at me.

If I'd known the reason for that empty stare back when I was a kid, maybe everything would've been different.

CHAPTER 2

◆

Reign in the Desert

"Morning, Gail," I panted, my leather messenger bag falling off my shoulder while I clutched an armload of papers to my chest. I swigged some lukewarm coffee from the commuter mug in my left hand as I scanned the countertop for a pen to sign in with my right.

"Hi, bubbeleh," Gail replied, a grin illuminating her face even as she scanned some official-looking letter. I loved Gail. Humble and cheerful, she was also a brilliant educator, a kind human being, and an unflappable multitasker.

Finally spotting a pen, I scribbled my initials on my time card and glanced at the clock on the wall. *Three minutes until the bell rings.*

I had just turned on my heel to hurry toward my classroom when I felt a gentle tug on my elbow. I glanced over my shoulder.

"How's your father?" Gail asked, her smile suddenly supplanted by a grimace of concern and her eyes telling me she was poised to offer any support needed—in spite of our mutual morning time crunch.

The bag fell off my shoulder once more; I caught it mid-plummet. *Cue my sad face?* Nope.

Stonily, I met her gaze. "He's, uh…well, pretty much the same."

Gail's expression pinched tighter. "I'm so sorry."

"Thanks. Really, *thanks.*"

The bell rang, and we crisscrossed the office toward our cross-campus destinations.

After sending off my students at the end of the school day, I drove home to snatch a twenty-minute nap. Then, after awakening and brushing my teeth, I made certain the dogs had fresh water and headed out the door to my dusty black SUV.

Minutes later I was hurtling east through Los Angeles's evening rush-hour traffic, heading toward the skilled nursing facility in Glendale that had recently become my father's home.

A quarter hour or so into my commute, the brake lights on a gold Toyota Camry in front of me lit up like red neon, so I trounced my brake pedal and lurched to a stop. Quickly, I scanned the lanes next to me for a moving spot to sidle into.

But no one was rolling. *Shit!*

I felt my forehead flush, a sure sign that my blood pressure was climbing.

Relax. I dipped my eyelids for a moment. *Breathe.*

As I slowly released the deep breath I'd drawn, a horn blared behind me and my eyes batted open. Traffic had begun moving.

And as my right foot depressed the accelerator, a familiar hypothetical question buzzed through my consciousness like a wasp: *After working his ass off all day, would my father drag himself across the freeways of Los Angeles—at nearly four dollars a gallon—to visit me in a hospital or a nursing home? Better yet: Would he do it once a week for nineteen years?*

*   *   *

In 1999, my father suffered a massive stroke brought on by his lifetime of smoking cigarettes, along with his out-of-control blood sugar, beer drinking, and consumption of ice cream servings that resembled scale models of the Matterhorn at Disneyland...not to mention his roiling anger and sour marriage and what we now suspect is probable CTE: all ingredients that churned in a cauldron that had been bubbling since 1956, when the man and woman who would someday be my parents echoed the words *I do.*

"We call this a stuttering stroke," Dr. Anderson advised me out in the hospital's hallway, his voice hushed. "And the occlusion is inoperable; it's in the blood vessels inside his spinal column; if it were in the carotid artery, we could do a bypass, but in his case that's impossible."

I shoved my hands deep into my jeans pockets. "What're the—"

"His left side is completely paralyzed," Anderson interrupted. "It's doubtful he will ever walk again, but there's always a chance." He paused, leaning in. "More than likely he won't survive this; we can get him stabilized after this event, but then the pathway will become occluded again and it will kill him."

"Like…how long do you think he has?"

"Could be a week. Six months at the most."

But he's only sixty-nine. "Have you told my mother this?"

"I'm only telling *you* this—for now. I want to…well, wait a bit and see how he fares over the next twenty-four hours before discussing this with your mother. She's been through a lot already."

"Yeah, she has." In fact, my mother's own beloved father had passed away a mere three weeks earlier, at the age of eighty-nine, after a slow-motion slip-and-slide that began with him walking into this same hospital after a fainting spell but ended with him inexplicably— five months later—toe-tagged and rolling to the morgue. "Let me talk this over with my sister Miriam," I told him. "You know, the nurse?"

He gave me a barely perceptible nod. "She understands these situations."

"Thank you, Dr. Anderson."

The man nodded, turned, and clip-clopped away.

But Dr. Anderson had been wrong.

Against all odds, my father went on to survive the event and even regained some mobility.

But inevitably, he would wind up in the hospital again.

Head injury from a fall.

Bowel obstruction.

Spiraling/tailspinning blood sugar.

Intestinal resection.

Dehydration. Inexplicable fatigue. Kidney failure. Heart attack.

Another stroke.

And each time I drove to the hospital—just as each time a call came in from either of my sisters or my mother—I wondered, *Is this it?*

*   *   *

Over the past decade, my father has frequented a local skilled nursing facility, or what used to be called a nursing home. It's near my parents' house, so when he's there my mother visits him twice a day, occasionally three times.

But since it's the better part of an hour from where I live, I had to make peace with visiting my father only once or twice a week.

Upon a recent trip, I learned that he was stubbornly refusing to perform any of the exercises the physical therapist was prescribing.

During mealtime, he told the courteous staff, "I'm not gonna eat that shit."

He called the female attendants bitches, and he squeezed one's forearm so hard she thought it might be broken.

He even took a swing at one of the male attendants. With his "good" arm.

If all of this sounds like the reactions of a man living in depressing conditions, this isn't the case: The facility is actually pretty nice. Fresh paint. Shiny floors. Homey feel. No screeching patients or diaper stench. In fact, a plaque on the wall says Medicare rated it five stars. *This year.*

So it wasn't the facility that was eliciting such volatile behavior.

This was simply my father's narcissistic personality magnified by multiple brain infarctions and probable CTE and depression and physical discomfort; and although he was being more than a little difficult to deal with, to my sisters and me, the nursing staff was simply riding out the aftershocks of the childhood earthquake we called *Dad.*

But there had also been some benefits to having had him as my father…some moments when he'd been able to dig within his volatile persona to extract kind and thoughtful deeds worthy of my emulation and respect.

Like the summer evenings when we'd stroll through the better sections of an adjacent neighborhood and he'd ask which house I liked and why: I'd point out the shallow wooden balcony on the two-story 1920s Monterrey Spanish revival; or the arched Palladian window on the Italianate mini-villa that showed a spacious, artfully lit interior; or the carpet of lush emerald dichondra that was to our yellowed St. Augustine lawn what diamonds are to rhinestones.

Or when he'd take me to the Los Angeles Auto Show each year, and I'd gape at the concept cars or dazzle my father with my knowledge of horsepower, build quality, and top speeds.

And those awkward times when he'd patiently tried to teach me how to box...or hit a baseball...or catch a football, all of which—through no fault of my father's—was as successful as training a sloth on a trampoline.

Finally, there were those late nights when we'd watch *Monty Python's Flying Circus* together and laugh—sometimes to the point of breathlessness—at the silly, brilliant skits.

But occasions like these were like rain in the desert...ephemeral downpours that lent welcome relief to the coyotes and jackrabbits, and nourishment to the Joshua trees and wildflowers, until the furnacelike heat predictably returned, blazing hotter than ever.

And now like some "king" reigning over snakes and cacti, my father held court over a landscape of calloused caregivers and a family that was long ago toughened by his blazing anger and withered heart.

Thus grew our thorns.

*   *   *

Two weeks later I was driving to the hospital again, this time St. Joseph's in Burbank.

Whether from lackadaisical managerial decisions or a sinister conspiracy, most hospital parking lots in Los Angeles do not take credit cards—cash or checks only, which no one carries anymore. So after swearing a stream of profanities that would've impressed a rap star, I parked on a faraway side street, waited in the raging afternoon sun for the crosswalk light, and then signed in at the reception desk before pressing the elevator button for the sixteenth floor.

Inside Room 1621, I spotted my mother sitting in a chair by my father's bedside, her now familiar mask of weariness weighing heavily upon her features.

I padded in, kissed my mother's cheek, and stepped back. "How's he doing?"

"Not well," she replied. "In the nursing home he spiked a fever, so they did some lab work that showed an infection. He's also dehydrated again, and his right leg's bent into a ninety-degree angle."

"His *right* leg? But that's his good one."

"I know."

"Did he have another stroke?" I asked.

Mom grimaced. "I hadn't thought of that."

"Do they know what kind of infection he has?"

"Apparently just a bladder or urinary tract infection. He's on antibiotics. The nursing home was afraid it was going to be that MRDO he had last month."

MDRO, I mentally corrected. Multiple drug resistant organism, which doesn't even respond to vancomycin, the SWAT team of antibiotics. "That's good. Anything else?"

"High blood sugar," she sighed. "But I want him to get well enough that he can come to the restaurant on Sunday."

My mother's eightieth birthday was only days away, and this would be the first time in their nearly sixty years of marriage where it looked like she would be stag—or doe—on her special day. "Maybe if you had the party at a restaurant closer to the nursing home, we could all visit him after dinner?"

"He's not going back there," she stated imperiously. "I'm *through* with nursing homes. He's coming back to our house when he leaves this hospital."

Now, if my mother had been talking about coming home with hospice care, I would've been down at the front desk helping her fill out the paperwork. But it was clear that she believed he was going to get better. And I wasn't going to argue with her.

I appraised Dad lying in his hospital bed: pale and motionless but for the slight rise and fall of the sheet covering him, his mouth slack; and with neither upper nor lower teeth installed he looked like something the coroner had just slid out from inside a metal-sheathed wall.

I stood quickly. "Gotta go. Been a long day and I've got work at home."

"I want him at the restaurant on Sunday," Mom reiterated. "If his grandsons are there, we can probably get him out of the car."

It would be easier to bring the restaurant to him, I thought. *Roof, walls, windows, and ugly vinyl booths.* "It'll take me nearly an hour to get home with traffic," I said. "It's been a long day."

My mother glanced up at me, eyes mournful. "You're sacrificing a lot to be here."

I was touched. This was the first time my mother had acknowledged what it took to slide a hospital visit into my schedule, and it stunned me. I bent down and kissed her cheek. "I love you," I told her. "I'll see you Sunday at the restaurant." Mom nodded and smiled wistfully. "I appreciate you coming."

As I turned to leave, I glanced back at them once more: Mom slumped in that cheap chair, her face aged, fragile, and sad; my father's motionless head tilted chin-first toward heaven. And I thought, *Is this how sixty years together ends? A once bright and shining love tarnished by anger, regret, resentment, and disease?*

That sight of them pushed me to tears as I made my way along the unfamiliar hallways in search of the elevators that would transport me back to my life.

My *happy* life.

* * *

As I lurched toward my car in the blistering, airless September evening, my thoughts rewound to a text I'd received in my classroom some months back from my younger sister, Gwen:

Dad took another swing at Mom.

I reread the text and dropped my teacher's edition on my desk. "Um, I need to take care of this," I told my fifth graders.

As I crossed the room to open the door between my class and my room partner Cathryn's classroom, my students were uncharacteristically quiet; they'd become skilled at reading my facial expressions and body language, so they could tell something was brewing.

Through the doorway I signaled Cathryn—deep in a grammar lesson—by waving one hand and holding up my phone in the other. She nodded solemnly; we'd long ago developed our own semaphore for in-class situations that needed out-of-class attention.

I turned and made my way out to the ramp in front of my classroom bungalow.

Gwen answered on the first ring. "Hi."

"What happened?"

"She was changing his diaper and he swung for her jaw."

"Did he connect?"

"Not this time."

"What do you mean, *this time*?" I asked. "I also noticed you used the word *again* in your text."

"Mom swore me to secrecy, but he's punched her in the stomach."

"*What?!? When?*" I felt my face flush and prickle.

Suddenly I was four again. *D-don't hit her! D-don't hit her!*

"It happened a while ago—and he's been pretty good since then. I went over and put the fear of God in him."

"Ooohhhh, *please* don't keep things like this from me."

"OK." Gwen sounded harried, and I could hear two of her kids screaming in the background. "Could you call and talk to him?"

"I'll do better than that," I replied, knowing I couldn't postpone today's after-school tasks. "I'll head there first thing after work tomorrow and see him, man to bully."

"You'd better clear it with Mom first," Gwen warned.

"I'll let her know I'm coming. And…I want to hear it from her mouth—see if she'll tell me what he did or if she'll cover for him."

"You should know something else," Gwen began, sotto voce. "He's also been doing that forearm-twisting thing with the women who come to help, but only one of the men. The small one. He won't do it to Ryan."

Ryan was big. *Really big*. "So he's still the bully," I stated. "And he knows who'll strike back."

"Yep."

"I'll talk to her and see what's going on. Thanks for letting me know."

I ended the call and tapped my mother's number into the phone. "Hello?"

"Hi, Mom. Gwen just told me Dad took a swing at you."

Silence. Then a deep sigh. "I was hurting him. And I lost my patience. It was my fault."

"*What do you mean it's your fault?* Without you, he would've been dead a decade ago."

"We were arguing and I couldn't get his feet into position, so I threw them down onto the bed. I hurt him—and he reacted."

"Gwen told me about his twisting-the-arm thing he does. And now it's with the attendants?"

"Except for Ryan."

"What do you want me to do?"

"*Be his friend,*" she pleaded. "Come over more often. He's always in a better mood when members of the family visit—at least for a few days."

My temples throbbed. *So now his abusive behavior was my fault?* "Will you be home tomorrow? Around three?"

"Let me check." The phone went silent. And then: "He has a doctor's appointment at ten, but we'll be home by three."

"See you then."

I ended the call, not having any idea about what I might say, only knowing that the time had come for someone—in this case, me—to shake him up.

I went to bed that night without a plan and woke up baffled and emptyheaded, blinking at the brightening ceiling and walls, wondering, *What could I possibly say that might make things safer for my mother as well as for his other caregivers?* But even after making it through another school day and then navigating the jam-packed freeways to their house, I still had nothing.

*   *   *

I rolled my SUV to a stop in front of my parents' home, shut off the engine, and reached for the door handle.

Then—like a cartoon character with a lightbulb suddenly glowing over his head—I had an epiphany: *Do what no one's ever done before: Speak the truth. Stand up to him.*

I felt relief as I pushed open my car door, realizing that I didn't care how he might react.

He couldn't hurt me anymore.

But he was hurting others, and I needed to stop him.

CHAPTER 3

◆

Raging Bully

"I'm not afraid of dying," my father's mother—tucked inside crisp hospital sheets—told her son, "but your boy hates you, and I'm sorry that I won't be around to do anything about it."

It was the summer of 1964.

Nanny, as we called our grandmother, had just received news that her colon cancer was terminal, and her husband and children and friends were understandably devastated.

At fifty-nine, the elegant silver-haired matriarch of the family, who had once been runner-up to Katharine Hepburn in a Connecticut high school beauty pageant, was too young and too vital to her family to perish; indeed, her husband worshipped her, her youngest daughter was only fourteen, and she had five other grown children—and three grandchildren—whom she adored.

The following October, she passed away just a few days after her sixtieth birthday.

I was then but three years old, and true to Nanny's prediction, I spent the next five decades hating my father.

An Irish bull of a man who'd boxed and played football throughout high school and college, he'd been scouted by both the Rams and the 49ers but at five foot eight (and 220 pounds of solid muscle) had been told that he was too short to play professionally. As a boy, he was beaten by his own father, until at fourteen he was able to knock out the man (Dad relayed this to me several times as the happiest day of his childhood); then at the age of eighteen he had been paid one hundred dollars (a princely sum back in 1948) to spar,

14

on several occasions, in New York City with legendary boxer Rocky Marciano ("His shots to my head were like getting hit with bags of cement," he used to tell me); later, after joining the US Air Force, he boxed his way and taught hand-to-hand combat and jiujitsu through four years of the Korean War.

My parents began courting in 1952 and were married in August of 1956, after Dad was honorably discharged from the air force, permanently deaf in his left ear from a blow to the head he received in the boxing ring. He never saw battle overseas because "the officers kept me stateside because when I boxed, they knew I'd win." Only recently did two things dawn on me: (1) Those officers *probably had some cash riding on Nolan*, and (2) Dad's violent outbursts were probably attributable to all of the knocking around that his brain had endured.

But more on that later…

My sister Miriam—blond, blue-eyed, and adorable—arrived in August of 1957; early photos portray her as a diminutive, grinning toddler with Mamie Eisenhower bangs and an infectious, toothy smile.

Unfortunately, that smile was destined to be permanently changed.

Then in March of 1961, I arrived weighing almost nine pounds; I was *a difficult birth* according to my mother. She also blamed her significant pregnancy weight gain—seventy-five or so pounds—on me instead of on the chocolate she habitually consumed; she held on to that girth until diabetes took her pancreas hostage sometime in her late sixties.

I don't have a cozy first memory of my father. But there are photos of him holding the infant version of me. We're both smiling, presumably giggling; in those days, Dad probably imagined that someday I'd be just like him: athletic, good-looking, aggressive, swaggering.

Instead, it quickly became apparent that I was a "broken boy," and if there'd been an Olympic decathlon for childhood maladies, I'd have easily taken bronze. Maybe even silver.

Diagnosed with an extreme case of eczema at around six months, I was derided by my unsympathetic cousins as a *crawling scab*.

A year later, this chronic skin condition was linked to all-you-can't-eat food allergies, most of the earth's pollen, all mammal dander (goats, we learned, were inexplicably exempt), and even milk; so after my mother permanently banished our beloved dog, Danny, to the backyard (after providing him with a secondhand dog house) and severely limited the scope of my food intake, I developed rickets.

Then, just as I was learning to walk (pigeon-toed, which necessitated clunky, black, cartoonish shoes), I developed a suffocating case of asthma. This was *before inhalers were invented*, so each miserable attack lasted several hours and sometimes all night.

I wouldn't stop sucking my thumb, so my front teeth were gapped and buck.

I cried a lot.

My triple Salchow was the stubborn stutter/stammer I developed at around the same time that my grandmother began failing.

"You'd be talking just fine," Mom relayed to me years later, "then Dad would walk into the room and you couldn't spit out a single word."

I'm guessing Nanny noticed this is as well.

I should add that my father confessed that tragic opening vignette about his mother in the hospital room to me in my late teens—in the same conversation when I expressed my doubts about my masculinity to him—and my first shattering thought was, *If other people besides Nanny saw me as this horrified child, why didn't anyone do anything?*

But more on that in the chapters discussing the Look the Other Way, or LOW, parents.

At four years of age, and following Nanny's death, I attended speech therapy at Occidental College with a nice lady named Mrs. Reed; she wore tailored suits and cat's-eye glasses, and she spoke to me in near whispers. Mrs. Reed changed my life, because my stutter/stammer pretty much vanished by the time I started kindergarten, even though it occasionally resurfaces when I'm under duress.

Although my maternal grandparents had sold my parents their house at a discount—just before I was born—in a charming suburban neighborhood, so Miriam and I might enjoy *a real home and a big backyard* to run around in, my father was as disinclined to keep the exterior clipped, mown, and painted as my mother was to keep the interior sparkling, uncluttered, and gracious.

Grandad's precise, geometric privets bristled into chaotic blobs; the stucco's pink paint peeled, our windows' mullions blistered, the St. Augustine grass—as if it were wisely attempting to escape—stretched strawlike tendrils out onto the sidewalk, and the old, unwashed Rambler and Ford parked out front appeared to be waiting for the junkman.

Inside, smeared dishes teetered in the sink, carpeting stretched threadbare, and stuffing molted from the sofa; faucets leaked, drapes sagged, and ceilings were marbled with tea-colored veins, permanent reminders of last winter's rains. Our once elegant dining table— long ago my great-grandmother's—was surrounded by only one of its original companion chairs; joining it now was a motley gang of garage sale castoffs or trash-night curb finds.

More than once, I returned from school to find Dad snoring in the living room's green vinyl recliner, the black-and-white Zenith blaring, and my mother either hibernating in the far bedroom or gloomily stirring a pot on the stovetop.

"Why's Dad home so early?" I'd casually ask, masking my disappointment and fear.

"He's just off work," she'd reply, not wanting to let me know he'd lost his job again; money was always tight, and even when Dad was employed, *after payday* was the most-often-heard phrase of my childhood, next to *stop crying or I'll give you something to cry about.*

Only the arrival of a shiny, new company car heralded hope.

As a professional ball-bearing salesman serving a large metropolitan territory, Dad sought jobs that supplied a late-model American car to replace the rusting, dented Rambler.

But almost as soon as the new car appeared, it would vanish:

The appliance-white 1966 Buick Wildcat. One week.

The manila-beige 1967 Chevy Chevelle. Three weeks.

The cocoa-brown 1968 Plymouth Satellite. One month.

The sapphire-blue 1969 Plymouth Fury wagon. Three weeks.

Then the much-loathed 1965 Plymouth Valiant that Dad bought because the only job he could find didn't provide him with a company car: This six-cylindered, three-on-the-tree gem featured pogo-stick shock absorbers, vinyl benches that roasted (or froze) our backs and thighs, an AM radio perpetually blasting KFWB News and Traffic, and the gag-inducing toxic reek of Dad's Tiparillo smoke, a brimming ashtray, and a glass Listerine bottle leaking under the front seat. On weekends, my parents reliably argued as we all sped toward church; it's easy to understand now why Miriam and I referred to the color of any car with oxidized blue metallic paint as Headache Blue. We still do.

During this era, I began attending elementary school in a middle-class neighborhood where all the other boys' fathers held *real dad jobs*: ophthalmologists and dentists and advertising executives and so on. So when asked about my father's profession, I half lied, knowing he'd served, years ago, in the US Air Force. "My father is a Blue Angels pilot," I announced to the class during show-and-tell one day, while holding up—*as proof*—a glossy postcard I'd dug up somewhere; I pointed to the sleek blue plane with its yellow trim as bright as dandelions against the dazzling, cloud-dappled skyscape. "This is a picture of his plane."

It wasn't until April of 1970, after the arrival of baby Gwen, that things began to change: With three kids and a wife to support, Dad hunkered down and found a better-paying job that provided him with a newer Ford LTD (celery green with a white vinyl top; 429 V-8), and Mom was able to trade her two-hundred-fifty-dollar junker for a late-model Plymouth Sport Suburban station wagon: understated ivory with glossy fake-walnut panels slabbing its flanks.

Our house was on an avenue with a fairly steep descent. When I came home from elementary school each afternoon, I would round the corner at the top of our street and gaze down at all the sequential emerald-green rectangles of grass separated by driveways and bordered by a ribbon of cement sidewalk.

But smack in the middle of this tidy suburban block was a rectangle unlike the others.

It was as yellow as a haystack.

So I decided to do something.

When I was about ten, my father was more than happy to demonstrate the proper use of our old gasoline-powered lawn mower. After I mastered this, I figured out how to fix the sprinklers. Finally, I dug a ladder out from behind our garage, found some garden shears, and began trimming our hedges.

Emboldened by my success and the way the house was shaping up, I hefted out the large extension ladder we kept in a shed, scavenged the garage for some dented cans of paint, found a scraper and some paintbrushes, and proceeded to paint the areas of exterior stucco that resembled shin scabs ripe for picking.

"That looks nice!" came a voice from below. I turned to see Mrs. Waller, the only person on our block who drove a Cadillac—and whose home was a showplace in its own right—standing on the sidewalk, arms akimbo.

"Thanks!" I shouted from atop the ladder, my chest swelling.

I don't remember if my father noticed anything different when he came home, and my guess is he didn't...or maybe he rationalized my hard work as a manifestation of simply being *too thing oriented*. But I cut him some slack, because he had as much aesthetic acumen as I had athletic ability. My point is I learned that if there was something I wanted, I had to stretch my limits to find out if my reach was long enough—and usually it was for just about everything...except feeling loved by the pair who brought me into this world.

*   *   *

One day after school—much to my joy—my mother drove us to Seeley's Furniture in South Glendale. There I convinced her to buy a tuxedo-armed, channel-back sofa and a pecan-wood coffee table with book-matched veneers. Soon after, my parents splurged on an antique dining table and chairs that could be spied each evening through the lace curtains (Sears Best) that I helped Mom hang.

Dad continued with his gainful employment and was seasonally outfitted with some new wide-lapel suits; Mom, despite still hefting that extra seventy-five pounds, began dressing more stylishly and getting her hair *done* every other week; Miriam—now a *foxy* young lady with a stunning figure, azure eyes, long blond hair, and an indefatigable smile—could be seen speeding away with her many high school friends; and Gwen was a chubby, giggling toddler with a plethora of brightly colored plastic toys.

I was...well, the sort of awkward teen who would've made Napoleon Dynamite look like Nick Jonas by comparison, but I still made futile attempts to blend in with the other boys: Hang Ten shirts, Ocean Pacific shorts, flip-flops and puka shells, and hair edging down over my ears.

Yep, the Nolans were finally beginning to look like the other families in our neighborhood, at least if one were ambling by.

But Mom still slept too much. She ate compulsively and then dieted haphazardly.

Miriam usually fled our house before dinnertime, her blooming anorexia eclipsing the need for anything more than an apple and a yogurt past breakfast.

Gwen, too young to stay awake past her seven thirty bedtime, enjoyed the armor of sleep.

And I crept into my bedroom and closed the door. I had geometry to flummox me, a clarinet to practice, and Joni Mitchell to keen with. And like someone living next to the railroad tracks who grows accustomed to the clanging and rumbling, I acclimated to our *House of Sad.*

But with Dad, there was little variation to the grayscale of his personality; he'd go from coal-black detachment to ashen indifference to white-hot rage: One minute the house would be calm, but then something would set him off that caused both parents' voices to be raised until my father's insults bullied my mother's protestations into quiet sobs.

His rages made me jump for cover: As a child running from his knock-the-wind-out-of-me smacks (*Your father doesn't know his own strength,* Mom used to tell me), I dove for the backs of messy closets and the undersides of the bushes in our front or backyard; then as a sullen teen, my preferred camouflage became my accommodating and compliant personality.

Up until this year, I figured Dad was simply an unlikable bully.

But now I suspect that his hair-trigger rages and extended depressions and sullen moods and excessive drinking and crippling anxiety attacks and flat affect were manifestations of what's popularly called concussion syndrome, and more specifically known as chronic traumatic encephalopathy (CTE).

This knowledge has changed everything for me.

Because now I know that some of it wasn't his fault, even if I'll never forget what he did to us.

CHAPTER 4

◆

The Past and the Furious

Entering through the kitchen door, I needed to take only a few steps before I found my father in his wheelchair at the dining table awaiting his lunch.

I went over to him and shook his hand. "Hi, Dad."

"Hi," he grumbled unsmilingly.

"How're you doing?"

"OK."

"Where's Mom?"

"Around somewhere."

I pulled out a chair and sat. "I heard you took a swing at her."

Just then, my mother sprang from my father's bedroom, her expression pinched. "*Oh, not now,*" she groaned at me. "We were having a good day today, and he was looking forward to your visit." She shot me an exasperated look that said, *You're ruining everything.*

I ignored her fury and faced my father. "You took a swing at Mom," I repeated.*

"What have you been telling him about me?!" Dad snarled as he turned to her, his face that all-too-familiar Jackie Gleason* mask:

—————————

* *Comedian Jackie Gleason's character Ralph Kramden, in the 1960s comedy* The Honeymooners, *would—when furious with his wife, Alice—shake his fist, bug his eyes, and roar his infamous catchphrase, "Someday, Alice…to the moon!!" This told her that if she wasn't more quiet/obedient, he'd deliver a right hook so hard she'd become airborne and defy Earth's gravitational pull; the studio audience reliably cackled and hooted at these "hilarious" moments, but whenever my family watched these episodes, none of us cracked a smile. Even today, the opening theme for* The Honeymooners *makes me run from the room.*

crimson complexion, taut neck cords, bulging eyes. "I did not try to hit you!"

"Yes, you did," Mom countered dispassionately, settling back into her chair. "Two days ago. When I was getting you into bed."

My father's glare met mine again, and I saw that his expression was indignant. I pressed on. "I also heard that you've been twisting the forearms of the caregivers. Only the women and the small guy. But not Ryan. You're a bully."

"They hurt me," he countered.

"*You need to listen to me,*" I began with a slow, steady baritone, my eyes holding his eyes, alpha to alpha. "The people Mom hires to take care of you aren't from an agency. So they aren't insured. If you injure them, they can sue you for their medical bills and charge you with assault. Then they'll own this paid-for house and whatever savings you still have."

The look in his eyes suggested my words were registering, so I continued.

"And if you hurt Mom again I'm going to call Harry and Bart, the only friends you still have, and tell them you're physically abusing your eighty-year-old wife. Then I'll tell them that you knocked out Miriam's front teeth when she was six years old."

His eyes bulged bigger. "I did not!"

"Yes, you did!" I yelled back. "You were driving up to Granny and Grandad's, and Miri was bouncing up and down on the back seat, so you hit her in the mouth and knocked out her teeth!"

He stared at me wide-eyed, and I could see that he didn't remember any of this, so I changed the subject.

"You're in this condition because you refused to stop smoking; even after your heart attack, six-way bypass, and stroke, you kept on smoking. And if not for Mom, you would've been dead a long time ago. She checks your blood sugar and gives you insulin twice a day, cooks for you, shops for you, drives you to your doctor's appointments, and changes your diapers. So if I hear one more word about you twisting arms or trying to hit someone, I'll call the police and have you arrested. And they'll put you wherever they put people like you. *Do you understand what I'm telling you?*"

"I understand."

"Because this is your only warning, Dad. *Do you believe me?*"

"I believe you."

"Now, apologize to Mom."

My father turned to my mother. "I apologize for trying to hit you."

Thus ended the confrontation.

More than a week passed without any word from my mother.

Her silence stymied me, because I'd just tried my best to protect her, just as I had as a little boy when I stood in the no-man's-land between them during one of their arguments, where Dad was shouting and Mom was sobbing, with my arms spread wide—as if my sapling arms could deflect crashes from his tree-stump fists. "*D-d-don't hit her!*" I pleaded, tears streaming. "*D-don't hit her!*"

But no words of gratitude came.

I mentioned this to Doc Reed, my therapist friend (and no relation to my childhood speech therapist).

"The cycle of abuse usually goes like this," Doc explained. "The abused person ratchets up their nagging or pokes a finger at the abuser until he or she explodes. Then there's a heartfelt apology and a period of contrition followed by a honeymoon, before the apathy settles in again, so the abused individual begins—consciously or not—picking another fight. They somehow need that contrition and honeymoon, in spite of the physical and emotional injuries sustained."

I mulled this over. "I guess that's why my mother didn't want me to confront to him that day, and why she tried to blame his behavior on me when we spoke about it over the phone."

"She what?"

I explained to him about her supposition that if I visited more often, my father would be nicer to her.

"It's amazing that you turned out as functional as you did," Doc told me. "The abuse you experienced and the mixed messages you received would be enough to drive any child into an adult personality disorder."

*   *   *

When I arrived home that evening, I broke down for what seemed like the first time in a decade.

I blubbered—for about twenty minutes—like a child whose puppy vanished through a hole in the fence onto a freeway on-ramp.

And Jay listened and soothed and supported me as only he can.

Then we opened a bottle of wine and made dinner, and we talked about our days.

Luckily, his had gone pretty smoothly.

That night as I rested in bed, listening to Jay snore in concert with the dogs, a scene returned to me:

1964. Sunday evening.

We're in Dad's 1952 Nash Rambler—daffodil yellow with a kelly-green roof. Miriam, now six or seven, is perched on the back seat; I loll unfettered next to her, making my way from the seat to the car floor and back again. Miriam, impatient with the nearly hour-long drive, begins bouncing up and down on the seat, making its springs squeak annoyingly.

"Stop that!" Dad bellows from behind the wheel, as he motors up La Crescenta Avenue toward Tujunga.

Miriam stops bouncing and we continue, my father's cigarette smoke billowing out through the lowered window, my mother silent in the seat next to him.

Ten minutes later...

Miriam, having forgotten our father's warning and being excited by the thought of visiting with her loving granny and grandad, begins bouncing up and down again as I continue exploring the car's thick rubber floor mats.

The signal at Honolulu Avenue turns from yellow to red, and as the Rambler slows to a stop, my father jerks his hand back over his right shoulder and delivers a jiujitsu chop to his daughter's face.

Miriam's two front teeth are knocked from her mouth and she lets loose a scream, my mother cries out in surprise, and I dive for cover below the front seat.

The light turns green and my father pulls over and Mom jumps out and yanks back the front seat to grab her daughter and see how bad the damage is and if there's anything she can do to repair the little girl's mouth and to soothe her son, who's also crying and terrified.

Ten minutes later…Dad pulls the Rambler into Granny and Grandad's driveway, where Mom ushers Miriam—sobbing and toothless, with the front of her pretty new dress streaked with blood—into their house to get cleaned up in front of her horrified grandparents.

Reliving this, I'm now fully awake.

Dad works out in his backyard gym every night, bench-pressing 350 pounds, then performs a set of curls, then squats, and finally military presses, before hitting his peanut bag—a punching bag the size of an eggplant that's designed for speed. I hear DAH-da-da-DAH-da-da-DAH-da-da as he pummels the ballooned leather; and just to make sure his hands and wrists stay tough enough to cave in someone's head, he smashes his bare fists into the wooden four-by-fours that hold up the open beamed roof of the structure, which in more gracious years served as a lattice-walled summerhouse, complete with built-in brick barbecue; now it's like a Victorian tea room that's been relegated to public storage.

The memories start hitting me in waves:

"Stop it!" Mom yells from across the room, knowing how important it is to maintain her own distance. "You're hurting him!"

Like a terrified mouse in the jaws of a cat, I try to escape.

But it's no use.

Dad twists my arm and throws me back atop the bed and holds me in a wrestling lock so tight I can scarcely breathe. He'd started gently—grabbing my arms, then pulling me around the shoulders and waist as I tried to run off—but then his grip became a vise. He always starts gently, but then it's like he doesn't know when to stop.

Laughing maniacally, Dad pushes my face into the coverlet. My neck hurts.

He lifts me into the air and then drops me onto the bed with such force that the air punches out of my lungs—my asthmatic lungs.

Crying now, I extricate myself and Dad chases me through the house from bedroom to bathroom, so I fling open the kitchen door and sprint outside. Is he behind me? I hear his heavy footfall. I leap toward one of the safe zones I've discovered for times like these—in this case, it's the space behind the privet hedge lining the driveway. I crawl inside and hunker down, throwing a hand over my mouth to quiet my panicked wheezing.

I watch in silence as his legs amble by, and then I hear the door open and close.

I'm safe. For now.

I blink at the ceiling, wondering, *How old was I?*
I can't recall.
How big was I?
The answer comes immediately: doorknob height.

Both of my tiny hands grip the doorknob—it's at eye level—with all of the strength I can muster, while Dad—the unseen monster—slowly twists the knob from the other side. I'm crying and trying to hold that knob steady. My hands are no match for his.

I've done something wrong, so Dad pushes the door open. I'm terrified. He grabs me, puts me over his knee, and spanks me. His hand whistles, cutting the air, and the smack on my scrawny butt kicks the air from my lungs. How many will I get? Three's minimum, but it could be eight or ten…Sometimes he doesn't know when to stop. The pain is blinding. Then he stops at last and I'm sobbing, snot trailing down my nostrils like snails from cracked shells. "You're lucky," he tells me. "My father always used a belt." I go to Mom for comfort, and she says, "Don't blame Dad for hitting you so hard. He does it for your own good—and he just doesn't know his own strength."

A word comes to me…*repose.*

"Your father always looks angry," Mom tells me. "Even in repose."

It's 1974 and we're strolling down the aisle at Sears looking for some back-to-school clothes for me. I pick up some plaid bell-bottoms and begin riffling through a nearby ringer, searching for a vest to match; I'd recently watched a Partridge Family episode and was now determined to look like David Cassidy. "What's repose?"

She fixes a disparaging look on the pants in my hands, so I refold the bell-bottoms and place them back on the shelf. "When he's relaxed. Asleep. Even asleep he looks mad. And, well, you know what he looks like when he's angry…" Her voice trailed.

"You mean his Jackie Gleason face?" I ask.

"Yes, his Jackie Gleason face."

"Why does he get so mad?"

Mom shrugs, picks up some straight-from-the-factory Levi's, and checks the leather size patch. "I have no idea. But he's always been that way." She hands the stiff-as-cardboard jeans to me. "Here, go try these on."

So I grew silent and compliant; I anticipated every move I made so as not to incite his wrath. And like the dog that's been kicked quickly figures out whom to cut a wide circle around, I ascertained that my father was best avoided.

But sometimes a boy needs his dad.

Especially for things he can't talk about with his mom.

Like when my body began to unexpectedly mature, and adolescence hit me harder than my father ever could.

CHAPTER 5

◆

Growing Up Ken Doll

During elementary school I assiduously dodged my father, whom I remember as sullen and silent when he wasn't complaining about something or snapping orders.

He did, however, make some efforts on my part—presumably at my mother's behest: We joined Indian Guides (*Pals Forever!*) when I was in fourth grade, and eventually I became a Boy Scout and Dad drove occasionally on the weekend outings.

But by the time I quit Scouts after several years of attendance, I had attained only the meager rank of Tenderfoot (that's one rank up from Scout, which you're assigned upon showing up in uniform to your first meeting).

Why?

Because any of the merit badges my father might've been able to help me with focused on athletics (physical fitness, swimming, etc.) and were simply out of the question due to my lack of strength and coordination, and there was no one else to walk me through the other nonathletic processes (woodworking, bookbinding, and so on). I recall thumbing repeatedly—futilely—through the *Boy Scout Handbook* trying to find *something* I could master on my own, but I'd consistently come up empty-handed, so Tenderfoot I remained until finally convincing my mother that there was no point in proceeding further. (As I perused the list online while writing this, seeing that the Scouts now have badges for things like theater, world brotherhood, and sustainability, I felt a surge of unexpected grief, thinking, *I'd have loved to have earned those!*)

So in the end, the Scouts taught me something invaluable: *If there's something I want, I'd better get it myself, and if I can't figure out how, I should go after something I can tackle.*

Thus began the countdown to the launch of my adult life—which blasted off when my voice changed at twelve.

This physiological, *audible* change is nature's smoke alarm, and it should compel a boy's father (or another trusted male elder) to alert the clueless kid about the other parts of his body that are shooting sparks. There's a lot to be made aware of: pubic hair, grooming, deodorant, erections, masturbation, sexuality...even *love.**

Contrarily, the extent of sex education I received from my father was—while showing me one of his old Norelco electric razors—instructing me to first splash hot water on my face. And then: "This is where the cord plugs in," he mumbled. "And you flip this back to open it up and clean it; just knock it on the sink." Then he pointed to his Old Spice aftershave on the shelf. "You can use that if you want."

Everything else I learned the hard way:

I welcomed the emergence of my pubic and armpit hair the way any middle-aged golf pro might welcome melanoma.

Then, my first orgasm was with another boy my age during a sleepover.

We were both about thirteen, and sometime during that dark, restless night our hands found each other and we brought each other off; but when I felt the wet stickiness on my belly, I assumed it was blood and cried out, "You broke it! You broke it!"

Nearing hysterics, I ran into his bathroom, where I saw that everything looked OK.

*Author's note to the adult males reading this: Whatever discomfort you as a dad, other relative or other adult have about being open about these physiological changes is nothing compared with the unease and confusion a boy feels when no one's explained to him what the hell's happening to his body...so please reach beyond your comfort zone and be a pal. Your son/grandson/brother/nephew will be forever grateful.

Taking it as a good sign that I could still urinate, I went back to my sleeping bag on his floor and told him all seemed OK.

The next day on a local hiking trail—camouflaged by the heavy foliage of some native scrub oak—we repeated what we'd done the night before.

"You're a *fag*," Mike chided after we'd finished.

I continued buttoning my jeans. "At least I wasn't the one saying, 'Oh, that feels so good, oh…don't stop,' last night." I laughed into his reddening face. "*So who's the fag?*"

Thus ended both our sleepovers and our friendship.

But not my consternation.

Secretly, I began gathering information. I rode my bike to the local library and found books on anatomy, checked the index, and read what I could about puberty. Furtively, I flipped through the pages looking for anything that might placate my guilty conscience, curiosity, and self-loathing.

There were keywords I'd scan for:

Masturbation, which was cheerily defined as *self-flagellation* or *self-abuse*.

Circumcision, which described the surgical removal of the prepuce (*What's that?!*) from the head of the male sex organ. (I was oblivious to the fact that I'd long ago been circumcised, so the thought of having anything surgically removed from my penis terrified me more than I can express; the reader can only imagine the relief I felt when someone—most assuredly *not* my father—brought me up to speed a couple of years afterward. But why didn't my father explain anything like this to his son? And what's more, what does it say about the parents who raised me that I knew *it just wasn't OK for me to even bring up the subject of my penis*? It's as if I were growing up as a Ken doll fathered by GI Joe: We were males, our arms and legs bent, we wore appropriate clothes, but there was nothing but empty space between the legs. Nothing.)

And the granddaddy of all buckshot-loaded words when one is thirteen years old: *homosexuality*.

Crouched in one corner of the Grandview Branch Public Library in Glendale, I gained comfort after learning that the ancient Greeks were guiltless participants in the celebrated custom of male-male love. I also learned that just one year prior—1973—*homosexuality* was removed by the American Psychiatric Association from its seemingly endless list of mental disorders. Finally, I read columns penned by Ann Landers in which she stated unflinchingly that homosexuality was not something to be changed; in addition to this, she proffered the revolutionary point of view that homosexuals should be accepted for who they are. (While writing this just now, I felt my eyes dampen as those long-ago emotions of relief and gratefulness swelled once more.)

But true to my upbringing as well as societal norms, I fought it. *Hard.*

After all, I could never devastate my mother, and my father would kill me.

One Sunday at church, I found a neatly typed slip of paper stuffed into the pew next to the missals:

"Dear St. Jude, Please beseech our Heavenly Father on my behalf to change in me that which I have not the power to change, and through His mercy and His forgiveness it will be done!" Say this prayer ten times each day for ten days in church and you are promised the change you seek!

I figured this was too good a deal to pass up, so I secreted the paper into my pocket and made the resolution to ride my bike to church for the next ten days.

And I did so for five or six days but finally gave up. Why?

One reason was because the bike ride to St. Robert Bellarmine Church in Burbank was about five miles, mostly uphill, from our house in Glendale. And my bike was an eleventh-hand ten-speed with mushy tires and a frame seemingly forged from lead water pipes.

But more than that, I suspect that even after day six I felt no ebb in my attraction to males: how my heart beat faster in the locker room after gym class in middle school, or how riveted my eyes were to a shirtless Robert Conrad in *The Wild, Wild West* or to sublime teenage Sandy and his über-handsome dad on *Flipper*, and how I couldn't glance away from tanned-and-blond water polo jock Richard Armstrong—in Latin class—and the way his white puka shells encircled his muscular neck, and so on and so on.

And all through this, even though I had an "intact family" at home, I had nobody to help me gain answers to the questions that chainsawed through my deteriorating psyche each day.

After all, Mom was barely making it through her own days: still overweight, depressed, friendless, and educated yet lacking a career. (And if a housewife is *married* to her house, Mom had been *unfaithful* for years.) But she enjoyed cooking and was an expert; the dining table boasted a delicious, steaming meal almost every evening of each week.

Miriam was working part-time, finishing high school, and dating tan, well-built, long-haired surfers.

Gwen had started kindergarten.

And Dad, well, he went off to work most mornings.

And when his car rolled up in front of the house in the evening, the Ford's wheels crunching the uncollected gutter leaves, my stomach would clench into a fist.

Then he'd hold court at the dinner table, unsmiling and gruff.

My assigned chair—where I chewed my food in silence each night, head down—was next to his.

Then sometimes after dinner, I'd be treated to one of Dad's lectures:

"Yoouu," he'd begin, looking up at the ceiling as if divining parenting tips from God's teleprompter, "want everything the easy way. Yoouu aren't willing to pay the price. Yoouu decide you want something, you start a project, and as soon as it gets difficult you give up and move on."

Or:

"Yoouu…are too 'thing' oriented. All you want is nice cars or a nice house. But you don't have the self-discipline to make these things happen for yourself."

And so on. And it's not that he was wrong—it's just that I was only thirteen, so spending time with my father was tantamount to visiting with *insert here the name of the teacher you dreaded most in middle/high school*; there was never a fuzzy/warm upside, only an immense sense of relief when the encounter was over.

Of course the irony of his words was never lost on me: the beer and the tobacco he was addicted to, even as a cigarette burned in his hand during his parenting lectures, indicated that he had some issues with *giving up when things got difficult*, just as the only reason our house looked as presentable as it did was because I took over the maintenance as soon as I was old enough to balance atop a ladder.

*　　*　　*

Then the next morning, I'd wait in my bedroom until Dad's heavy footfall along the hallway indicated he'd pulled on his shoes—which concluded his dressing for work—signaling his imminent departure. Finally, when those heel thumps were followed by the slam of the kitchen door, I knew it was safe to emerge.

*　　*　　*

I was fourteen when my own depression bloomed charred petals…probably after surmising that my attraction to guys wasn't going away. It was at this same time that middle school was becoming more challenging and my academic workload was increasing, not to mention the chores awaiting me each day upon arriving home, or the carefully penned list taped onto the kitchen cabinet each Saturday morning: laundry, cleaning bathrooms, dumping trash, washing windows, mowing lawns, walking the dog, pruning hedges and trees, pulling weeds, fixing sprinklers, washing and drying dishes, and so on. And as teenagers will do, I became argumentative—at least with my mother.

"Marky and Johnny just passed me on the sidewalk on the way to the park, and they didn't even ask if I could go with them," I told her as she flipped a ground beef patty in a sizzling pan atop the stove; she was back on low-carb and this was her lunch. "It's Saturday, and I've worked hard all week at school. I got all my homework done and practiced the clarinet and I did chores!" I said, eyes brimming. "Why can't I just have some fun like every other kid my age?"

"Because these things need to be done," Mom replied coolly. "After you're finished with your list, you can do whatever you want."

"But it's too much!" I cried, exasperated with how muleheaded she was.

"I'm not talking about this with you anymore." She turned off the blue flame, placed her spatula in the spoon cradle, and made her way toward the living room, where Dad sat in his recliner watching a football game, the volume full blast. "Your father can deal with you from now on."

Uh-oh.

Dad was red-faced as he pushed himself up out of his chair and spun around, pointing at me: "*I'm tired of you and your mother arguing so much. Yoouu should listen to her!*"

"But I—"

"You think you've got it hard, buster?!" Dad roared. "*Huh?!*"

I hung my head.

"When my father had had it with me, we put on gloves and settled it in the ring," he growled. "I shoulda done this with you a long time ago."

I brushed my tears away before looking up. "Done what?"

"Get in the car!" he barked, tossing his head toward the driveway where the new Ford Gran Torino Squire station wagon was parked: refrigerator white with fake walnut paneling; navy blue vinyl seats with fancily embossed headrests; ersatz spoke hubcaps with ruby plastic hubs. "We're going downtown."

"*Why downtown?*"

"Main Street Gym."

Moments later, I slammed myself inside the wagon as my father went inside to don his workout gear: baggy gray sweats, a T-shirt, and some shitty old athletic shoes—*sneakers*, he called them. Minutes later he returned and we began the silent sojourn downtown.

After the streaming freeways narrowed into litter-strewn streets with graffiti-scrawled walls, dusty storefronts, and lurking silhouettes huddled beneath their makeshift Quonset huts, it dawned on me:

35

Will I survive? I'd seen Mom's yellowed newspaper clippings of Nolan in the ring, so it was easy to imagine my stick-figure form quaking across from Dad's hulking physique; a modern-day David shrinking from Goliath because his mother had purposely hidden his sling.

At last my father slowed before swerving into a parking space. Then, like a prisoner from the French Revolution who takes his first glance at the guillotine, I saw the sign: MAIN ST. GYM. (Scenes from *Rocky* and *Rocky II* were later filmed there, and Cassius Clay as well as Dad's old pal Rocky Marciano had sparred inside its storied ring.)

The front wheel bumped the curb, and my father switched off the ignition.

I watched as he swaggered to the entrance and then tried the gym's door.

Locked.

He pressed his face to the glass and then banged on the glass with his knuckles.

Moments later a man opened the door.

They chatted, occasionally glancing over to where I sat, cadaverlike, in the car.

An eternity later, the man closed the door and my father turned and strolled back toward me. He opened the driver's door, sat, and twisted the ignition key.

The rev of the engine was a "Hallelujah Chorus."

"Training some new hotshot," Dad muttered under his breath, "so they're closed."

He yanked the gear selector into drive and gunned the engine.

Finally exhaling as we headed up Main Street toward the Harbor Freeway, I wondered, *What if the place had been open? Would I already be in an ambulance?* Or would my mother have burst into the place, waving her arms and yelling, *Don't hit him! Don't hit him!?*

Nope.

Mom hadn't objected to the idea of his taking me there, and she hadn't even tried to persuade him to take it easy on me. She just watched from her kitchen window as I got into the station wagon, probably thinking that I was finally getting what I was due, *and boy could she use a toasted, buttered English muffin and a nap.*

Still today, I wonder if the gym was really *closed for some new hotshot* or if my father had changed his mind; I've speculated upon the humiliation Dad might've imagined he'd feel by unveiling—to his old barbell-tossing, tobacco-spitting pals—that his only son was a mincing and fragile adolescent; and what did this imply about Nolan, that his *chip off the old block* was molded out of bone china instead of stone?

Or, like the schoolyard bully whose sinister leer is all that's required for lunch money and cookies to be cast his way, perhaps Dad figured that from now on I'd be cheerily compliant, because he'd proven his point.

Or maybe the guy at the gym's door recalled my father's rages and sensed the clouds of disaster gathering, and he didn't want a boy's tears, bones, and blood on his hands.

Whatever the reason had been for our outing's truncation, Dad's intent to profoundly wound me had been successful.

And he'd done so without even raising a hand.

But the real tragedy was that at this very moment in my life's development, when my pubescent canoe was taking on water in the storm of manhood—and I couldn't imagine my self-esteem… or hope…or prospects for the future sinking lower than they had— instead of throwing me a rope or even a pail, Dad tossed me cinder blocks.

Looking back, I think it was as much a catastrophe for him as it was for me…until what I could only imagine as the worst thing in the world happened:

I fell in love for the first time.

CHAPTER 6

◆

Skid Marco

Where the hell is this classroom?

I double-checked the crinkled slip of paper in my hand to verify the number.

Why isn't it right here?

It was my first day of eighth grade, and after discovering I couldn't locate my next class, I found myself sprinting first up and then down one of the building's numerous staircases looking for Mrs. Winslow's journalism class.

The bell rang just as I located Room 8.

I stopped in the doorway, shifting from foot to foot while scanning the classroom for a place to sit at the same moment Mrs. Winslow began addressing her new students.

I caught her eye and smiled apologetically, and she pointed to an empty chair.

After sidling over to it, I lowered my backpack onto the floor and sat as Mrs. Winslow began running through her syllabus.

"You didn't miss anything," whispered the boy next to me. Then he jerked his head upward, as if a fly had landed on his nose. "Marco."

I spotted his ragged jeans with both bony knees poking through, his strawberry-blond hair, and his pale skin and freckles; he looked like a cross between Huckleberry Finn and Rolf from *The Sound of Music*. I mimicked his head jerk. "Hey."

Weeks later, after churning out a couple of assignments that Marco and I coincidentally wrote on automobiles, we discovered our shared obsession with foreign-built sports cars: Triumphs and Jaguars and Morgans and MGs and Austin-Healeys and Porsches, instead of the plebian Chevy Chevelles, Dodge Chargers, and Corvettes most of the boys our age were pining for. And because we spoke the same language—horsepower, skid pad results, quarter-mile sprints—our friendship began accelerating.

One day, while each of us was trying to outshine the other's knowledge of cars, I told Marco, "My sister's boyfriend just bought a '67 Fiat Abarth 1300. Know what that is?"

Marco smirked. "A base Fiat 850 that's been reworked from the ground up. Little shop in Switzerland blows out the engine and the suspension; it'll outcorner just about anything." He paused. "Do you know about Briggs Cunningham?"

"British bodies with Cadillac engines," I murmured dreamily, "although they also pack the Chrysler Hemi in some of them. Don't they have a museum in LA somewhere?"

"In Costa Mesa. My brother's taking me there this weekend."

"*What?!*"

Marco cocked a smile. "Wanna come?"

Thus, our friendship shifted into high gear.

Marco was the youngest of five brilliant, nonconformist siblings who inhabited, with their parents and flat-coated retriever Cleo, an old Spanish villa situated in a tree-lined Burbank neighborhood; their genteel, Ivy League parents watched PBS, drove Fiats, smoked, and drank (lots of) wine in front of their kids. And if that weren't progressive enough, his eldest brother was openly gay, his sister looked like Joni Mitchell, and another brother was married to an African American woman.

On weekends, after I'd earned my learner's permit, Marco's eighteen-year-old brother allowed me—as he copiloted from the front passenger's seat—to (foolishly...so foolishly) race their mom's Fiat 124 sedan through the winding suburban hills, blowing through stop signs and whipping around corners like a stunt driver on a movie set.

In the meantime, at my parents' home, Dad and I were living under the same roof but rarely—thanks to my silent compliance and skillful lies—interacted, and Mom was occupied with taking

Gwen—now seven—to Girl Scouts and gymnastics, and teaching Catholic catechism, a (nonpaying) job she truly enjoyed. Miriam, in the meantime, had found a boyfriend, so she was pretty much MIA every day.

And I was pretty much free to come and go as I pleased…as long as I stayed out of trouble and respected my curfew; I'd accumulated more yard maintenance jobs than I could handle, so I enjoyed a little spending money for the extras that caught my eye.

Over my sixteenth summer, Marco and I spent many hours together enjoying long walks while discussing religion and philosophy and his favorite book, *The Little Prince*; then, after we'd both attained our driver's licenses, we took turns squealing around the precipitous curves on Mulholland Drive or cruising to the old revival theaters around Los Angeles to watch anything that was obtuse, intellectual, or foreign (it was then that I became adept at reading subtitles—a skill I still enjoy). We shared shiny boxes of Dunhill cigarettes, and Marco sometimes lifted a bottle of whiskey from the local store, or we passed a joint back and forth.

All the while wrenching our friendship closer.

During this time, I began "going steady" with a beautiful Sicilian American girl named Martina, and one balmy evening in the back of my mom's Plymouth we surrendered our virginities to each other; Marco, meanwhile, spent his summer nights either running amok or tinkering with his brother's Austin-Healey Sprite.

After Martina's and my passions cooled along with the heat of summer, Marco and I became nearly inseparable. We feasted on each other's teen cynicism, laughed at each other's sardonic reflections, and seldom ran out of provocative ideas to discuss.

Then one night, while sitting on my bed, across from where he slouched in a grimy club chair, I *really* noticed Marco for the first time: the gleam in his green eyes…his crooked grin…his languid, lean physique…his arrogant Germanic nose.

His scent.

I was suddenly overcome by the desire to trace a finger along the hollows of his cheekbones; to lean forward and *kiss his mouth*.

And then it hit me: *I'm in love with my best friend.*

The hopelessness and helplessness I felt was dizzying. Terrifying. Stultifying.

And there was *no one anywhere* to help me process this.

After all, I'd grown up in a house where my brutish father referred to overtly homosexual men as *fairies* or *fruits*; for instance, after our Catholic parish recruited an easygoing, soft-featured, thirty-something priest who preferred to be called "Father Gary," Dad preferred instead to call him "Father Fairy." Similarly, we were watching the Santa Clause Lane Parade one December evening, and actor Robert Conrad floated by in a convertible flanked by his two handsome teenage sons. "Couple of fairy-lookin' kids," Dad muttered, as I sat across the room from him in silence.

Mom, on the other hand, simply referred to gay men as *icky*. "That man is icky," Mom whispered as we exited the convenience store, where the polite, lisping, toupee-wearing gentleman working the register had just rung up her half gallon of milk and jumbo Hershey's chocolate bar. "I don't want you coming back here alone."

Thus, I—at sixteen—had rotted into an *icky fruit*.

So I hid my heart, and I tethered my desires.

And that autumn, I began swirling within the worst depression of my life.

Then in December of 1977, I started drowning.

And *drowning* is exactly what each progressive week felt like, where every day I treaded water while dressing for school, drifting off in class, paddling off to my yard jobs, and then sinking like a stone to eat at home and then wade through my homework, the waters of self-hatred lapping at my shoulders, neck, and earlobes.

During this period I don't recall either of my parents even once taking the time to ask what was wrong, when even a falling-down drunk could've ascertained that very little was right with my demeanor: I shuffled, I slouched, I slumped, and I stammered, and I most likely didn't make eye contact with anyone in my family for weeks at a time.

"You need to get out of this house and do something," I do recall my mother snapping at me once or twice, as if *do something* were adequate guidance to pull my rudderless boat back into the shipping lane. And today I wonder: Was she simply too deep within her own depression to notice mine, a mother impervious to her son's forlorn forest for the sagging branches of her own trees? Or did she see and just not care?

Look the other way, indeed she did.

And with my father I didn't even bother: His hair-trigger rages and endless lectures about every fault I possessed were enough to keep me quietly exiting through the back door of life as Dad stormed through the front.

Then in February 1978, while kicking through the flotsam of my home life and clinging to the jetsam of any moments with Marco, the fetid waters inevitably splashed into my mouth and nose. Depression nearly paralyzed me in a series of rogue waves, until— like an exhausted man kicking against a riptide as the shore shrinks farther into the horizon—I began weighing my options for the end.

On February 15, 1978, I wrote these words in my journal: *If I'm not happy in one month I'm going to kill myself.*

I kept dogpaddling, but nothing changed.

Then the day came when I—like Dorothy spying the dwindling sands inside the Wicked Witch of the West's hourglass—saw that only one week remained before D-Day.

Having determined I had nothing to lose, I decided, *I'm gonna tell Marco how I feel.*

It was nearing my midnight curfew as Marco and I sat in Miriam's VW Beetle on the quiet street opposite his family's villa, with the tiny engine rattling in the rear.

"So…since you and Martina broke up," Marco began, peering out of the windshield, "what kind of girl are you looking for now?"

Also staring forward, I fiddled absently with the Bakelite shift knob. "I'm not really sure I can look at someone that way again—at least not for a while."

Marco snorted amiably while turning to me, and my side-eye caught how the streetlight harshly illuminated the right side of his face while his left was cloaked in shadow, a real-life *Phantom of the*

Opera mask. "You? But you're always dating this girl or that one; you've gotta have someone you're thinking of."

My heart raced. The silence between us crested. My mouth was dry.

Say it! Say it! You've got nothing to lose because you'll be dead next week. Say it!

I turned slowly toward him. "You." My heartbeat thudded inside my ears. "You're who I'm thinking of."

A sigh escaped Marco's lips. "Are you…saying what I—?"

"Yeah."

Then Marco—like a robot in slow motion—turned to face the windshield again as a smile curled up the edges of his mouth. *That wonderful mouth.* A sudden calm descended upon me.

"I've, uh, felt the same way about you," Marco whispered. "For a while. But I was too afraid to say anything." Then he turned to me, pulled my face to his, and kissed me. *Hard.*

So hard my ankles tingled.

Driving home that night, I felt rescued.

If only I'd known how perilously the waters ahead churned.

CHAPTER 7

◆

Tsunami

"Your father went into one of his rages last night," Mom told me, wiping her eyes. "And I don't know why. He does it every time we're coming back from somewhere, especially when he's driving. It frightens me, and I just don't know what to do anymore."

I listened to my mother—while flipping through my high school yearbook, its scrawled-ink sentiments barely dry—report this to me for the umpteenth time. "I don't know how you put up with him."

Mom squared a look at me. "He's my husband."

My mind rewound to all of those times I'd witnessed their arguments: something seemingly insignificant (*should've turned right instead of left; spilled some coffee; etc.*) would become escalated, and moments later my father's features would twist into that snarling Jackie Gleason mask. "*Shut up, Maryann!*" he'd bellow, his arms and shoulders taut and ready to spring; and then Mom would withdraw into silence interspersed with sobbing.

"He doesn't have to be your husband," I reminded her.

"I was going to have the perfect marriage," Mom muttered. "But no one tells you what it's like being married to an Irishman."

"How so?" I asked, knowing half of my DNA waved the green-white-and-orange-striped flag.

"His temper. His impatience. His drinking. All of that. And how he denigrated me for being fat. *But especially the rages,*" Mom explained. "I had no idea." She paused, absently pinching her double chin. "And the intimacy, or lack of it."

"*Mom*—" I groaned.

"I had to beg your father for intimacy—"

I pushed my chair back from the table and stood. "*Waaay* too much information."

She looked up at me. "I only say this because it illustrates how he doesn't allow anyone to get close to him. He's always had this wall"—she held up her hands—"around him that no one could get through, not even his wife."

"Except Gwen," I reminded her.

Mom nodded thoughtfully. "Yes…he was gentle with her. And very loving."

I leaned back against the wall, crossing my arms. "I used to get so angry seeing him hold her and nuzzle her and laugh with her when she was a baby and a toddler. It's like he did it just to throw at me what I could've had *if I'd only been the son he wanted*."

"I can understand why you felt like that," Mom said. "I used to feel the same way with Granny and how she doted on my brother Freddy."

"But you knew Granny would never smash her fist into your face or snap your neck."

I glared at her and then trudged toward the door.

By mid-June of 1979, Miriam had moved out and was waiting tables at a restaurant in Old Town Pasadena, Gwen had just turned nine, I had graduated from high school and was working full-time delivering furniture while taking night classes at our community college, and Mom was as depressed as ever because Dad was pushing fifty and pulling no punches: He'd clambered into a vice president's position with an international industrial supply company, and his unexpected success had bestowed upon him an especially smug arrogance bolstered by an even greater sense of his own power as a breadwinner, a man, and *an authority on everything*: Russian history, mechanical engineering, American economics and politics, and every character flaw possessed by both his wife and his son (at least *those of his son that he knew of…*). During those two years before I moved into my own humble digs, I don't remember much interaction with my father except for this: I was cordial—as was he—in much the same way two employees who loathe each other manage to pass each other in the parking lot without breaking into a fistfight.

In the meantime, Marco and I were perfecting our Lucy and the Football* routine: After we'd spent one magical, intimate, gasping night together, he was so freaked out he wouldn't speak to me; thus I ascertained that any discussion beyond Porsches and MGs would catapult him from my life. Contrarily, whenever I'd swear off him completely, he'd magically reappear, as if I were the only one he ever wanted.

Which was bewildering, to say the least.

Especially because the compass needle of my sexuality was spinning like a propeller: Over the years, I'd dated and had satisfactory sexual relationships with six young ladies, and I wanted kids someday. But when it came to kisses that made my ankles tingle, Marco was the one.

What was I to do?

Where might I turn?

My father and I faced each other in the driveway as night approached. Mom's ivory Sport Suburban station wagon, to my left, glowed lavender in the twilight, and I could see the blue, strobelike flashes from the television inside our neighbor's darkened living room next door.

"I'm...um, having, um...*d-doubts* about my m-masculinity," I confessed, prepared for anything: the jiujitsu chop to my mouth, the Jackie Gleason face, the silent rage...the lecture starting with *Yoouu*... And as much as I objected to that trite euphemism about 'doubting my masculinity' (I was about eighteen and had bedded—and been bedded by—more than a handful of women and men), it was the only intro I could think of; but in reality, I had few doubts about being masculine: In the manner of Rock Hudson, I'd already developed sufficient physique and swagger and lispless enunciation to dupe even the most observant sexual-orientation detective.*

I even drove a boy-next-door 1973 Mercury Capri sport coupe that I'd purchased with my own money: It was Crayola yellow with

* Please Google or YouTube *Lucy Football Charlie Brown* when you get the chance.

flat-black accents, lowered suspension, Cragar mag wheel rims, fat BF Goodrich radial tires, and a V-6 motor with dual glass-pack exhausts braying out the back.

So how did I gather the courage to tell him?

Not sure.

But I do recall having been goaded by my mother, who'd finally acknowledged my scowling features upon returning home each day…and the silent hours spent sequestered in my room and my long naps and my tense silence at the dinner table each night—as my father smacked his lips over his blood-rare slab of beef or pontificated politically or criticized my mother's cooking or raised his empty Coors can to demand *more hooch*—and then lumbering back to my bedroom, where I stayed until lights-out, only to awaken and repeat the previous day's activities. "You can tell your father anything," she said at last, drowning segments of iceberg lettuce under the running faucet.

I laughed. "No, I can't, and you know it."

"You need to trust him. You rejected him, but he still wants to help you."

"I rejected him?" I asked. "I was the child, remember? I think it should've been up to him—the adult, the parent—to patch things up."

"Tell him what's on your mind. I've talked to him. He wants to help you."

"I'll think about it."

So I thought about it.

My father drew heavily on the cigarette in his mouth and then flicked it toward the street gutter. It burned out on the sidewalk, having missed its target.

"Yoouu were always a mystery to me."

I turned my head so he wouldn't see me roll my eyes. *Fuck. Here it comes.*

"If I hadn't known your mother better, I would've sworn you were someone else's son."

And I wish I had been.

"When your grandmother was dying of colon cancer," he continued, "she said she wasn't afraid of dying, but she could see that you hated me and it bothered her that she wasn't going to be around to do anything about that."

She WHAT?!

"Then at one point," Dad went on, "Mom said I was too rough with you kids, so she would take care of disciplining you both; but when I was a boy and did something stupid, my mother locked us in the woodshed to wait until our father got home. And he would beat us. With a belt, with some wood, with whatever was close by. It wasn't until I got big enough to knock him out that things changed; up until then, we'd put on the gloves, like I told you, and he would smack me around pretty hard."

"I can't believe Grandpa was so tough on you," I said, recalling how rewarding our own father-son outing to the Main Street Gym was. "You must've *hated* him."

"I loved my father," Dad replied. "He did the best he could with what God gave him. He wasn't the smartest man. But I loved him." He pulled another cigarette from the pack in his shirt pocket and sparked it with his Bic. "Yoouu were just so different from me," he said, looking off down the street, while his words made a white cloud—like a cartoon bubble—over his head. "I couldn't figure you out. So I guess I...left you to your own devices."

"You mean, you abandoned me emotionally," I corrected him, shocked by my honesty. "Because that's what it felt like."

Dad mulled this over. "You could say that."

"*Why?* I could've used a father. I remember driving to church with you, just the two of us, and asking you question after question, trying to make conversation. All you would say was 'yes' or 'no.'"

"We just...didn't have anything in common. The only thing I knew was athletics, and your asthma made that impossible. You were talented in areas where I couldn't help you. Music, art, mechanical things." He dragged deeply on his cigarette. "I decided to stop forcing you to be athletic because you didn't have any talent there, and I figured you needed to find your own way with what you were good at."

This sounded reasonable, so I let it drop. "What about what I told you?"

"About being a homosexual?"

I stiffened. *That word.* "I'm not sure if I am or not."

"I've never known a happy homosexual."

"And I know very few happy heterosexuals," I countered.

"Good point." He dragged on his cigarette again and leaned against the Plymouth's fender. "What would help you?"

"Probably seeing a therapist."

"If that's what you need, I'll help you out with it. The money."

I smiled, feeling very much relieved. "I'd appreciate it."

"Just don't say anything about this to your mother," Dad warned me. "You know she has mental illness in her family—her grandmother was a schizophrenic; crazy lady saw and heard things that weren't there—and Mom's been worried about this, about you being a homosexual. *It would send her over the edge.*"

"Mom's been worried?" I asked, shocked at how she could apparently read the signs on my Gay Trail, especially because I'd been very, *very* careful about covering my tracks.

Had I inadvertently bent some willows along the way?

"If she finds out about *any* of this, like I said, it could send her over the edge." He sucked in another deep drag, shaking his head. "*Nervous...breakdown.*" His words evaporated in an ominous white cloud.

A day or two later I filled out a form at the Verdugo Mental Health Center, which was about two miles from my parents' house. I checked the boxes for depression, suicidal thoughts, low self-esteem, sexual identity issues, possible alcohol addiction (although I'd only been drunk half a dozen times, both my father's drinking and his telling us kids, *Nolans are very well-traveled; we've died in skid rows all over the world,* spelled "impending disaster" for me), and whatever else I can't recall.

A young woman named Melanie became my therapist. She was working at the VMHC as an intern *getting her hours*, and she helped me bridge what could have been the most treacherous—and possibly fatal—chasm of my young life. Facing her in that chair each week forced me to peel back the invisible, weeping bandages covering my emotional wounds, and in her care I began learning about my feelings, my desires, my fears, and my history.

So I began walking back to myself…on a long road that stretches into today.

Of course my father conveniently forgot about his offer to help me with the cost of therapy. But thankfully the VMHC charged on a sliding scale, so I think my sessions with Melanie only cost me about five dollars a week, the same amount I charged for the weekly maintenance on a front and backyard.

Nevertheless, it would've been nice if he'd at least *tried* to honor his promise.

Melanie also helped me see how toxic my relationship was becoming with Marco, and how Marco appeared to be even more confused about his sexuality than I was. "Have you considered seeing someone who's actually *out* to his family, and maybe even a little older?" Melanie asked during one of our sessions. "This might reduce some of these confusing variables—like sexual identity—and help you focus on your overall compatibility."

This sounded reasonable.

A week or two later, I met Kenny.

Kenny was a waiter who worked with Miriam; he was twenty-five, fit, funny, and handsome, and he lived in a spacious mid-Wilshire duplex along with two roommates.

And Kenny was unapologetically gay.

In the span of that next month, Kenny confessed that he loved me and urged me to move out of my parents' home *so we could spend more time together*.

A few weeks later, just before my twenty-first birthday, I found a cheap studio apartment in an old brick four-story walk-up in Koreatown that was centrally located between my work, Glendale

Community College, and Kenny's lovely duplex. I drained the cash in my checking account that I'd been hoarding for more than a year to pay for the apartment's first month, last month, and security deposit.

Then I began packing my belongings.

Upon leaving my parents' house, after bidding farewell to my mother, sister, and father on that first evening—and knowing I had neither food nor money and it was days until payday—I asked my mother if I could borrow something to eat; she was standing by the oven and I was leaving by the back door, which was off our kitchen, and I stopped and opened the fridge and palmed a single egg. "Mom, would you mind if I borrowed one? I don't have anything to eat."

She glared at me. "No."

I laughed, thinking she was joking. "Really, Mom, I don't have a thing to eat. Nothing. Could I just borrow this for tomorrow morning?"

"No," she told me again, her eyes two cold marbles.

I opened the fridge and placed the egg back in the wire basket along with well over a dozen others. Then I said goodbye once more and walked out the door.

And that was that.

Childhood officially over.

A couple of nights after I moved in, Kenny came to visit and then stayed for breakfast: coffee and an Entenmann's fat-free (but packed with sugar and carbs) pastry I'd purchased after payday.

After he left, I congratulated myself: It had been tough, but somehow I'd managed to work for—and provide myself with—my own apartment, my own car, some decent furniture, and a doting boyfriend.

I was ecstatic.

Exactly one week later Kenny unexpectedly blowtorched our relationship, while bestowing upon me this charcoal briquette of wisdom: *In the gay world there are no long-term relationships, and the sooner you accept this the happier you'll be.*

I didn't sleep after he left that night, and even though it was nearly forty years ago, I can still see myself lying in my lumpy, squeaking Murphy bed watching the darkness thawing under the sun's unwelcome heat lamp. *Today is my first day without Kenny,* I thought as I hugged my pillow and squeezed shut my eyes. *But I can't tell my family, and I can't tell my friends. I'm alone, confused, down to my last dollar, and completely depressed.*

What the hell do I have to live for?

Only weeks later, the explosion of something called *gay cancer* would make me ask myself that question again.

CHAPTER 8

◆

Sabotage?

Right about the same time I was lugging my boxes up the stairs of that walk-up in Koreatown, the *New York Times* published a story by physician and medical correspondent Dr. Lawrence Altman titled "Rare Cancer Seen in 41 Homosexuals."

It was AIDS. But they didn't call it that, yet.

AIDS was *gay cancer* then, or *gay plague*.

One journalist even dubbed it *the Disease of the Century*.

And gay men everywhere were scared witless; some even jumped out of windows.

Shortly thereafter, *People* magazine wrote the headline: "AIDS: Fatal, Incurable and Spreading."

Life magazine used the title "Now No One Is Safe from AIDS" for their investigative piece.

What was I to do? Where could I turn?? The authorities said the incubation period for AIDS was five to ten years, and I'd begun sneaking into gay bars when I was seventeen…so I probably had it.

But more on that later.

*   *   *

Fast-forward three years. With Kenny now a speck in my life's review mirror, and after working full-time selling furniture and accumulating just over sixty college credits taking night classes at Glendale Community College, I set the lofty goal of attending Occidental College in Eagle Rock: not only the location where dear Mrs. Reed—wearing her cat's-eye glasses and tailored tweed blazer—had effectively tamed my stutter, but also the prestigious private Quaker college that today counts former US president Barack Obama among its luminary alumni.

After bricking together a respectable GPA and garnering recommendation letters from three of the most highly esteemed professors at Glendale College, I submitted my application to Oxy and waited; I knew tuition was more than I could afford at ten thousand dollars per year, but the school's brochures stated, *With our endowments and foundations, no worthy candidate has ever been excluded from Occidental College for their inability to pay* (or words to that effect). And seeing as I'd already been independent from my parents for nearly three years and only needed to have been for two, I figured I had at least a chance—albeit slim.

I was called in for an interview with Dr. James Montoya. He was smart and personable and inquisitive, and toward the end of my interview he asked about my ability to pay their tuition. So I advised Dr. Montoya of my independent status and said I'd be applying for financial aid, if so fortunate as to be accepted.

Dr. Montoya ended our interview with a smile and a handshake.

Then, much to my shock, a letter arrived in the mail announcing my acceptance to Oxy for the spring semester of 1984.

Gleefully, I registered for a history class, which cost about a thousand dollars out of pocket (I was taking home nearly eight hundred dollars per month working full-time, so after paying rent and my car note and insurance and expenses, there wasn't much remaining). So I asked my parents if I could move into their garage to save more money, even though their garage had neither bathroom facilities nor running water nor heat.

Because nothing mattered except attending Occidental.

My parents agreed, so that June I moved out of my apartment and stacked my belongings inside their garage next to a used sleeper sofa a friend donated to my cause.

In the months following—and with no more community college classes to attend—I spent the summer and fall of 1983 working full-time while restoring my childhood home: I stripped, patched, primed, and painted the thirty-odd (decrepit) mullioned windows with their rotten sash trims dating back to 1927. I pruned nearly half an acre of bushes and trees, and I planted flowering shrubs; I installed new porch lamps and wiring. I primed, painted, and fitted wooden shutters around each of the windows, I repaired sprinklers and fences, and the venerable St. Augustine out front bristled as green as Italian parsley.

All while peeing at night into an old green flower vase I kept under a table, and stuffing my old socks around the garage door's openings to keep out the winter drafts.

"Your father said our house used to be the eyesore of the neighborhood," Mom told me one afternoon. "But now he thinks it's the showplace of the block."

All work done for free...not only because I thought my folks would appreciate it, but also because I'd always wanted my family to live in a pretty house.

Then one afternoon—about five weeks into my first semester—I returned home from the history class at Occidental that I'd been able to scrape together the cash for.

"Hi, Mom."

"Hi—oh...this came for you," Mom said, handing me an envelope with a return address from the financial aid office.

At last! Gleefully I tore it open, thinking, *I'll finally be able to attend full-time!*

I stood, blinking at the letter in my hand. "You...you...*claimed me as a dependent* and negated my *independent status?*" I asked, my voice shaking.

"You're living here," Mom replied sharply, "so I have the right to do that."

"But I pay you rent! I pay all of my expenses!" I yelled. "My car, my insurance, my medical bills, my clothes, even the braces on my teeth! Not to mention that your house is nearly paid off, and Dad drives a company car! *You don't need the money!*"

"We were going to have to pay too much in taxes otherwise," Mom said, gently stirring a pot of dumplings.

"How much?"

"About two hundred and fifty dollars."

"*I would've paid you that to keep my status!*" I nearly screamed. "*Didn't the last six months of free labor count for anything?!*"

"You're living here," Mom stated coolly. "I have that right."

The next week, knowing that my mother and he had beheaded my academic unicorn, Dad and I met with a friend of a friend at UC Irvine who happened to be a college financial aid specialist. "You're a perfect example of *exactly what not to do*," the nice man mumbled while reviewing my documents. "And it's too bad, because with your grades and SATs you could've gone anywhere…Occidental, UCLA, UC Irvine." He paused. "Hell, you could *teach* at UCLA with grades like these."

I felt ashamed, not realizing that his estimation of my bureaucratic witlessness had been meant for my father's ears and not mine.

Reluctantly, I withdrew from Occidental and moved out of that garage.

And I've always wondered: Did my mother purposefully sabotage my dream?

Mom, can I borrow an egg?

*   *   *

I was feeling especially courageous the first time I went in for my HTLV-III antibodies test—now commonly known as HIV antibodies—which signals that one has been exposed to the AIDS virus.

I'd become engaged to a woman with whom I'd been involved over the years (one of the aforementioned six young ladies), but because I'd been honest with her about what I'd done and whom I'd done it with, we put the announcement on hold until I could verify my status; *positive* meant there would be no wedding, but *negative* indicated there would be.

Alone one afternoon, I drove to the Edmund D. Edelman Health Clinic at the Los Angeles Gay and Lesbian Center, in those days down on Highland Avenue in Hollywood, where I filled out the anonymous forms that contained only an identification number (heinous Lyndon LaRouche wanted us all quarantined, not to mention what those panicked medical insurance companies might do if they found out), waited in a lobby that resembled an old Greyhound station, and was called in, at long last, to give a vial of blood to a nurse.

Three agonizing weeks later I received the results.

Negative.

So my fiancée and I made the grand announcement to our families, and we began making plans.

Somewhere at the end of the first month, she let me know she didn't want children.

None.

And I thought, *If I'm swearing off ankle-tingling kisses for the rest of my life, I'd better get some kids out of this.*

We discussed it some more, and then we reluctantly called off the engagement.

And I began dating guys again. And practicing safe sex.

In the meantime, I watched my friend Richard die by inches: the diarrhea, the fevers, and finally the Kaposi's sarcoma—like squished Concord grapes peppering his skin—that rendered him nearly unrecognizable.

Then Christopher; I sobbed at his bedside while he lay in a coma.

Other friends simply vanished: Carlos and Mark and David and Paul and Steven and Tim and Clayton...sweet, funny, handsome, blue-eyed Clayton with the button-down collared shirts.

I still don't understand why I was spared.

*   *   *

"Mom...um, can I talk to you? *Outside?*"

She looked at me, her eyes searching mine. "Why?"

"Gwen's here"—I nodded to my younger sister doing her homework in the living room—"and I don't want to discuss this in front of her."

My mother clutched her stomach as her face turned paper-towel white. "Oh God…"

"I'm fine. I just need to talk with you about something." I tried a smile. "Come outside. Please?"

The following Saturday, my father strolled into the furniture store I was managing, his face grim. "Mom's been crying for three days," he stated calmly, although his eyes suggested murder.

I was taken aback by his presence, primarily because as a career salesman and general manager, I considered any commissioned territory—sales floor, car lot, factory office—hallowed ground. Hence, his confronting me *here in the store I managed* was an act of war.

I looked around.

Seeing how I had another salesperson tending to a handful of customers leafing through fabric samples, poking at nightstands, or trying out dining chairs, I led him out the entrance door to the sidewalk, where we faced each other as if participating in a *Hamilton*-esque duel. "Yeah, I kind of expected this, although I was hoping she'd take it better."

"I told yoouu not to tell her!"

"I'm not going to lie to my mother forever," I said, backing away (and knowing that even if he could outpunch me, I could easily outrun him). "Better to tell her now than to have her find out by mistake, later."

"She can't stop crying," Dad repeated, his Jackie Gleason building steam. *"Did you hear me? Mom's on the verge of a nervous breakdown, and if she loses her mind it'll be your fault! I TOLD yoouu this would happen!"*

"Then as her husband," I said, reciting the lines my therapist and I had practiced in case this exact scenario presented itself, "it's *your responsibility* to get her the help she needs."

I waited for a retort, but he had none.

I left him seething next to a parking meter, so I could get back to a woman who'd asked me about glass-top coffee tables: *not too modern…maybe with a whitewash Santa Fe finish?*

From the safety of the display window I watched my father linger on the sidewalk for a few moments, turn around, and then limp away (by this time he'd begun favoring one leg, an ominous barometric drop for the CTE storm that was brewing).

*　　*　　*

Weeks slid into months without contact.

During this interlude, I upended my life: I quit drinking and smoking and began jogging compulsively; traded my well-paying manager's position for a seven-dollar-per-hour sales job; moved from a remodeled Silver Lake hillside bungalow—replete with hardwood floors, three patios, and a deck with sparkling nighttime views of Hollywood—into a forlorn downtown loft; sublet my year-old Merkur XR4ti sports coupe (you'll need to look that one up...) to a recovering alcoholic with rotten credit; unloaded the sacred 1956 Packard I'd lovingly stored for ten years for five hundred dollars to buy a sturdy 1969 Dodge pickup truck for six hundred dollars, and reenrolled in community college to begin accumulating the few lower-division semester units toward my BA degree I still lacked (the pursuit of which I'd abandoned after the sad Occidental College fiasco).

I was broke and alone, didn't have medical or car insurance, owned no glasses and only one contact lens, and barely had enough cash at the end of each week for gasoline and what was to become my staple diet: canned stewed tomatoes, onions, and frozen beef patties (I dropped during this period from 175 pounds to 155). But I was *out*, clean and sober, exercising like a fiend, and on track for a career I'd previously felt too unworthy to deserve.

Three months into my ascetic's existence I met (through some *very* odd coincidences) Jay, who was as handsome as he was funny. We shared the same taste in movies and music, and we dated on Saturday nights and spoke every evening by phone. On my half-hour lunch breaks from the sales floor—when I usually had nothing to eat—I'd lean back into the tiny breakroom's dusty old love seat, close my eyes, and dream of the life Jay and I might build together.

But wait: In the gay world there are no long-term relationships, and the sooner you accept this, the happier you'll be.

Fuck you, Kenny.

Then one day in late August, I returned to my loft to see the red light flashing on my answering machine: "Hi, Nicky. It's Mom… Could you…come over for dinner sometime, maybe next week?" She sounded tired, apologetic. "Please give me a call back if you can."

My pulse quickened. Had her heart mended? What about Dad's anger? I'd already resigned myself to navigating my new life's highway as an orphan, so this could be an unexpected off-ramp.

I tapped her number into my phone.

"Hello?"

"Hi, Mom."

Silence. "Oh. Hi."

"Um…you left me a message about dinner. Would Monday be OK?"

"That would be good," Mom sighed. "What time?"

"I get off at six thirty, so around seven?"

More silence. "We will see you then."

* * *

Dinner—spaghetti and meatballs alongside cherry tomatoes atop iceberg lettuce drenched in Thousand Island—started out amicably enough: *How's school? How's your new job?* But then our conversation morphed into an orchestrated ambush about how ashamed they felt at my refusal to cast off my sexuality, as if it were some turd-stained bathrobe:

"I ran into Mrs. Waller in the market and she asked if you were married yet. What'm I supposed to say?"

"Why do you refuse to find a therapist who'll change your perversion?"

"How could you do this to us?"

"Don't you know you're going to hell?"

"How long do you expect us to keep *your problem* a secret from your sisters?"

Now, hell and nosy neighbors and Catholic guilt and calling me a pervert I could shrug off.

My two sisters were another story.

"Um…yeah, Miriam introduced me to one of my ex-boyfriends—his name was Kenny—so I guess you won't need to shield her from the *awful truth*. And my relationship with Gwen has nothing to do with you," I stated calmly, even though I was raging inside. "She's eighteen, so she can handle the truth; I'll tell her when the time's right."

In an instant, my father's fists clenched as his face Jackie Gleasoned. "If you tell Gwen you're a gay," he began, "you won't need AIDS to finish you off, buster, 'cause I'll kill you!"

Knowing what was coming, I jumped back from the table and snatched my backpack from the couch, and then I banged out through the front screen door and sprinted across the street to my rusting truck.

I started the engine and floored the accelerator and sped to the nearest phone booth to call Jay, while fully realizing how risky it could be to run to a freshly minted boyfriend—especially one whom I was falling in love with—for a hug and a willing ear.

But my intuition was a powerful GPS.

"Can I see you?" I groaned into the pay phone's mouthpiece.

"My God, are you OK? *What happened?*"

"I'll tell you when…I see you. My father just said—" I choked back a sob. "*I'm sorry.* If it's a bad time, I totally understand."

"I'm here. *Just be careful.*"

It's dangerous driving a ramshackle pickup truck—with bald tires, no power brakes, and no power steering—at night when its windshield is blurred by tears, because for some reason the wipers don't do any good. But somehow I made it across town to Jay's.

I parked my truck and rang his doorbell.

"Are they showing *Old Yeller* at the drive-in again?" Jay deadpanned upon seeing my blistered eyes in the glare of his porch light.

"I'm *really* sorry to hit you with this." Sighing, I straightened myself. "I just kinda needed a friendly face."

"I'm guessing you could use something to eat, too." Jay opened the door wider, arms outstretched.

"Just no spaghetti and meatballs," I told him, stepping inside. "Please?"

"I'll warm up some tamales."

And as Jay embraced me, my father's threat once again echoed in my head: *You won't need AIDS to finish you off, buster, 'cause I'll kill you!*

It would take thirty years—and some wise, kind words from a talented neurologist—to make peace with those words...and the man who barked them at me.

CHAPTER 9

◆

Mother, May I?

The decade between 1987 and 1997 is a smeary blur except for these milestones: I graduated with my BA in psychology and quit my furniture sales job; was accepted into a program to earn my Marriage, Family and Child Counseling license; and got a position with the GLASS (Gay and Lesbian Adolescent Social Services) agency, working with homeless and abused LGBT teens in a residential, clinical setting. But after four years I burned out, so I became a public schoolteacher on an Emergency Credential while earning my California Clear Multiple Subjects Credential.

In the meantime Jay and I continued gaining momentum on the life we'd dreamed of: We moved from our apartment and acquired a mortgage and two rescued dogs. And my mother continued mailing me thick, neatly sealed manila packages from (Catholic) Father Joseph Nicolosi's Reparative Therapy, which ostensibly transforms homosexual males into (real) heterosexual men by focusing on the emotionally lacking relationships between fathers and their homosexual sons (I should add that his "therapeutic process" even today relies on studies published in 1958, 1969, 1978, and 1996).

So Mom and I argued, mostly over the phone, until a conversation in 1995 ended the debate: "Did you read those booklets I sent you?" Mom asked.

"Nope."

"But they gave me hope."

"I threw them out," I told her. "They always go straight into the trash [this was before curbside recycling in Los Angeles], so you're wasting your postage; I believe I've mentioned this before."

"Why won't you just read them?"

"Because they're selling false hopes to people who're miserable. *And I'm happy*, Mom. Jay and I've been together for eight years now, and we're happy. Doesn't that mean anything to you?"

"But it's a dead kind of happiness," Mom stated, her tone flatter than usual. "And you don't know what it's like for me when people ask me if you're married. You don't know how hard *your choice* has been on your father and me! Dad says your being *that way* is harder on him than when his parents died!"

My choice. I saw myself kneeling in that mahogany pew, the solitary soul in an empty church: *Dear St. Jude...* "Have you ever considered what it was like for me, going through all of this on my own?"

"That's why I've been sending you those brochures," Mom explained, "so you can finally get the help you need—it's not too late. But you won't even read them!"

"Because it's all lies."

"How do *you* know?"

"Uh, well for one thing…Jay's always had a *great* relationship with his dad. His father's a kind, gentle, loving, supportive man—so there goes your theory about the cold, horrible ways Dad treated me causing me to be gay."

Mom's tears began leaking through the phone. "You don't know what this does to me!"

My thoughts suddenly spooled back to the funeral Jay and I had recently attended for his good friend Chris, who'd just succumbed to *the Disease of the Century*, and watching Chris's devastated mother, Jan, as she valiantly stood guard next to her son's shiny blue coffin, its chrome handles gleaming in the sun. "I happen to know a mom who'd gladly trade places with you," I told her. "Jan just buried her only son, who died after four years of battling AIDS. And Chris didn't even get to see his thirtieth birthday! He was only twenty-nine, Mom. *Twenty-nine!*"

There was silence.

And then: "Sometimes I think it might've been easier if *you* had died of AIDS."

Easier for who? I wondered, hanging up on her.

It was many, many months until we had any contact.

* * *

Years later I confronted my mother—*calmly*, I should add—with her having said those words to me, and she promptly denied it. But she's also denied many things, such as my father hitting her, even though these incidents were recently witnessed by someone (*four times*, according to her once-a-week housekeeper: *several times*, said another of my father's caregivers). The only rationale for her denial that makes any sense is that just as Mom can't fully comprehend that she allowed herself to be an emotionally and physically abused wife, she also can't fathom being a verbally abusive, cruel mother.

It's occurred to me that my mother might also suffer from CTE; after all, my father hits hard with the arm that still functions, and he always aims for the head or the gut.

But I know what I heard. Her anger simply got the best of her.

Just as my father's anger still gets the best of him.

No Place Like Home

Ironically, it was my father who came forward first with the proverbial olive branch: He called me one day out of the blue and asked if Jay and I wanted to meet Gwen and him at a restaurant called Barone's in Toluca Lake.

Of course I said yes, and we met the following week, while Mom sat at home.

We had a nice, cordial meal together; by this time Gwen was about twenty and preparing to transfer to UC Irvine, and my father was sixty.

I don't recall anything special about that night other than the event feeling more like a business meeting than a family reunion;

the four of us were on good behavior, and it was *Conversation Lite* during the meal…probably similar in mood to that final gathering at Appomattox.

I still don't know what possessed Dad to reach out back then, but I like to think that this was the type of behavior—thoughtful, compassionate, generous—that he might've regularly demonstrated had his probable CTE not stained so much of his personality.

But I'll always be grateful to him for that evening.

Always.

CHAPTER 10

◆

Giving Thanks

"The stuffing's gotta be ready by now," I told Miriam, as she stirred the turkey gravy steaming atop the stove. "Be right back." I headed out the back door to the garage (my former digs), where my mother's microwave sat mostly unused; due to Mom's quasi-hoarding behavior, every flat surface inside their home was crammed: papers and Depression-era tchotchkes and framed pictures and copies of the *Conservative Chronicle* and medications and notes to herself.

Hence, room for the microwave there was not.

Miriam and I were there because we had received an impassioned plea from Gwen to spend some time with our parents due to the impending presence—in Gwen's small house—of out-of-state in-laws. So, after texting each other several times, Miriam and I constructed a traditional carb-heavy menu, and then I called our mother to let her know she and my father wouldn't be alone on Thanksgiving.

Once in the garage, I discovered that the corn-bread stuffing and the macaroni and cheese I'd brought were both steaming and bubbling, so I lifted them from the contraption with pot holders and made my way back into the main house.

Just inside the back door I was stopped by Naiara, the kind Salvadoran woman who'd been cleaning my parents' home once a week for the past decade. She clutched my shoulder and insistently pushed it down, so my ear would be at her mouth's level. "Meester Nolan hits your mama," she whispered intently.

"What?" I stood up and turned to her, eyes wide. "He hits her?"

She replied with a single, deliberate nod, her mouth a grim line. "In de face. Four times I see it."

I closed my eyes and sighed. "You've seen him hit her in the face four times?"

"*Sí.* Four." She held up a hand with four fingers extended. Then she mimed what she'd seen by squeezing her own forearm and then backhanding herself in the face.

"I saw him squeeze her arm once," I said. "Hard."

Her eyes bugged. "Yes! So hard she cries out! Then he hits her face. I tell him, *Why you not be nice to Miss Nolan? You want to go to nursing home? You hurt her and you go to nursing home!* Then he cries and he say he don't want go there." Naiara's face hardened into a mask of indignation. "I tell him, *You be nice,* but he still hit Miss Nolan. *Four times.*"

"Thank you for telling me, Naiara."

"I so sorry. Your mama cry when we talk about it."

"She told me he's never hit her." And I wanted to add, *So she's lying to me,* but I didn't.

At that moment Miriam rounded the corner and Naiara scurried off.

Miriam caught my expression. "What?"

"Naiara just told me she's seen Dad punch Mom in the face. Four times."

"God, no." Miriam grimaced as she crossed her arms and propped herself against the counter for support. "What do we do?"

"It's Thanksgiving, so we won't speak of this anymore today. Let's talk tomorrow. OK?"

"OK." Miriam turned but then swiveled back to face me. "I could kill him," she stage-whispered.

"I could help you," I replied, and we each went back to our food prep.

During the meal I looked my father in the eye anytime we spoke, and I saw that his gaze was clear. He asked me how things were going at school, and when I told him how much I liked the new principal, my voice was cheerful.

But inside I was seething. *Your mama cry when we talk about it.*

We made it through dinner and Miriam volunteered to stay longer with my parents, because I needed to make an appearance with Jay at his family's across town and then stop by our neighbor's house to have a glass of wine.

Much to my surprise, I fought angry tears all the way home. Anger that my father would do this after all my mother had sacrificed to keep him alive, and after my threatening him with arrest.

And anger at my mother for lying to me and protecting him— for how long was anyone's guess.

So I wondered once again: What had I witnessed as a child that had made me stand in front of Mom crying, *Don't hit her...* or chatter comfortably until Dad walked into the room, causing me to launch into a stream of stammering and stuttering so severe I made Porky Pig sound eloquent?

I'd questioned my mother about this several times through the decades, and she always gave me the same response: *Of course I was afraid he'd hit me, but your father never did. He came close, though.* This became one of the few things I respected about him, because at least Dad was somehow able to stand behind the most universal line of decency—if not for his children, then at least where his wife was concerned.

But Naiara's revelation changed everything.

And now I realized that the line I'd imagined him hanging ten on was written in chalk.

That night during our neighbor's party—where I was predictably slamming chardonnay—my phone rang, so I sprinted to an area in the yard where no one could overhear me.

"Do you have a sec?" Miriam asked, her voice noticeably meek.

"What's up?"

"I lost it with Dad. I totally blew up at him."

I began pacing in a wide circle. "*Tell me everything.*"

"After Mom and I watched *South Pacific*—which was totally cool, and it's been so long since I've seen that side of her—we went in to check on Dad and saw he had diarrhea again, so after cleaning him up he started complaining about how I was moving him and he started making all these noises and I got frustrated and said, *Are you going to hit me now like you hit Mom?* And he tried to deny it so I just laid into him. I was mean. And I told him I knew everything, but I didn't say who told me. I even reminded him about knocking out my teeth when I was six and how I've always had trouble with them, including the four-thousand-dollar implant I needed recently. All thanks to him."

"Miriam, I'm so proud of you!" My pacing was frenetic now, so I looked over at the other partygoers to see if anyone was watching me. *I must look like a madman.* "This needed to happen!"

"*But I was mean.* He could see the hatred in my eyes. I was practically screaming at him. Maybe I shouldn't've done it. It's Thanksgiving."

"That's what he gets. It was coming to him, no matter what day it was. And if it's the truth, it's not mean. *Truth heals.* You did the right thing."

"Do you think so?" Miriam asked weakly. "Really?"

"Yes. And I'm just so proud of you. I think his soul needed to hear this from you. He's heard it from Gwen, then from me, and now from you. What did Mom say?"

"She denied that he'd hit her but admitted about his twisting her arm. She was really strange. She seemed really neutral about it all. I don't get it."

"It's because she was lying," I told her. "Again, I'm so proud of you. You stood up to the bully."

"What do we do now?"

"Let's talk tomorrow."

The next morning I was awake by four, my mind hamster-wheeling until a bleary-eyed Jay brought me coffee at six.

By eight we had the dogs leashed for their morning walk.

The late-November morning was brilliant and clear: an arching sapphire sky; trees with leaves the colors of red and yellow and orange balloons; a refreshingly brisk chill in the air. Jay and I chattered nonstop about the events of the day before, about work, about the immunology he'd just begun for his allergies, all while correcting

Romeo's wild antics: barking rabidly at other dogs, lunging at squirrels half a mile away, pulling like a Clydesdale on his harness.

Three blocks from home I felt my phone vibrate: Miriam.

"Good morning. Are you OK?" I asked.

"Yeah…" Her voice trailed off. "But I think I've got a problem."

"What?"

"As an RN," Miriam explained, "I'm a mandated reporter. If I don't meet my mandate I could lose my license. This feels sticky to me."

"Who are you mandated to call in a situation like this?"

"Adult Protective Services."

"Then let me call," I told her. "I'm a mandated reporter as well, but only when it comes to kids…I think."

"Would you? I had to take a Xanax last night. This really has me twisted up inside."

"I have no trouble calling it in, and after they give me the report number I'll give it to you. Mandate met."

Miriam sighed. "Are you sure?"

"I'll call as soon as we get home from our walk."

Unfortunately, I'd needed to call in Suspected Child Abuse Reports many, many times over the course of my tenure as a public school teacher, so I was familiar enough with the process that I knew the 800 number by heart.

But the number to Adult Protective Services necessitated a quick online search.

Less than a minute later I punched the numbers into my phone.

It rang twice.

"Adult Protective Services, this is Carmen speaking. Are you calling to report elder abuse or neglect?"

"Yes," I told her. And then I relayed my account.

Carmen was articulate and professional. I figured she'd heard it all. She asked me a few questions; then I asked her specifically about my sister meeting her RN's mandate. Finally, we both had everything we needed, so she gave me the six-digit report number and a contact telephone number to call if I had any further questions.

"Thank you for your time, Carmen," I told her.

"It's no trouble," she replied. "I'm so sorry this happened."

I could tell from the tone of her voice that she meant it, and I felt sudden tears pushing the backs of my eyes. "I appreciate it. Have a good day."

"You too."

It was done.

I called Miriam, relayed the information to her, and asked her to please keep Gwen in the loop. Sounding relieved, she told me she would.

About twenty-four hours later, with Jay and the dogs up in the mountains, I received a voicemail from Alexander, the social worker assigned to our case. He would be available only for the next hour at his number, but I could also reach him on Monday from eight to five. And because of my circumstances—at our cabin where cell service was scant—I decided that waiting to return his call was my better choice.

Jay and I went about our day: brunch with two of our best friends, Art and Claudine, and their best friends Joe and Liz, a delightful retired couple from Arizona. And though our ages spanned thirty-plus years, our conversation was spirited and the laughter rocked and rolled steadily.

Two hours later we said our goodbyes, took our dogs on their walk, and then settled down to make a relaxing evening.

Around dinnertime my phone rang. It was Gwen. "Mom said the police showed up at her house this afternoon: two big officers. They grilled her for some time, and then they went into Dad's room and scared the bejeezus out of him."

I looked over at Jay to see if he was listening, but he was deep inside his laptop. "What did the police tell him?"

Jay looked up.

"They said if Dad hit Mom, he'd go to jail. And apparently, they were pretty convincing." Gwen's voice was giddy, and her evident happiness took the twist out of my shoulders. I felt myself relax.

Jay was still staring.

"I'm glad they said he'd go to jail next time," I said, watching Jay's eyes widen. "Did Mom tell them the truth, or did she lie to them?"

"I know she didn't tell them about him punching her in the stomach."

"Stomach? When did he do that?!"

"She swore me to secrecy not to tell you or Miriam," Gwen confessed. "She wants you both to have a relationship with him—"

"—and she figures if we knew he was hitting her, we would hate him even more than we already do."

"Yep."

"Was this recently or a while ago?"

"I think it was recently."

"I *knew* she was lying. I just wonder for how long. Months or decades?"

"I don't know," Gwen answered. "But remember, it was after his arrest for DUI that he stopped drinking for good. Being in jail is something that scares the hell out of him."

I'd forgotten about him being arrested for drunk driving: Back in 1987, when coming back from a meeting with clients, he sideswiped a car about two blocks from home. The entire episode had cost him about four thousand dollars and a night behind bars.

That night, after Jay and I finished dinner and were sitting in front of the fire with Romeo and Princeton, my mind began sinking into a dark place. *A very dark place.*

I realized that so many of the standards—and the shame—I was raised with were shams. *A man never hits a woman,* my father told me repeatedly. *Always tell the truth,* my mother drilled into my head. *You rejected him.* The masks of respectability our family wore. The smiling photographs of us as kids. The cardboard stand-ins for love and support that were my parents.

The fire dancing inside the brick hearth hypnotized me as I imagined myself yelling at my father and confronting my mother.

I sank deeper.

"I need to talk this out," I mumbled to Jay. "And I need you to dig down into that wonderful bag of compassion you have, because I know you're sick of hearing this, but I need to get this off my chest."

"Got it."

"I've got this screaming in my head. I'm thinking thoughts I've never had before. I hate them both so much for lying to us. It's all crumbling, the last bits of any good I was raised with. I want him gone. This just has to end."

"I know. I've had those same thoughts. And he'll be gone soon. He has to."

"We've been saying that for years—"

"He'll be gone soon," Jay interrupted. "And you know it."

I sighed. He was right. "What amazes me is how perceptive I was as a child. That even as a toddler I steered clear of him; I understood, somehow, that inside him was this demon, this unlovable monster. I knew it even back then, Jay. *I knew it!* Yet my mother always blamed the failure of our relationship on me, saying *I rejected him.*"

"I think that's one of the most horrible things she ever told you," Jay said, his eyes reaching into mine. "And it points to how sick she is. How evil she is. They deserve each other."

I thought, *No one deserves my father,* but I could see his point. Jay had been raised in a Mexican American family that was as big as it was loving, with two parents who built a real estate empire literally with their bare hands and made certain—through copious self-sacrifices—that each of their seven children entered adulthood working, and excelling, in the career of their choice. Stories about our family had given Jay nearly three decades of headaches and head scratching.

"But you know what's great?" I asked. "I don't want to hurt myself—it's not like the old days when I would get so angry at them I used to take it out on myself."

"Like when you'd imagine yourself crashing your VW van into their front yard's tree?"

"Exactly." I smiled. "I think my anger's in exactly the right place now."

"That's great to know." Jay stifled a yawn.

"I know it's kinda late," I said. "I think I'm ready for bed."

"Me too." Jay held his arms wide and I fell into his embrace. He held me for a few moments, and then we released each other. "Are you OK?"

I nodded. "Thanks for listening."

"You're welcome."

CHAPTER 11

◆

Self-Pity Is Better than None*

"They scared the hell out of your father," my mother reported to me. "I really wish you'd asked my permission before calling them."

Asked your permission? "But you aren't honest with me," I argued. "You lied to me. And you told Gwen not to tell Miriam or me about him socking you in the stomach."

"It was partially my fault. I'm mean to him sometimes—but *I do not lie*," she added.

"You told Gwen not to tell me or Miriam that he hit you, so you were lying by omission, which you always taught me was *wrong*."

"He's never hit me," she insisted. "He's swung at me, but I ducked."

"What if next time you don't duck fast enough?"

"I know how to gauge him. When he's like that, I stay away."

"But you can't stay away!" I shouted. "You're changing his diapers and checking his insulin and giving him injections. And I don't believe *he's never hit you*." I thought back to my childhood. "Remember me standing in front of you waving my arms? *What did I witness?*"

"We all knew what he was capable of. But he never hit me."

"I don't believe you."

Silence.

"A social worker is going to show up in the next few days," I told her, trying to move the conversation forward. "They only want to offer some suggestions to help you, maybe find a way to get Dad some better care."*

---

* From *Housekeeping Hints* by Phyllis Diller.

76

"You should've asked my permission," she snapped once more.

"I've gotta go."

"Goodbye, then." She hung up.

I walked back to my classroom shaking my head: *On some level she wants this.*

A few days later my father was admitted to the hospital again. This time for skyrocketing blood sugar—590—and dehydration. He'd also been vomiting.

"Maybe he had another heart attack," I suggested to my mother over the phone one afternoon.

"I hadn't thought of that. Why do you think so?"

"Because he always vomits when he has one. Remember when he was admitted to the hospital back in 1999, the first time? He was throwing up like crazy and his head was rolling back on his neck."

Mom was silent. And then: "Yes, I remember that. Are you going to visit him?"

I ran through my mental checklist. "I can stop by there on Sunday. But not until then."

"That would be nice."

I hesitated. "Mom, you know I'm a better son to him than he was a father to me."

A heavy sigh blew through my phone. "I know you were. And you still are."

"I'll talk to you later."

Sunday arrived, so Jay and I decided I'd run my errand to the hospital, and then afterward we'd begin our relaxing Sunday with a champagne brunch.

I made my all-too-familiar journey to Glendale Adventist, checked in at the front desk, and rode the elevator up to the fifth floor, where I found Dad asleep in his bed, a tangle of tubes and wires attached to every patch of exposed skin.

I stood looking at him for a minute or two, trying to decide if it would be worth the trouble to wake him.

Finally: "Dad?"

No response.

"Dad?" I repeated, louder.

My father opened first his left eye and then his right, took one look at me, and closed his eyes again.

Had he fallen asleep? Or was he just pissed off and telling me to *get lost*?

I waited, shifting from one foot to the other. And then I left.

Riding the elevator down to the lobby, I was giddy; I'd done my duty, and Sunday was now mine.

Two days later, my father was released to my mother's care.

"I can't believe she's doing this again," I told Miriam.

"That's not the worst part," Miriam began. "She canceled his caregivers again; when I went over to watch a Christmas movie with her, she told me she sent Bryan home."

"*Why?*"

"Because she thinks I'll clean his diaper and put him to bed." Miriam chuckled. "But not anymore. I told her if she does that again she's on her own. I'm done."

Two weeks went by and I heard nothing back from the social worker from Adult Protective Services, and I wasn't going to ask my mother if anyone had visited. So I put it out of my mind, knowing I'd done what I needed to.

On some level she wants this.

Three days later, my father was back in the hospital again—this time with *low* blood sugar.

I went over to my mother's and found her disheveled and surly, the drapes in their house drawn tight against the daylight.

She looked even frailer than I'd remembered; it seemed she'd aged five years in the few weeks since Thanksgiving. Bracing myself, I asked how she was doing.

"Horrible," she replied. "I'm completely exhausted."

"You look it," I told her. "There was a woman down the street whose husband had terminal cancer. She was his primary caregiver and died six months before he did."

Mom fingered the wattle under her chin. "I've heard of things like that happening."

"He can't come back here," I told her. "It's clear that you can't care for him anymore."

"If he goes to a nursing home, it'll devastate him emotionally and he'll die."

"You need to make a choice Mom. It's either him or you."

She laughed.

*   *   *

"She's got bags of candy in the house," Gwen told me over the phone. "She bought them at Walgreens; with the holidays, all the candy's on sale."

"I'll call her," I said.

"Are you sure you want to do that?"

"Of course I don't *want* to," I said, chuckling bitterly, "but it needs to be done."

I ended the call with my sister and called my mother.

"Hello?"

"Hi, Mom, how are you?"

"*Sur-vi-ving,*" she slurred.

"Gwen said you've got Halloween and Christmas candy hidden all over the house."

"So…what if…I do?"

"You know when your blood sugar gets high your kidneys shut down and you can't think straight. And Dad's supposed to be coming home from the nursing home. How can you supervise his care?"

"My thinking is perfectly fine," Mom snapped. "And it's none of your business if I want to eat candy and die."

"But you won't die," I argued. "You'll wind up in the hospital, and your kids will need to drop everything and visit you and talk to your doctors, and you'll be on dialysis. Is that what you want?"

"It's my business—and you'll just need to accept it…just like there are things about you that I had to learn to accept. The way you went in *that* direction."

Oh, so she's still pissed about Joseph Nicolosi and his sham therapy.
"Mom, this isn't about my being gay. It's about you and your blood sugar and Dad coming home."

"I don't appreciate the way you're talking to me with such anger."

"Can you at least promise me you'll do your best to monitor your blood sugar?"

"I'm not making any promises to anyone."

"Can you promise me, yes or no?"

"No."

"Then I'm communicating this to my sisters."

"It's my business if I have candy hidden in the back of my freezer. And if I die tomorrow from my blood sugar, that's my business too."

"But it becomes everyone's business if you mow down some nice Armenian family in a crosswalk because your blood sugar is 560—"

She hung up on me.

That evening, with dinner in the oven and the afternoon sun tucked behind the bristled, brown hills, Jay and I steeled ourselves for the coming week inside the healing waters of our Jacuzzi, while the dogs scampered off to retrieve tennis balls for our usual game of fetch.

After sipping sauvignon blanc from his plastic, long-stemmed wine glass, Jay tipped back his head. "Have you given any more thought to writing that book you're considering?"

With the foaming water now reaching up to my neck, the scalding bubbles worked their magic on my perpetually aching lower back. "You mean where I interview other people who've dealt with an abusive parent who's dying?"

"Yep."

I waved my hands in the air. "*Too depressing*—and the last thing this world needs is another Jonestown."

Jay laughed. "But I'll bet lots of other people are going through what you and your sisters are experiencing."

"Doesn't mean anyone would want to read about it."

"But…what about a book that could be informative, in a *self-helpy* kind of way?"

I thought about Jay's proposition. "Only if I could interview therapists…or other professionals who're practiced at helping people get through this insane process with their sanity intact."

"Then do that." Jay took another airy sip as Princeton dropped the ball into the fizzing water near my shoulder. "You know more therapists than anyone I've ever met—*I can't imagine why*—so it's not out of the realm of possibility."

I snatched the tennis ball and lobbed it over onto the far strip of grass; and as I watched Princeton scamper off to retrieve it, I made a mental list of the licensed clinicians I knew. "You're right." Excited, I gulped more chardonnay. "Doc, Terry, Carol…Adrian, even Cissy might be interested in the project. And each one has contacts with other qualified people; like, maybe someone knows a neurologist who's familiar with CTE. Maybe I…I could even interview Brandy from high school—we used to call her mom *Vlad the Impaler*—and Jake; with what they've all gone through with their parents, maybe they'd benefit from sitting for an interview." I paused. "I'll…put together some notes tonight."

"Think it over." Jay raised his glass to me. "But it *could* be a great read—and it might help *a lot* of people."

"I'll email Brandy and Doc tonight to see if either would be interested."

With darkness graying the yard and flattening the tree branches into silhouettes, we turned off the water jets, toweled ourselves dry, and—with our beloved boys trotting at our heels, tennis balls clenched between determined jaws—made our way back into the house.

CHAPTER 12

◆

A Shot of Brandy*

I double-clicked Brandy's email (her actual text is included here): I know I have a toxic parent who never seems satisfied with anything I do, but being the only child I still have to do everything the way she wants which is insanity... there is so much anger in me that when I come home from being her "whipping girl" I usually unleash it on my husband...if you want to hear shit like that...I got stories!!! I was bulimic for 10 years trying to be the perfect skinny daughter for her I could never be...I am wondering how I am going to deal with her passing...will I be relieved and feel the ultimate guilt for the feeling of relief??? Call me...lets go away for a weekend???

I snatched my iPad and trotted into the kitchen to show Jay, who was pushed up to the kitchen counter bar meticulously examining an *Architectural Digest*, with both dogs curled in opposition around the base of his barstool like a Pisces symbol.

I slipped my iPad under his nose and tapped the glass. "Look!"

Jay scanned the message as a Lilliputian rock slide emanated from the ice maker inside our freezer. "That should make you happy."

"But it's going to be a tough interview; I remember Brandy's mom from when we were teenagers, and she made my father look like Jimmy Stewart in *It's a Wonderful Life*."

Jay laughed. "No one's that bad."*

---

* Broken into two chapters to spare the reader excessive grief.

"Brandy mentioned getting together for a weekend. Would you have any objection to us going up to the cabin?"

"Of course not. I think you should do it."

"Maybe she could take the train…up from Orange County to Chatsworth," I suggested, thinking aloud, "and I could pick her up from there?"

"Sounds good—when's dinner ready?"

The timer beeped on cue, and I made my way over to the oven. "This is going to happen," I said, peering inside at the crusted salmon. "This book is going to happen."

*   *   *

As Jay and I fell into bed that night, I recalled those melancholy teen years and the evenings Brandy and I spent together: It was 1978…the era of *Saturday Night Fever* and Farrah Fawcett, Chemin de Fer jeans and Frye boots, sluggish Corvettes and exploding Ford Pintos.

We met in Latin class. Her name was Brandy.

Brandy's parents had emigrated from Romania in the early 1960s, so Brandy spoke Romanian fluently, but you'd never suspect this, because she also spoke English like a typical suburban teenage stoner. She had green eyes and that natural shade of chestnut-with-blond-highlights hair that made other girls seethe; she was also wonderfully athletic and lean, and she sported a pug nose, straight teeth, and a *fuck you* attitude.

Brandy was as irreverent as she was hilarious, and we spent *lots* of time together.

The last time I'd seen Brandy was at her massive country club wedding—in 1982—to a man I didn't particularly like (the feeling was mutual). Eventually, Brandy discovered she didn't like him either, because—as I was soon to discover—after bearing him a son and daughter and building a career for herself as a prep school educator, Brandy began an affair with a younger man and filed for divorce.

The years churned along and we lost touch.

Then Facebook came along.

* * *

The streamlined commuter train slowed to a stop at the Chatsworth Metro station, and Brandy leapt off the platform looking—at fifty-four—exactly as I'd remembered her at twenty-one—with a crease or two added around her eyes for good measure.

"You look fantastic!"

We gripped each other in hugs.

"I'm so happy to see you!"

* * *

An hour or so later, with our groceries unloaded inside the cabin's fridge, and the sun inching behind the western mountaintops, we were ready.

"Sure you want to be sober for this?" Brandy asked, settling herself atop one of the countertop's barstools and holding out the tiny marijuana pipe she'd brought along.

"Work is work," I replied. "But I brought plenty of wine for afterward." I fiddled with my voice recorder. "Ready?"

"No."

"Then let's get started: What's your first memory of your mom?"

"Oh *Jesus*," Brandy groaned, leaning her elbows on the countertop. She paused, looking around uneasily. "OK. I'm…a little girl picking flowers in the backyard and trying to spell out M-O-M in the driveway with those flowers; I'm so proud of myself, and I can't wait to show her, so I run inside. *Mommy, Mommy come!* So she sees the flowers and says, *Brandy, what kind of a mess did you make here?! You clean this up right now!!* Then she goes back into the house."

"Nice," I said.

"And that's my first memory." Brandy sparked her lighter, took a hit off her pot pipe, and then offered it to me again.

"Chardonnay is my drug of choice," I told her. "Tell me more."

"I was trying to show her my love," she continued, blowing out her words in a plume of white exhaust, "and I got stepped on. That's pretty much the way it's been ever since. There's always been something wrong with whatever I do: She says, *Why did you do it that way?* Or, *That's stupid,* or, *Who does things like that?* It's rare that I ever get a compliment, and if I do there's always a *but* attached."

"Did she hit you as a child?" I asked, snapping open a bottle of sparkling water.

"*Yes!* And she'd always come back for more. She'd start spanking and then go away, but then she'd come back; I'd lie in bed knowing she wasn't finished. She'd hit me with her hand—on my butt—or she'd slap my face with both hands. But as I got older, she saw I was a physical girl and could punch back—"

"So it was all with the mouth?"

"And how she could one-up me and prove herself better. *Just wait 'til you're a mother.* And I'd say, *Being a mother was the best thing for me, and I raised two wonderful kids.* Then she'd tell me, *Just wait 'til you're fifty!* And I'd I tell her, Mom, *I'm fifty! And I'm loving it!*"

"Does she still try to one-up you?"

"When she talks about me to other people it's *allegedly* complimentary," Brandy replied, "and she says lots of good things; people tell me, *Your mother's so proud of you.* But for me it's the opposite."

"Why?"

"Maybe because she didn't want to be a mom. In fact, before I was born my dad told her, *All you got to do is have the baby and I'll take care of her.* My dad loved me so much that she got jealous. He's been devoted to me for fifty-four years, and he tells me, *You are my gold.* But my mother calls me *swine. You are swine.* That's the word she uses for me. *Swine.*"

"Since you're swine," I said, "tell me about your accomplishments."

Brandy stopped fiddling with her pot pipe and looked up, her jade eyes shining. "Should I brag about myself?"

"Tell me how wrong that label is."

"I've raised two fantastic kids," Brandy began. "I put a man through college. I was head of my department at Faraday Prep, where

I've been teaching for thirty-two years; I have a master's and a math degree, I graduated third in my high school, and I got straight As in college; I play the drums, and I play volleyball at fifty-four like I did at twenty-two. I do horseback riding, and I snowboard like a guy; I started surfing at thirty and got OK at it; I've bought and paid off four houses, and I have a hundred and fifty thousand dollars saved in the bank."

"So how does it feel when your mother looks at you and says, *You're swine?*"

"All that other stuff doesn't count," Brandy muttered, visibly deflating. "And as a mommy myself, I could never imagine saying that to my children; I celebrate everything they do."

"Does she ever ask you about your life?"

Brandy slammed down her fist, and my water glass jumped. "*Never!* The minute I start talking about myself the topic gets changed, or she'll find something wrong with what I said; when I got divorced, she even took my ex-husband's side. My dad says, *Let it go in one ear and out the other.* But I can't, because she's my mother.

"Of course she reminds me, *I never wanted to be a mom.* Dad was the only parent. He's the one that would come home from work and help me with my homework."

"Your mother didn't help you at all?"

"She was too busy running from store to store so she could save three cents on grapes. She was never tender; she used to complain about how much trouble it was to brush my hair. And she shamed me; when I was thirteen, she smelled my panties and said, *Oh, so stinky. You have discharge.* And I thought, *Well, how should I know about puberty? Of course I have discharge on my panties.*"

"What about when you had your first period?"

"She got so mad, because she had to wash the sheets! But she had her own hang-ups about sex: She'd say, *Just because you're getting fucked doesn't mean you're pretty; a pussy has no face.* That's the mother who brought me up. I used to ask, *Mom, do you think I'm pretty?* And she'd say, *No one's gonna kill themselves over you.* I used to have to wrap up my own Christmas presents.

"And on my wedding day," Brandy continued, "she came to my house and tried on four different outfits to check out which one looked best...*four different outfits* that I had to buy for her, and she wouldn't try them on the week or even the day before. My wedding day was all about her."

"Would you describe your mom as a narcissist?"

Brandy coughed, laughing. "And a *sadist*. She's cruel, and she revels in the unhappiness of others. She's envious and jealous and gossiping and always talking about how bad other people are."

I stepped to the freezer and retrieved the Trader Joe's eggplant Parmesan I'd brought up. "Did you ever have any nice moments with her?"

Brandy sparked her lighter and inhaled another hit. "We both loved movie stars. That was one of the few times we could bond: talking about the stars and who's married to who and who's going through problems. We connected through that."

"But that's also focusing on the negative," I pointed out.

"Mom *always* focused on the negative! She'd compare me to other girls and say, *Look how skinny she is.* Or, *You have such big calves, such short arms.* And I used to be a chubby girl, so she'd say, *You so chubby.* I had to wear 6X clothes; if you're a little bigger, it's the husky version for girls. And I *was* a chubby girl; I had broad shoulders. She'd say, *Why you have to wear 6X? They don't have good clothes in 6X.* And my favorite: *You don't need a top for your bathing suit. People will think you're a chubby boy. Just go.*"

"If you'd been the physical ideal of the daughter she wanted," I asked, "would she have treated you differently?"

"No, because she saw me as competition from day one."

I retrieved a jar of marinara from the cupboard and twisted off the lid. "She's eighty-seven now, yes?"

Brandy sipped more water. "Yep."

"Do you think she's faltering with her mind or body?"

"She can't get off the couch, and she has a caregiver because she can't go to the bathroom by herself. She'd call me in class and say, *I can't get to the bathroom! Get over here!* And I'd say, *I'm teaching second period!* I'd been taking care of her for three years before I found the caregiver.

"But even with the caretaker," Brandy continued, "she blames me for everything. She has such a *distorted* view of the truth. Her doctor told her, *Find another doctor because you don't listen to me.* Her health is terrible: She can't walk, she has swollen feet, and she was really, *really* heavy for a while, in spite of her being so critical of my weight. So now she's critical of my husband because he's sixty pounds overweight. She says, *What kind of wife are you that you can't get your husband to lose weight?*"

"Have you ever talked to your father about her?"

"Often," Brandy said, smiling wistfully. "He says, *Brandy, it's only a few more months that we're here. Just nod your head. Let it roll off.*"

"So he's never confronted her," I said. "He's allowed her to bully you all along?"

"It took me a long time to realize it was bullying behavior, and I never stood up to her. But I finally told her *fuck you* for the first time this past year."

"What was that about?" I began peeling and then slicing the yellow onion I'd brought.

"I took my dad to the beach and he got dizzy, *really dizzy* with the spins, so she yelled, *You're trying to kill your father.* So I said, *That's the opposite of the truth! Fuck you!* So now every time I see her, she says, *You gonna start with the fuck you? Well, fuck you back! Fuck you! Fuck you!* She can't hear, so she takes her hearing aid out so it's harder to communicate. She even sticks her fingers in her ears.

"The new thing is her caregiver Juliann spills my mom's poison on me. *Your mother wants her bracelet back.* My grandmother gave Mom this beautiful bracelet when she turned fifty, and Mom gave it to me when I turned fifty, but now she wants it back. She gave my son a car and now she wants it back. So now I hear it twice: once from mom and another from Juliann. So I said, *Mom, if you've got something to say, talk to me,* so she put her fingers in her ears and I tried to pull out her fingers and she started screaming, *She's hurting me!* And Juliann walked in and—*oh great*—I had my hands on my mom. But I've lived by *Honor thy father and mother* for fifty-four years; it's so ingrained in me. I would never physically hurt my mother.

"So now she has a whistle, and that's how she calls Juliann: She whistles and Juliann sees me with my hands on Mom's wrists."

"What else do you remember?"

"She said, *You were loose when you were young. You were fat and ugly, and you went out with any boy who liked you.* And the sad part is there's a grain of truth in that: I was chubby. I wasn't really popular. And if a boy gave me a second glance I'd look back at him, too. My mom said, *You'd sleep with anybody.* But I've only been with maybe ten guys in my entire life! She even called me a whore and said I was whoring with my dad! That I'm a coquette, and that I'm flirting with my dad! I said, *Are you kidding? I don't know how to coquette with a man, much less my dad!*

"She used to wake me up in the middle of the night because she counted the cookies and saw one was missing. *Did you eat that cookie?* One night she woke me up and said, *Did you eat my Cheetos?* I said, *Yeah I had some,* and she said, *You want some more?* And she smashed them into my face!"

"It's no wonder you had food issues." I shook my head. "It's even more amazing that you survived that."

"I had my dad. Thank God."

"And yet he allowed her to continue," I pointed out for the second time. "Are you angry at him for never shutting her down, for not protecting you?"

"She'd browbeat my father into doing everything for her," Brandy explained. "He'd go off to work; then on the weekends we'd get out while she'd clean. My dad and I would go skiing, go to the beach, go to the racetrack, or up to the mountains. They didn't spend any time together; he'd come back from work, eat dinner, watch hockey, and then go to bed.

"When my parents came to visit us, he'd talk to my husband, and she'd bring bags of candy and doughnuts and cookies and Twinkies and all the shit she never let me eat when I was a chubby little girl, but she'd bring it for my kids and leave it at my house, and it would torment me; I'd feel like shit and eat everything she brought and feel even worse."

"She was setting you up for failure."

"Yes!" Brandy exclaimed, clutching her pot pipe. "Setting me up for failure! She'd say, *I could not eat a cookie. How come you could not eat a cookie? I brought them for the kids. I'm not somebody who has to go to Weight Watchers for the rest of my life, like you.*

"*This past Monday she said she wants the camera my dad gave my son. I want the camera back or I want five hundred dollars. I said, Mom, I don't know where the camera is. Then she roars, LIAR! I want it back! And the car! I'm running out of money. You stole that car from me. You made me give it to your son!*

"And I've been telling myself, *I'm not going to fight with her anymore.* But on Father's Day, I had to come inside and play chess with my dad, and the whole fucking time she was criticizing me. And I didn't want to play chess, because I didn't want to take any of my dad's pieces—his rook—and I'm not that good at chess, but I couldn't kill my dad's pieces. I couldn't make him lose. Isn't that pathetic?"

I dug inside the lower cabinets, looking for the frying pan. "It's noble."

"And then my mom yells, *You got no patience! You can't even play a game of chess!*"

"My God!" I shouted, bolting upright. "Every word that comes out of her mouth is *poison*. How do you feel knowing that you were cheated out of a mom?"

Brandy's eyes spilled sudden tears. "*I wanted a mom so bad! So bad. It's gonna come,* I tell myself. *She's going to see that I'm her baby girl, that I'm part of her.* Last Christmas after twenty years of not spending it together—because Mom hates Christmas—I said, *Let me try to make a Christmas like my dad remembers.*"

"Oh no," I groaned, handing Brandy a paper towel. "Oh no..."

Brandy dabbed at her eyes. "I tried to make Christmas like I remembered, and we were going to open presents at night with cutlets. Mom used to make us eat carp before we could open our presents—do you know how many bones are in carp?"

"Um...no?"

"*Bleh!*" Brandy grimaced. "But one year she made cutlets. So I made cutlets, and potato salad, and peeled tangerines, and Parisian cake—*eight layers*—and that night, while we were having the cake, my dog ate half of it...but he was OK. My son and his fiancée and my daughter came, and it was a *beautiful* Christmas. And I couldn't believe my mother's response.

"The next day my mom called me and said, *I had a dream about you. In my dream, I felt like you were OK, you were OK.* She wouldn't even say *good. But everything you did was OK.* And I hung up and started crying, because *Jesus Christ, it was a compliment!* I was OK! Like she was saying, *I realize that part of you is me. And you're OK.* And that was my Christmas.

"But it's been downhill ever since..."

CHAPTER 13

◆

A Second Shot of Brandy

"I got her a caregiver because I couldn't take her to the bathroom anymore," Brandy continued. "I couldn't go to the doctor three times a week or do their shopping. Do you know she checks the receipt to make sure I didn't pick up ·the wrong milk? It's *Walgreens* for milk, *Ralphs* for food, *Albertsons* for the goddamn whatever…all because that's where she likes it from. So my whole free time is spent on them.

"But I thought, *That's how it should be, I'm an only child, and my dad has given his life to me. He's the best dad possible. I want to pay them back.*"

"You want to pay *him* back," I interjected, turning on the oven to preheat. "But she comes with the deal."

"They're my *parents*," Brandy clarified, while carefully pinching more weed into her pipe, "and *Honor thy father and mother* is part of me, like I said. I'd see them and then I'd come home and take it out on my husband, so my husband started fighting back; and I'm so egocentric that I believe everything bad is my fault; I take the blame for everything."

"Do you find it comfortable to be the victim?"

"I do…and I like to play the martyr. But I'm an overachiever, and I can do ten things in the same time someone else does two; I carry heavier burdens than most."

"You were well trained," I reminded her. "Has your mother had any hospitalizations?"

"She had a hip and a knee replacement and was screaming so loud in the recovery, the staff couldn't take it and sent her home!" Brandy touched her pipe to her lips and sparked another hit.

I switched on the burner atop the oven. "So what's it like taking her to the doctor?"

"It's a goddamn four-hour process," Brandy answered, exhaling a smoky plume.

"How do you feel during those doctor visits?"

"Like I'm her bitch and I can't breathe…and I know she's going to say something crazy, and people will look at me like, *How do you deal with this?* Then on the way home I'll be berated the whole time, and I dread it for days before we go.

"One time my husband stood up for me. He said, *You can't talk to her like that! She's always doing her best for you!* So she told him everything that she's been holding back: *You're fat, Brandy should be in jail for smoking pot, and you should be in jail too.* Stuff like that. She laid into him so much that when we got into the car, he actually started crying. He said, *Your mother is so mean! She knows exactly which buttons to push.* And when I saw him crying, I thought, *There's no way this is happening again. It's my burden to carry.* I didn't want anyone else to go through this."

Brandy paused while tracking a squirrel outside in the fading light, as it bounced along the deck railing and then scampered up a pine. "Every gift I ever gave her she returned. I'd say to her, *You return everything, Mom.* And she'd say, *I wish I could return you!* I swear to God she said that! *I wish I could return you.* How'm I supposed to feel after my mother says that to me? I'm a sensitive person who comes from sensitive people; my father cries reading kids' stories, and I cry at Subaru commercials—you know, the ones with the dogs?"

"I cry almost every day." I tossed sliced onions into the sizzling pan.

"So my mom says, *You're so stupid and childish. You love to cry.*"

"How did you stay sane?"

"Maybe I'm not sane; ask my husband, maybe I'm not sane." Brandy fiddled with the pipe in her hands, nervously screwing and unscrewing the chamber lid. "I…I don't want to risk being happy, because I'm afraid God will zap me," she whispered. "If I ever get dressed up and look in the mirror and think, *I'm beautiful,* the first thought that follows is, *God's gonna make you ugly. God's gonna punish you.* It's her voice in my head."

"It goes beyond toxicity," I noted, stirring the now sizzling onions. "She's *radioactive.* And I'm angry at your father for not protecting you! Yes, he overcompensated a lot, but still—"

"My dad got the same shit I got, and he stuck up for me when I lived at home, but since then she's attacked me covertly, and I wasn't gonna run to my dad, because it was between Mom and me. I didn't want to bother him, only to protect him. He just wanted to be Grandpa.

"My father is a saint," Brandy went on. "He did *everything* for her. But I don't blame him…except to wonder, *Why the fuck didn't you get out of there? Why didn't you find someone else?* And I know why: Romanians don't get divorced."

I stopped stirring and glared at Brandy. "So the million-dollar question is—"

"How will I feel when she dies?" Brandy looked away, gazing at something inside her mind. "My first thought is *relief.* The second is *regret* that I'll never get what I want. But it could've been worse…I could've had *two* bad parents." She caught my eyes again. "Why don't I focus on the good that my father was?"

"Because your mom's the turd in the punch bowl," I replied. "You can't enjoy the sweetness of the punch or the maraschino cherries or those delightful slices of fresh pineapple with that turd floating around; she's polluted everything."

"And she's the one telling me *the turd is my fault!*" Brandy exclaimed. "She points to me and screams, *She should be taking care of us! Not the caregiver!* So I told her, *You think I'm ungrateful? Go ahead and hit me! Is that what you want? I can take it.* And she says, *Hitting you would not be good enough for you! You need more!*"

I clutched my stomach. "That makes me nauseous!"

"*So I'll feel relief and regret,*" Brandy stated. "One time, if you can believe it, I asked her, *Why didn't you die already? I can't wait until you die.* That was when she was saying, *You're whoring with your father. I said, What do you mean I'm whoring with my father? She said, You flirt with your father like he's your boyfriend."*

"There's no shred of humanity in this woman," I stated, seeing now that my onions were burning. "So after she's gone?"

"Part of me—and I'll be honest—thinks my mother will come back to haunt me."

"Because you've never known life without her evil ghost?"

"Yeah, yeah." Brandy nodded. "And I'm afraid her voice in my head will stay after she's gone: *Look at that double chin. Look at how bad you look from the back. Look at your wrinkles. How is it that your husband is so fat! He's a piece of shit!*

"But thanks to my therapist, Mom's voice in my head is actually fading; maybe because I've been in therapy since I was twenty: five years for bulimia; three years for my mom; and counseling for my first marriage. My husband would go in and complain about my mother and why I didn't have the guts to stand up to her. It was all true. I was brainwashed."

"I'm amazed that you're so functional," I reiterated.

"As bad as my mother is? That's how *good* my father is. *I'm functional because of him.*"

"Did he ever play victim?" I asked.

"No, no, no." Brandy waved her hands. "When he could hear, he stood up to my mom. But when he lost his hearing, that's when he got depressed and became childlike, and that's when Mom became the monster she is. She held the money, paid the bills, planned vacations, but she didn't say shit to him, except to complain: *You know your father makes poops in his underwear?* she'd ask me. *I hate to clean his dirty pants!*

"*I'll clean his dirty pants,* I told her. And I'm so afraid he's gonna die first. But if my mom dies first, he'll live with us and have chickens in the backyard, and the first thing I'll do is take him to Romania for ten days. I'm not scared of anything…except that he'll die and not get a chance to enjoy the beach. He says, *You know the beach? Always different, always beautiful.* She yells at me when I take him there, but I don't give a shit no more.

"But Juliann doesn't want me to stir Mom up, because it makes her job harder. She tells me, *All your mom talks about is how bad you are, all day long! I know everything about you. All morning your mom's been preparing for you to come over, so she can say these things to you.*"

"It's like sport for her," I suggested, dumping a blob of marinara onto the charred onions.

"I think it's like sex," Brandy countered, "so she can *feel* something. I had a dream once that I was in charge of my mother's orgasms; that I was playing with her clitoris so she could get off. How sick is that?"

"But it's a perfect metaphor," I told her. "Giving your mother pleasure in the sickest way possible."

"And she lives for it…but what makes her unhappy is when I don't engage her; when I walk away, it makes her crazy."

"So how about walking away more?" I asked, covering the frying pan.

Brandy cracked a smile. "I just started. But then she summons me: She wanted her old bracelet back, she wants her car back… an old camera, whatever. So I gave her this bracelet back. And you know the witch from *Snow White*? The one with the googly eyes? I printed out a picture of that witch and taped it inside the box with her bracelet, so she opens it and says, *See how childish Brandy is?* I told my son what I did, and he started crying and said, *Mom, it's never gonna end! She wants you to fight her! You're fighting back just like her. You need to stop!*

"And my son is right." Brandy sighed. "When I fight with my husband, I turn into my mother; I go for his jugular, and any praise I've given him I can snatch away. That's why my mother is my burden to carry: I'm the only one strong enough."

Her words knocked into me like a wrecking ball. "There it is. *There it is.* Oh, there…it…is."

Brandy fluttered her eyes. "There's *what?*"

"You said, *She's my burden because I'm the only one strong enough.*"

"But I am," Brandy stated. "*Nobody's* as strong me."

"Have you always felt this way?"

Brandy tapped her pipe into the ashtray and then began reloading. "I've known for a long time that I'm the strongest one in the family. I'm even stronger than my mom."

"Of course you are!"

"I guess…" Brandy drained her water glass. "Even as a kid…I knew she needed help."

"Do you feel protective of her?" I asked. "Especially now, in her old age?"

"No— Well, I shouldn't say *no* that quick. I don't want my mom to suffer…" Brandy's face reddened as she choked on a sob. "If I could only make her happy, I would! When I found Juliann, I thought her life would be better and she'd calm down. *But she got worse.* Even still, I wouldn't want her to suffer."

"Even though she's made you suffer beyond the moon and stars?" I asked, transferring the frozen eggplant into a casserole dish.

"I don't want *anyone* to suffer," Brandy said, wiping away her tears. "Unless I'm mad; and my husband will tell you I'm the meanest person he knows; I know how to say *exactly* the thing you're scared of hearing."

"Because you had expert training."

"And the more I love you, the more I know about you, so the more I can make you feel like shit." Brandy began sparking her lighter again. "But when I was reading my high school journals a while back, I was surprised that there was no hate on those pages for her!"

"That's because you still believed you could grow up to meet her standards; you were still willing to mold yourself into what she wanted you to be."

"Yes."

I slid the casserole containing the eggplant inside the oven, closed the door, and leaned back against the counter. "You know what I found recently? A box filled with letters and cards that my mom saved…greeting cards I'd given them: Father's Day cards and things like that where I wrote, *Thanks for putting up with me.*"

"But you were a good kid," Brandy pointed out. "I remember."

"But I figured that if I apologized for myself—denigrated myself…and supplicated myself enough—that I'd be someone my dad could love. But there was *never* that love."

"I denigrate myself too." Brandy twirled the pot pipe atop the counter. "When I meet someone new, I expose my faults because I don't want anyone else to figure them out; I'm always putting myself down, and I play the idiot."

"Did it ever occur to you that if your second marriage fails, your mom wins?"

Brandy suddenly sat up, pointing at me. "She's laughed at me, saying, *You thought you could be happy with that second man!* And, *You don't love Joey anymore, do you?* I have moments of weakness, when I spill my guts to her, hoping she'll be the mommy I always wanted; she knows how to trick me to open up, and then she uses those words against me." Brandy's eyes searched mine. "If you asked her, *Who's the worst person in the world?* she'd say it was me. *A slap in the face is too good for you,* she tells me. So I asked her, *Mom, why do you hate me so much?* She says, *You know why.* I said, *Why? I don't know.*"

"What does she say?" I asked while retrieving my bottle of chardonnay from the fridge; I'd heard all I could without reinforcements.

"She says, *You know why.* She puts it back on me so I need to figure it out. Maybe it's because I'm not pretty enough or I'm looking old and haggard. *You're looking old and haggard; you got things hanging off you.* That's what she tells me now."

"Did you ever consider killing yourself just to get back at her?" I asked, knowing how often that thought had occurred to me.

"No, I love my life too much: I love my job, my husband, my children, my activities, my body. I love my strength and what I'm still gonna do."

"Are you hoping she'll die soon?" I uncorked the wine and poured myself a generous glass.

Brandy wiped her eyes with her sleeve and then picked up her pipe. "Yeah."

"But she's not even in a care facility," I pointed out. "And it sounds like her health is holding steady, so this could go on for—"

"Ten years, which makes me feel trapped, very trapped, and like time is passing me by, and my therapist says, *You go to a dark place when you're sad,* and sometimes I can't get out of bed—like, when Dumbledore in *Harry Potter* died, I couldn't get out of bed for a day, because he's pure good and he dies. I also can't get out of bed when I think my father's losing his grip on the earth, that he's not enjoying life because he's stuck with her. I can't take him to the beach or the racetrack, and he goes to sleep talking about Romania, and I could take him there, but he won't leave my mom." Brandy lit the pipe and sucked a hit. "So if my mom wasn't around," she squeaked, blowing out a cloud, "Dad could live with me, because he still smiles and walks and takes a shit by himself; did you know that my son won't go see his grandfather, because he's afraid of his grandmother?"

I pushed the corkscrew into the top of the wine bottle. "Now, *that's* sad."

"I've asked God, *Please let my mother die.* Not in a cruel way, but *Just let her go.* She's not happy and she's taking everyone down with her. So is she gonna go to hell?"

"It sounds like she's created hell for herself, and she's missed out on every opportunity to find happiness—and to make her daughter and her husband happy."

Brandy laughed. "You think?"

"Do you fear the joy you'll have when she's gone?" I asked. "Do you fear any happiness you might feel?"

Brandy paused. And then: "I never considered the happiness or joy I might feel; I think it'll be more like *relief.* Not joy. And *freedom.* I look forward to the *freedom to be my own person.* But if there's any possibility for spirits to haunt their loved ones, she'll do it; to this day, she threatens to *pay me back* for all of the unhappiness I've supposedly given her. *I'm going to get you!*"

"Well, that remains to be seen," I said, and then something occurred to me. "Do you think you'll be able to forgive her, either now or after she's gone?"

"I don't know," Brandy said, picking up her pipe. "Just like everything else, it remains to be seen."

"And in the meantime, *here's to you*." I held up my glass of wine, and she clacked it with her water glass just as my phone pinged.

Brandy smiled. "Here's to us both."

I swigged a gulp, looked down at my phone, and spotted a text from Doc Reed:

For interview: How about this Friday 3PM my office in Pasadena?

CHAPTER 14

◆

Maul In The Family:
Interview with Edward F. Reed, EdD

With my final professional task for the week drawing to a close, a sense of relief overtook me. I'd been helping the school's chorus teacher, and I loved watching her teach my kids—for the upcoming winter concert—the harmonizing strains of "Do You Hear What I Hear," a song that stirred my own emotions, having memorized those simple lyrics nearly half a century ago as an awkward, hopeful fifth grader.

When the bell finally sounded at two twenty-eight, I waved goodbye to Mrs. Spaulding and my students, hefted my leather satchel over my shoulder, and made the trek across the schoolyard to my car.

The better part of an hour later I was in Pasadena, lurching up the steps to the second floor, where I would interview Dr. Edward Reed, a clinician known to his clients as "Doc."

An imposing yet somehow ageless figure approaching his seventh decade, Doc escorted me into the cramped therapist's room that would serve as our recording studio, his six-feet-plus towering over my five-eleven. Looking equal parts Socrates and Midwest farmer—with a dash of Burl Ives—the doctor radiated a homespun sensibility as he listened to me highlight my goals for this book and then made the suggestion that I also include a section about how a teacher, such as myself, might recognize the signs of toxic parenting in his students.

I fiddled with the recorder's settings. "Can you tell me what your qualifications are and how long you've been practicing?"

"I'm licensed as a psychologist in the state of California," Doc began, his velvet baritone filling the room, "I have a theoretical clinical EdD in counseling psychology, and I've been practicing for about thirty-five years."

"That's impressive," I replied, meaning it. Then I checked my notes. "How would you describe effective parenting?

"Effective parenting," Doc began, "is the ability to know when you're *developing* a child versus *raising* a child. Few parents *develop* children. And I think it's not so much their fault, because they're only emulating what they experienced as kids, where being raised was more centered around the parent than considering first what the child needed to develop."

I'd never thought of that. "So what do you consider bad parenting?"

Doc looked away from me, his attention focused on the Chinese elm sweeping the air beyond the window. "That's huge, you know...*big*. I think if a child doesn't have a safe environment, or if the environment isn't made to *feel* safe, that's bad parenting."

"As a psychologist, do you think the long-term effects of bad parenting can be overcome?"

"When I've worked with children who've been abused, they tend to gravitate toward someone who listens, and they know if you're authentic and you care. And those kids—as young people and also as adults—tend to respond well to therapy; they can make significant changes."

"Do you think the term *toxic parent* is fair?"

"Oh yeah, because in this sense *toxic* means *crippling*...it's going to do something bad to you. And it does. *Toxic*—and I'm not sure who came up with that term—but it's just so appropriate. But we tend to only see it in a particular light, and I think you have to look at the many different forms of toxic parents." Doc nodded. "They kill the *emotional you.*"

"What commonalities do you see among adult children who're dealing with a parent who's killed—intentionally or not—their emotions, and now this same parent is dying?"

Doc paused, shifting in his chair. "Their natural instinct is to avoid," he began, "because they know the zingers won't stop. The adult child suspects their biggest hope is going to be smashed once more...and reality will destroy the magical thinking that *somehow this parent is going to make a miraculous change to validate the adult child's worth.* But I've only seen this happen once or twice in my career when that toxic parent was dying.

"But I think this is an extremely important time for the adult child of a toxic parent," Doc clarified. "It can be a beautiful time to rectify how they were impacted. And it's a truth-telling moment. Unfortunately, most people won't take advantage of this, but if they could, it would not only help themselves; I think it's even positively impacting on the parent. *You know, Mom or Dad*—or whoever it is— *you really harmed me when you did this...or when you hit me here...or were so unloving, and I really hate you for it.* Whatever those emotions are, to state them in a factual and clear way is healing, because the parent on some level *knows* they didn't do right by their child. And this *honesty* heals...*truth* heals...*transparency* heals. And my job is to try and get this work done prior to that death-scene experience. By the adult child being transparent, the parent will take that truth into their death, and hopefully something positive will come from it for the adult child. When you face yourself, that's when we grow."

"But what about when the parent has dementia," I asked, "and there's so little cognitively for that child to reckon with?"

"If this is a child who was abused," Doc explained, "to me there's nothing wrong with the one-act play—or soliloquy—when they can finally confront and tell them how they feel. It's very empowering... just as it's also empowering when the parent still does have those mental faculties, because the parent has the opportunity to come to terms with it. But either way, I couldn't care less about the condition of the parent; it's more important to heal that inner abused child so this individual can finally move on."

"It's more important to be authentic than to worry about how it's being received?" I asked.

"Exactly," Doc stated. "This authenticity is something really good. We tend to make people better in death than they were in life, and I never understood that. For example, my uncle Smokey was a jerk in life. And when he was dying he was still a jerk. And most people at the funeral were talking about this wonderful Smokey, and I was wondering, *Where the hell is he?*" Doc laughed. "Where's he at?"

"Which reminds me," I interrupted. "What if someone has already lost that parent, and the adult is still suffering from the parent's toxicity and there's no chance for a confrontation?"

Doc paused, reversing the cross of his legs. "You know there's a recent film, *Nebraska*, when the characters visit a graveyard and the old woman flashes the headstone and has a dialogue with someone who's six feet under; she blurts out what she was feeling about them all along. This is a practice that we use in therapy all the time; not the flashing part, of course"—he laughed—"but having a dialogue with your dead relatives.

"There are some lethal types of parents who can kill you *even after they're dead*, so we have techniques like writing a letter to them and perhaps tearing up the letter or having a ritual burning to end the relationship. This means, *yes*, you can end the relationship with toxic parents. But it's important that the adult child ends the relationship *on their terms*.

"They can say things like, *I've tried to deal with you for the last ten years as an adult, and you're just too much for me. I'm leaving.* And psychologically you *can* leave. However, most children *don't* leave; they're still emotionally attached. But there's nothing wrong with finally saying, *Fuck you, I'm outta here.* Because you know that anything further will damage you."

"So it's an act of self-preservation to accept that *you* are never going to change, and I need to live life on *my* terms?" I asked.

Doc smiled. "They might need to tell themselves, *I'll learn to live with a wounded heart, because I'll never have the mother or father I deserved.* And this makes that person more inclined to be a better parent with their own children by cutting it off; by never cutting that umbilical cord, you see people duplicating how they were raised. They become violent, or drinkers, or drug users, or they act out and abuse. There's intense anger in having been abused. But one of my favorite sayings is, *There's no problem too big that you can't walk away from,* and I think there're some parents you'd *better* walk away from."

"But what about the ensuing guilt?"

"The way you control people is by shaming and *guilting* them, and kids with toxic parents receive a tremendous amount of both—so the adult child will need to be certain that walking away is the only self-protective option.

"Frankly, shaming is one of the most destructive parenting behaviors, where the child is made to believe he doesn't count..." Doc paused. "Then again, parents should teach guilt in an *appropriate* way: If a child steals, he needs to feel guilty and to know he'll be held accountable. That's *healthy* guilt, so there's a place for guilt if it's balanced and used in a constructive way."

"Do you think a narcissistic or toxic person can change?"

"Um...*minimally* is probably the best you're going to get; more if it's treated early, because it's hardwired in the brain. I've seen change, but these were long-term patients. Toxicity is heavily ingrained... kind of like trying to get a Republican to think like a Democrat or vice versa."

"Is this ingrained because it's a child-rearing style they were brought up with?" I asked.

"Oh yeah," Doc replied, his deep laugh rumbling the room. "But if you have one loving parent and one that's destructive, at least you get a little sense of having value. But if you've got two crappy parents, you're probably not going to make it, to be frank—and if both crappy parents are there from the child's infancy, by the time therapy takes place, it's often too late."

My thoughts peeled back to what was going on with my father and what his death might mean for my sisters and me. "What feelings might an adult child feel when that toxic parent dies?"

Doc leaned back in his chair. "It's really mixed, because on some level there's genuine relief, but on other levels—especially if they haven't had therapy—they're going to feel conflicted because deep down, they'll want acceptance from Mom or Dad…they still want their love. And even after they die it can stay an open wound, a stinging wound."

"What about a year—or ten years—later?"

"That open wound is always part of you. And it gets projected out unless you become aware of it."

"So it's the awareness that matters?"

"You can't change anything without awareness."

"What advice would you have for an adult child of a toxic parent who's anticipating the death of that parent?"

"Take some time to process what you need to do for yourself to let that parent die—but don't focus on what's best for them; focus on what's in *your* best interest. You're going to still be around. So have that honest dialogue with your parent, and even if he or she tells you to get the hell away, at least you got a response and you got it off your chest."

"But what if my mother's got dementia or my father's terminally ill and I don't want to add to their burden? Or is this one of those *overloaded lifeboat* situations, where the parent is going to die and this is the final opportunity to act in what might seem like a selfish manner?"

"A *self-caring* manner, not a selfish manner," Doc clarified. "Big difference. It's *self-caring* because otherwise the adult child is doing what they did all their life, trying to protect their parent, or seeking their approval by *not dredging up all that old stuff.* But eventually you've got to start doing some work. Otherwise you're doomed."

"Might the adult child think, *I'll just suffer through this, and soon they'll be dead and I'll be fine once they die?*"

"That's rationalization—you're still protecting the parent." Doc paused. "And you know it's much harder to hit an invisible target than a visible one," he added, chuckling.

"Do you think a toxic parent is capable of love?"

"That's a…tough one"—Doc cleared his throat—"but I'll tell you what just hit me: *No.* Because I think a child can be affected so badly, so early in his life, that his spirit is killed. His soul. We see this in sociopaths, where they weren't developed at all, or their development was arrested. Those kids under two from really abusive families where no one shared love or made them feel safe missed out on a critical period and can't pick it up again. Like language, if you don't learn to *goo-goo* and *da-da* by two or three, you're not going to be talking. Development—in language as well as love—is critical.

"But today, children are so much more exposed to ideas and thoughts from people other than their parents, for better or for worse. And this could be a saving grace for those who're abused; they might find people outside of their families who could validate them, educate them, and care for them. This gives them an opportunity for change."

"And for love?"

"Well, yeah. That's a good way to say it. Because they can actually see love."

"Do you think the adult child of toxic parents realizes at some point that they really weren't loved?"

Doc nodded. "They finally get it. And it's our job as therapists to assure them, *It wasn't about you;* it was about their parents. Because as youngsters they imagined that if they were *better* kids…if they did things *more properly*, were more intelligent or better-looking, better athletes—whatever—then Mom or Dad would be nicer, more loving."

This struck a chord with me. "What about the difference between feeling loved and feeling controlled? The child of toxic parents might feel controlled—*you can't do this or you must do that*—and the child thinks, *My father or mother cares about me because I have all these rules,* but in reality they're only trying to control behavior, to raise a child and not develop a child."

Doc shifted in his chair. "But if a parent is *authentic*—even if they are controlling—the child can distinguish between the control that's trying to suppress them versus the control that's protecting them."

"The child knows the difference, deep down?"

"Absolutely. I once worked with a hit man who'd been totally controlled and abused by his parents: physical abuse, emotional abuse; as a kid he would come home with no one there, or when they did show up they'd be drunk, bringing in other people who abused him physically, mentally, and sexually. He never developed a sense of conscience or any kind of compassion, so killing people was easy to do. He had no feelings for others, so he was a lost cause."

"Do you think when his parents died he felt anything?" I asked.

"Nope," Doc said. "There was nothing. I don't think he even knew when his parents died. He lost all contact, lived in a car in a junkyard because he'd been booted out when he was thirteen or fourteen.

"But the flip side of that *control coin* is the *do-gooders*, the community activists or the religious zealots coming out of toxic, controlling families, and they're doing all of this free work for their own gratification because they can control people who're sick or ill or whatever, and they get to wield their own control. It's all they know."

This didn't sound right to me. "But what about the Florence Nightingales who're always trying to please? They have this bottomless pit where their self-esteem should be, but whatever they do it's never enough."

"Of course," Doc agreed, "that *need to be needed* compulsion originates in a toxic upbringing, and it can be manifested in many different ways. That's why adult children of toxic parents blend so well into society. But once I start talking to them and getting their background, it's like *holy mackerel.*" He laughed. "And because toxicity manifests itself in so many ways and spreads like sewage in so many directions, we need to fight this war primarily on two fronts: abusive *and* helicopter parents…but the helicopter parents are trickier because they look so good. *They love their child.* But to me, loving a child is only measured by the ability of the parent to let go of those children once they become adults.

"But most parents don't let go," Doc continued. "They hold them by inheritance…because they need to be needed; they need to give them the right advice, and so on. But what they *really* need is to let that child go be themselves."

I glanced down my list of crossed-off questions. "Finally, there's this expectation that everyone should have and raise children. What do you think of this?"

"It is the most ludicrous behavior and expectation," Doc stated. "So I'm always impressed with people who say, *I wouldn't be a good father or mother so I don't want to have kids.* Kids don't magically make you a better person."

"So what happens to children with parents who weren't prepared, where there's toxicity that permeates the home…and then time goes by and suddenly that parent who was never ready to parent is now in a nursing home. And the kids' wounds are still oozing."

"It's amazing how long those wounds can gape," Doc added. "And in those cases, I think the whole concept of family, at least for that individual, needs to be redefined. And that's another myth we perpetuate, that blood is thicker than water. But most of your trouble comes from blood. Ask any therapist."

"Do you think this varies across cultures," I asked, "or are the dynamics pretty much the same?"

"Good question," Doc replied. "And if you're interested in a point of view from someone who'd know, I've got the perfect guy." Doc retrieved the iPhone resting inside his shirt pocket, which he tapped and swiped and then slid back into his pocket.

Moments later the device dinged, and Doc drew it out for examination. "He'd be happy to read more about your project," Doc told me, his glasses threatening to slide off his nose. "Let me send you his contact information."

Moments later, I had the email address of Dr. Lawrence J. Martin.

CHAPTER 15

◆

Color Me Blank:
Interview with Lawrence J. Martin, PsyD

A few weeks after my interview with Doc Reed—while padding down the carpeted hallway to Dr. Martin's office in nearby Santa Clarita—I found myself hoping that I'd prepared sufficiently for this interview; as a male Caucasian, the last thing I wanted was to present myself to any person of color as someone who suffers from *white savior complex*: a white guy or gal who wants to "help" disenfranchised African Americans or Latinos or Asians or Middle Easterners while (knowingly or not) acting in a self-serving manner. (For a hilarious take on this, search Google or YouTube for comedienne Catherine O'Hara's depictions of Lola Heatherton interviewing Andrea Martin's Mother Teresa).

But apparently, I had little to worry about.

Dr. Martin greeted me in the waiting room of his office. Younger than I—early forties at most—with a handsome smile and a tall, athletic frame, he was well dressed in casual business attire: imposing yet friendly.

"I read what you sent me," Dr. Martin told me once I'd taken a seat across from him inside his comfortable, well-appointed therapy room. "It's very moving—and it sounds like you've been through a lot and come out the other side transformed."

I grinned. "Thank you; it's been quite a journey, and I can't thank you enough for being part of this."

He settled back in his rolling office chair. "I'm hoping it helps."

I double-checked my voice recorder. "May I ask your qualifications?"

"I'm a licensed psychologist in California," Dr. Martin began, "and have been working in the field for twenty-five years; I hold a PsyD [doctor of psychology degree], and I trained as a clinical psychologist and a school psychologist, so I have a good understanding of learning disabilities, ADHD, and behavior problems. I help teachers and families, and I worked in a medical clinic for six years as a health psychologist helping patients with chronic illnesses. I also worked with ob-gyns to assist their patients with postpartum depression, and I treated my patients' husbands. I've done work in pediatrics, as well."

"Where have you practiced?" I asked.

"Before Southern California, in Visalia and the Central [California] Valley, south of Fresno."

"Could you say that you saw the gamut of the socioeconomic range, from A to Z?"

Dr. Martin nodded. "I worked with all ages in that clinic, so I had everything from seventy-eight-years-olds who wanted to quit smoking to kids; you name it. I also worked in the field with adolescents—boys in particular. I'm trained in family work, and one of my microspecialties is working with abuse victims and perpetrators."

"Early offenders?" I asked, recalling my early years working in the group home milieu.

"Yes," Dr. Martin replied. "Adolescents who've acted out sexually and physically. I've done a lot of legal work as well, so I've collaborated with probation officers and attorneys."

"Has your work with people of color been extensive?"

"It has," said Dr. Martin. "I had some early years working back east in Harlem, the South Bronx; mostly African Americans—near Rutgers, where I went to school—in a clinic with every population. But in the Central Valley it was mostly poor people, about thirty-five to fifty percent Latino; lots of migrant workers and their families, and sometimes we communicated through an interpreter. In college, one of my areas of strength was African American studies, so in practice I melded the two."

"When working with families of color," I began, after reviewing my questions, "particularly African American families, are there specific issues—and I know this is a loaded question—pertaining to the parent-child relationship?"

"Wow."

I cocked an uneasy smile. "I know."

Dr. Martin leaned back in his chair. "Well, let me ask you this: In the context of your book, some of the focus is preparing for end-of-life situations with parents who've been abusive?"

"Specifically where there hasn't been a nurturing relationship," I replied. "So there may be lingering anger and grief—even feelings of abandonment—and the idea that even though this parent wasn't there for me, now I'm inconveniencing myself on their behalf...so I need to mitigate that anger because it's eating me up."

"And you're wondering how this plays out in the African American community?"

"But also in other communities of color," I clarified.

"Um-hmm." Dr. Martin scanned the room. "Well...bad parenting happens, of course, in all cultures. But even when I'm working with my own folk, I never forget that we're [African Americans] a diverse group—just as white people are also a diverse group.

"I was trained by Dr. [Nancy] Boyd-Franklin—she's a prolific writer and researcher and family therapist—and she let us know right from the beginning that there isn't a plain vanilla white family: It's a myth, and everyone brings their culture and nuances and subcultures within the family. Many white families had to change their names and languages, just as blacks and Latinos had to.

"That said," Dr. Martin continued, "with many people of color in general, and with African Americans in particular, the family is commonly of critical importance; and there've been situations where a family member can't be present—not because of abuse or neglect, but maybe they're working a lot; and now decades later, when the child's grown up but still feels the old absence, the lack of parenting—even if they now understand *why* their parent was absent or limited in their parenting—[they] may have built up resentment, so it's important to recognize the pain and the loss.

"Oftentimes—when the child is hurting—they'll be told, *But Mom or Dad is putting food on the table,* which is true…but the pain isn't acknowledged. When I'm working with this situation I say, *Let's acknowledge the pain first; let's talk about the loss.* This person feels angry and sad—period. *Inhale, exhale.* Now let's move on to the circumstances…because usually within the family, there's acknowledgment of the pain, but only *with a comma and a 'but.'* It's qualified."

"What about in situations of abuse?" I asked. "And here's that abuser in the hospital bed, and the adult child who's now middle-aged has to deal with that person. How might you guide them to do what they need to do and still be able to have their sanity?"

"It depends on the severity of the abuse…the length of time, and whether or not it's continuing; sometimes that person is in a wheelchair and they can still be abusive—to the end. So that's a situation where the adult child needs to find a way to take care of themselves; my training says: *You've got to protect yourself and make sure you're whole.* When you're a productive adult—especially with a family—your life can't stop."

"So one should prioritize," I summarized, hoping I was hearing him correctly, "knowing certain things in *my life* come first, and if I have any time or energy left over, I need to spend it wisely?"

"*Yes.* It's critical to take care of oneself. Sometimes people overlook their needs when they're working with others; my brain and your brain work really well under certain circumstances, but we can overwhelm our brains: Get three hours of sleep or skip dinner, and see how well your brain works. We're all really adult toddlers, and when a toddler misses a snack or a nap, it's not pretty.

"We may not flop on the floor"—Dr. Martin chuckled—"but we become irritable, and we can't be good caregivers when we're off-kilter.

"What I've been finding is that many children who're raised by a narcissistic parent always learned when they were coming up to put their own needs as secondary. So now, as adults, when they're running off to the hospital or nursing home, they may have difficulty paying attention to what's going on internally; this can impair their functioning and result in an increase in anxiety and other mental health symptoms. And then their lives start falling apart and they *really start to become unglued*: anxiety attacks, things like that."

"How do you help them regain control?"

"I tell them, *Take care of yourself.* Write things down, and set an alarm in your fancy phone that it's time to eat. I don't ask if they're hungry; I ask if they've eaten. Because adrenaline shuts down the feedback loop of stomach to brain, and *I've gotta get here, I've got to get there,* and we're all caffeinated, and you'll say, *Jesus, it's two o'clock and I haven't eaten yet.* Maybe ask your partner to remind you at two o'clock to eat. Or set another alarm to turn the TV off, to shut down an hour before bed so you can go to your happy place. Let your body relax—put on some Enya, or whatever calms you down.

"Remember, other family members will also heap stuff on you, and even if you have a huge support system and know about self-care, you've got another voice when you show up at the hospital or pick up the phone that's conditioned to feel guilty or feel like *they should be first and you should be second,* and suddenly it's like you're seven years old again.

"Your parent may be one hundred and ten, and even if you're ninety, you still may feel seven; you might be the CEO of the company, but you're still the youngest of your siblings, and your parents or siblings may continue to enforce those old roles from childhood."

"So the family dynamic doesn't change very much, unless there's intervention like therapy?" I asked.

Dr. Martin leaned forward. "A ball will roll downhill until it's hit by an opposing force like a rock. That's a therapist; that's what we do. People usually keep going until something changes their direction; we don't change until the environment tells us to."

"So a therapist is that force for change?"

"Yes…or maybe for you it's consulting a spiritualist, or seeing the birth of your child, or watching *Oprah*—or maybe you saw a doctor who said you're at risk for something and it's time to make changes. Those are some of the events that make someone look like they magically evolved—but it's something they were exposed to."

"How does religion factor with families of color?" I asked.

Dr. Martin pushed himself up in his chair. "Reminder: *People of color* is an overly broad term, because it also includes Middle Eastern or Asian groups, and I'm not an expert in any ethnic area, but I do have some experience. Religion, and not just Christianity, but also Islam and the Alcoholics Anonymous communities, have played *huge* roles as protective factors. Again, many people don't believe in God and don't pray, but culturally it's important, and the Christian church has a very powerful role as a gathering place and a cultural center as well as a political force.

"If you think back to Dr. Martin Luther King, he didn't invent the church as a gathering place and political force; he was the result of what was happening in the culture before then. So the church can be particularly helpful, not only if you have external struggles, but also if you're dealing with a family member who isn't available, who's ill, or who's passed. Plus, it fits with AA's importance of family, extended family, community, and higher power."

"And with the influence of the church and that *Honor thy father and mother* credo," I began, "do you see someone saying, *I'm pissed off because Mom or Dad wasn't there for me, but if I don't attend to them I'll feel too guilty?*"

"Do I see that conflict?" Dr. Martin asked. "Oh yeah. Another piece is when you go back twenty, thirty, forty years when our parents and grandparents were coming up, there was segregation and discrimination, and the pressures on the parents were astronomically high; and in circumstances when a parent was flawed to the point of mistreating or being unavailable, or using drugs or whatever, it was conflictual to the family to hold that person accountable because of those other external pressures.

"I'm not trying to be overly specific and I may be missing clarity, but if you have a parent who was not there for their child in a healthy way, who's addicted, mean and hurtful, or absent, or is intermittently present—which is not uncommon—it often could have been hard to hold their feet to the fire, because everyone could see the other pressures on them from that bad job situation, where they were mistreated or underpaid or outright abused. They'd come home and were unavailable, and—if we use the stereotype—Mom might say, *You need to cut your dad some slack.* But the awareness of the circumstances and/or contexts of the parent's behavior doesn't erase the child's need for that parent to have been more present, loving, and supportive at the time; nor does it diminish the child's sense of loss for not having had those healthy experiences.

"With Latinos there are also linguistic issues, or they're working multiple jobs and they come home exhausted. Mom or Dad wants to be there for their kids, but sometimes they're under enormous amounts of external pressures.

"Families in all cultures will try to understand the perspective of the person in that position, but sometimes to a fault—where the child's taught to ignore what they aren't getting."

"So the family structure might be enabling?" I asked.

"Yes," Dr. Martin agreed. "Again, because accountability is critical in the work I do, this enabling is what we call cognitive distortions: *thinking errors.* One of the big things is thinking it's all black-and-white, all-or-nothing: *Your father's all good or all bad,* and it may be that he's trying but failing to meet the needs of his child. So in therapy, we elevate the perspective of the person who's been hurt to where it's *no longer less than [that of] the person who's inflicted the pain.*"

"How important would you say is forgiveness in dealing with that failing parent?" I asked. "For instance, let's say I'm making sure I'm taking care of myself, but I'm faced with this incapacitated elderly parent who wasn't there for me, and I'm still carrying a grudge."

Dr. Martin paused. "Forgiveness is mostly an internal process: Maybe it's gaining an understanding of circumstances; maybe it's tapping into a higher power; but maybe it's not about sitting down and trying to get them to understand your point of view, because they're flagrantly narcissistic or they have Alzheimer's, or they're simply not able emotionally to hear you. And thinking you're going to work it out sometimes reopens wounds that took years in therapy to heal; it's not necessarily healthy to go into the lion's den covered in bacon grease. So, yes, it's of critical importance to ask yourself, *How much is this hurting me to hold on to the anger?*

"When it comes to caring for one's family member who has a history of being abusive but is now elderly, disabled, or dependent, there is a significant change in the power dynamic, and that family member who was the victim—who is now the caretaker—needs to be cognizant. In some important ways the roles have switched, and if they haven't adequately addressed their own history of victimization, they risk being abusive themselves: physically, emotionally, sexually, or financially. *Dad owes me a thousand dollars,* or *Grandma was really a fill in the blank to me.* And these are actually crimes, but one can easily slip into that position.

"So, yes, I believe the answer is forgiveness, and don't take it out on them just because you can, even though it might even some score."

"But do you think there are situations where forgiveness isn't an option—where an individual is probably better walking away?" I asked.

Dr. Martin scanned the room. "There's a difference between forgiveness and trying to work it out, and forgiving *but still being able to keep a healthy distance.* I should've mentioned that even though self-care is critical, so are boundaries. When we've been abused, the abusive person didn't respect our boundaries—therefore, *we must set the boundaries so they don't trounce on us again*: *It's on my terms now, and I'm gonna write this letter and you can read it or not. I don't care.*"

"What do you think are the greatest stressors when that parent is failing and the adult child is put into that position of caretaker or decision maker?" I asked.

Dr. Martin tapped his pen. "Probably the conflict between having been disempowered and now being in a position of authority. *It can be tough.* We want to take care of people whom we like and not those whom we feel *forced to pretend* we like. There are lots of people who removed themselves once they turned eighteen, and they can't imagine how they'll feel in forty years taking care of that failing parent.

"That parent once had too much power over me," Dr. Martin elaborated, *"yet I went on to do successful things, but now I'm back where I was.* And that elderly parent may still act like they can overpower you, so the adult child has to ask, *How do I compartmentalize and not be taking my resentment out on this feeble, emotionally distraught person, who's the same person but isn't in the same position as before? How do I not allow them to hurt me and still take care of them?* And the answer isn't perhaps that I'm going to stroke their head and tell them everything's going to be OK, and whisper and hug and bathe them gently."

I laughed, shaking my head. "God knows."

Dr. Martin smiled. "Maybe it's paying someone else to do that, which hopefully you can afford. *Because sometimes it's just not doable.* It was never the nature of your relationship. But I'm going to make sure your human needs are met…even when the aged parent may *want* their child to be there and give up everything, but it's just not possible: *Maybe I'm self-employed or I've got kids or we're finally going on vacation.*" Dr. Martin sat back in his chair. "And sometimes it's appropriate to let them know why you can't, but sometimes it's not. It's case by case."

"When might it not be appropriate?" I asked.

"Like with Alzheimer's or CTE—in a similar way to interacting with other mental health disorders, brain diseases, or brain damage— if you're dealing with a severely narcissistic person, there's some sort of barrier that'll prevent them from understanding their impact on— or the perspective of—others; they may have limited or no capacity for empathy. But this doesn't work with everybody," Dr. Martin went on. "When someone has some sort of mental illness, perhaps they put you in situations you shouldn't have been in…because there's a chip missing, and Mom or Dad didn't know any better. Mom was a seven-year-old in a twenty-five-year-old's body; and this somewhat pathologizes the parent by saying they weren't capable, but different things can cause this."

"Like CTE?" I asked.

"Yes!" Dr. Martin exclaimed. "When we look back on all of the cases of football players and boxers with repeated head injuries, we say, *Holy cow!* That man lost his mind at forty-two, someone else at forty-five. But they don't come to you crying, saying, *I'm really sad and really hurt.* Instead, we see examples of decline in their personal and interpersonal functioning, in their difficulty identifying their own feelings or those of others, because their brains no longer function as they did prior to the disease or injury.

"They don't have the qualities they had before; their brains no longer access emotions like empathy. For many people, a diagnosis could be helpful…that the person is damaged. And if this is your father, you could've been the best kid in the world bringing home A-plus-pluses and scouring the house with your toothbrush, but it wouldn't have made a difference, because it wasn't you."

"So having a diagnosis and something to put a label on is helpful," I repeated.

"Good Lord, yes," Dr. Martin agreed. "And now we're seeing traits of CTE even earlier: I've seen traits in teenagers who're really going in this direction—but back to labels for those whose parents didn't give their kids what they needed: For some people the diagnoses are really helpful: *Wow, my mom's really borderline,* or *My dad's really narcissistic, and damn I wish they'd had treatment.* It's a mental flip I do with my clients, changing perspective; but if you're in the heat of the hurt, it's not going to happen. Hopefully with distance, and some therapy or a support group or reading self-help books, one's perspective can change."

"Can you think of any examples where you helped a client go through this process?"

"I've seen and helped people clear their own conscience, like putting some of what they've held inside out in the open: Sometimes it's on paper, which can be really therapeutic; others act it out or paint it out, so it's no longer something that's *festering.* I've also seen people read their letter to a parent—or even bring them into therapy—but again, this takes preparation, and it's not something I recommend they do on their own, because they can get reinjured.

"Sometimes I've even seen some of these parents get their own therapy, not because they wanted to, but because someone said, *No one wants to come visit you and these are the reasons,* like an intervention.

That's been fruitful…but again, if someone's flagrantly narcissistic, I'd never recommend this because they're setting themselves up for disappointment. But in the best circumstances that parent might say, *I can see the patterns, and I didn't want to be here, but I've had three marriages,* and no one's sat them down before.

"Dr. Ira Byock wrote a book called *Dying Well*. I saw him speak, and he has a multipoint approach when you're saying goodbye to someone who's actually dying. And every time I say it, it hits me here"—Dr. Martin patted his heart—"and the first point is, *Forgive me,* and it could be something minor, like I wasn't the son or grandson or husband I should've been. Next is, *I forgive you*—and this is optional, because if they don't deserve it, don't say it. Third is, *I thank you,* for whatever you were thankful for, and, *I love you,* and the last is, *Goodbye.* Dr. Byock has sections on how to manage it when the person is not able to be truly forgiven.

"I'm not a fan of lying to people," Dr. Martin added, "so I don't say we should say things just for the sake of saying them or letting people feel better; I think sometimes we let people off the hook too much. But I think there are ways of holding people accountable without giving too much…and still being able to take care of ourselves."

"Holding people accountable without giving too much, while still being able to take care of oneself," I echoed, wondering if I could accomplish this with my own parents. "So it's a balancing act."

Dr. Martin grinned at me. "Balance is crucial—especially around family occasions and the holidays—*like Christmas.*"

Christmas: Dread jabbed at me as I recalled it was only days away. "So you don't fall down?" I stood up, extending my hand.

"That's the idea." Dr. Martin grasped my hand and shook it. "Don't let yourself—or the life you've built—fall down."

CHAPTER 16

◆

Falling Down the Rabbit Hole

Four days later—in spite of my father being eligible for an extended Medicare-sponsored nursing home stay—my mother ambulanced him home for Christmas. And we all understood why: Perhaps the only thing more disheartening for Dad than spending his birthday in a hospital setting (which he'd recently done) would've been watching Christmas come and go from the confines of his linoleum-floored, polyester-draped, semiprivate room.

On Christmas morning, my sisters and their families and I assembled at our parents' house bearing savory casseroles and gaily wrapped gifts, and we had a nice enough time; Gwen had gone to the trouble of buying a fragrant Douglas fir for their living room, and her little ones had decorated it beautifully with all of Mom's ancient glass ornaments, some from her own parents' tree when she was growing up in the 1930s and 1940s.

But the event carried a practiced air, as if we were weary actors upon a festive stage: Each played his or her part well, reciting lines that had been rehearsed for years, and adhering to the family script and stage cues from our mother, who—like a director seated *front row center*—launched quiet signals to each of us with her smiles, her defensive gestures, or her frowns.

Lights! Curtain! Roll eyes!

Then as we were settling in to watch the kids open their presents, Mom took off her shoe to show everyone one of her feet. "It's turning black," she announced proudly.

"Grandmom, what happened?" Miriam's eldest son asked.

"I fell in the parking lot at Walgreens," Mom answered. "I also hit my head."

"You what?" Several of us gasped.

Mom began toeing her foot back into her shoe. "I was down on the ground for a while, and several men walked right past me, but finally a nice woman helped me up."

"No one called 911?" I pressed. "Have you been to the doctor?"

"I'm tired of doctor visits," Mom snapped. "My foot's just bruised. It'll heal."

"But it's *turning black*," Miriam added, frowning. "And you're diabetic."

"I'm fine."

Our discussion was sidetracked as little Danny squealed while tearing open another Lego box, so I settled back into my chair thinking I was prepared for whatever might come next; after all, I'd been a captive audience to this interactive Punch-and-Judy for more than fifty years.

How wrong I was.

*   *   *

A week after Christmas, I called my mother to remind her about the tickets I'd bought for us to see *Wicked* together on January 6 and to figure out arrangements for dining beforehand; I had given her the tickets along with a promise of dinner at the Smoke House restaurant in Burbank for her eightieth birthday back in September.

"I would have loved to go," Mom told me.

"What do you mean, *would have loved to*?" I asked, knowing I'd spent nearly three hundred dollars on seats to a show Jay and I had already seen. "Why can't you make it?"

"I'm having trouble walking," she replied. "And it's too late for me. I'm usually in bed by eight."

Suddenly relieved, I still did my best to persuade her to attend. "But we can take Dad's wheelchair. Everything is handicap accessible."

"It just won't work," Mom insisted. "You have Jay, and if he can't make it I know Gwen would love to go."

"OK," I said and changed the subject before she could change her mind; the idea of seeing this wonderful show again with Jay was beginning to appeal to me.

Days later, as Jay and I were speeding down the Hollywood Freeway toward the Pantages Theater, my phone rang: Mom.

I was driving, so I let her call go to voicemail.

Then as Jay and I were enjoying our martinis at Off Vine restaurant, which was within walking distance to the Pantages, my phone rang again. This time it was Gwen: "I'm on my way to take Mom and Dad to the hospital."

"What's going on?"

"Dad's blood sugar has been over 400 all week, and Mom's has been over 300. She just called me and isn't making sense. I'm going over there to see what I can do. Can you meet me?"

"Unfortunately, Jay and I are sitting down to have dinner before seeing *Wicked*."

"*Ohhhh*, I forgot that was tonight. Never mind."

"If it looks bad, you could call 911."

"Yeah, I might need to do that."

"She brought this on herself with the bags of candy," I reminded Gwen. "This is exactly what we've all been trying to avoid."

Gwen sighed. "I know....It's just that she was babbling. She wasn't making any sense."

"Thank you for taking care of this."

"You guys enjoy the show, OK?"

I ended the call as the waitress appeared with our entrees.

The next day after work, I drove over to the hospital to see them.

My father was alert and sitting up in bed.

But Mom was mostly comatose, drifting in and out of consciousness.

When she awoke, she had no concept of where she was. She kept asking me what the lights were doing on and telling me to close the refrigerator door.

Then she'd drift asleep again.

And I thought: *All of this from high blood sugar?*

"She was awake all night," the nurse told me. "That's why she's sleeping now."

"Was she making any sense?"

"No."

"Is her doctor around?"

"I'll see if I can find him." The nurse turned and stepped out of the room.

An eternity later Dr. Lee arrived. "Your mother has what's called *post-concussion syndrome*. She's got a brain injury from that parking lot fall your sister told me about; however, the injury didn't appear on the CAT scan, so it's on a microscopic level."

I grimaced. "Will she recover?"

"Yes, but it'll take about two or three weeks. We'll assess her for rehabilitation, and if she's a good candidate she'll be moved to the rehab floor. What she's experiencing is pretty much routine." He smiled at me, I thanked him, and he left.

I stayed with Mom for an hour or so, all the while being reminded of the cartoons where Tweety Bird bonks Sylvester the Cat on the noggin with a frying pan, and then tiny birds chirp in a circle over his head, and a wobbling Sylvester can't remember who he is or what he was doing.

Only this wasn't funny.

It was frightening.

Mom's slack facial muscles rendered her ten years older and nearly unrecognizable, her voice was a strained whisper, and her orientation to time and place had clearly been obliterated.

After five days Mom was deemed ambulatory, but because she flatly, adamantly refused to participate in any physical therapy, she was discharged to a local skilled nursing facility along with my father.

During the next several weeks the nursing staff at the new location became exasperated with her, not only because she was noncompliant with her meds, but also because she was argumentative and combative. She fought them while they tried to change her diaper or feed her, and she hallucinated that there were men trying to set fire to her bed.

Naturally, she refused PT there as well, so it was nearly a month before she was able to walk.

My father, however, just down the hall, was alert…trapped in his unresponsive body, in a scenario reminiscent of that old horror classic *The Brain That Wouldn't Die.*

The ensuing four weeks were spent teaching school and then driving across town to the nursing home after the dismissal bell rang, all the while remembering Dr. Martin's sage advice about setting boundaries for myself while making certain I ate well and got enough sleep. But the effort seemed worth it, because like a ship drawing closer to shore, my mother's view of her own mental coastline began slowly to reemerge.

Reality ho!

One sunny afternoon, I pushed her wheelchair out onto the nursing home's flowering patio.

"Not there," she insisted, pointing, "over here. I don't want them to hear us."

"Who not to hear us?" I asked, bewildered.

"The bad guys." She motioned toward an open door some ten yards away. "They are trying to kill us. Your father and me."

"They're trying to help you get better," I countered, sitting down on the concrete planter bed next to her wheelchair.

Her face morphed into a snarling mask as she turned to me. "You're one of them!"

"Mom, no, I'm not. I'm trying to help you, too." I decided to change the subject. "How's the food here?"

"Mediocre," she replied, straightening herself in her wheelchair. "But I must be one of the upper echelon, because they keep bringing me meals."

Wondering how to make sense of this conversation, I scanned our surroundings and spotted Miriam emerging from a nearby door, her features pulled into that strained smile-grimace I'd seen so much of recently. She raised her hand in a tentative wave, and I waved back.

"Hi, Mom," Miriam announced upon drawing closer.

"Oh, Miriam," Mom replied unsmilingly.

"How are you?"

"Terrible."

Miriam and I exchanged smirks. *Almost back to normal.*

"Did you eat lunch already?" Miriam slowly asked her.

"No, and I'm not going to eat lunch. The food here is mediocre."

"But you—"

"Don't tell me what to do!"

Miriam took a couple of steps backward, crossing her arms defensively. "Well, it seems like I'm being told I can't talk, so I won't."

Mom stared intently ahead, as if focusing on a juggler or unicycle rider only she could see.

"Maybe she'd like to see Dad," Miriam dryly suggested.

I bent down, released the wheel brakes, and pushed Mom into a U-turn. "Great idea."

We found Dad in the nursing home lobby in a wheelchair of his own.

We rolled each parent up to the other.

Neither one recognized his or her spouse.

I'll spare the reader the ensuing conversation, which I can only liken to having two televisions facing each other while tuned to two different shows: Sentences were uttered, but absolutely nothing related or made *any* sense.

Yet, one emotion was skillfully communicated by each person to the other: *anger.*

CHAPTER 17

◆

Wishing I Could Walk Away

It took a couple of months, but thanks to Gwen having arranged a tiny SWAT team of round-the-clock caregivers to look after them, our folks came back to Dolores Avenue.

Knowing my mother would attempt to drive her car before she was ready, I made a special trip after school one day to hide her car keys.

And somehow, as her memory and motor function returned— more or less—to normal, the mother we were accustomed to fully reemerged.

Show over. Curtain down. House lights up.

During this time, I'd made good use of the advice bequeathed me by Doc Reed and Dr. Martin: I was setting boundaries, maintaining authenticity, using my various support systems, and taking care of myself physically; Jay and I had for months now been exercising hard at the gym three times weekly, and weekends allowed us the leisure time to stroll into the nearby hills with our fur buddies.

Then a few days before Jay and I were to leave on vacation, I got a text from Gwen (this is the actual text; Marilu and Bill, at the time, were caregivers):

Dad punched Mom in the jaw this morning. Mom could talk but not eat, so went to GAMC emergency, and I have not heard results yet. Marilu and Bill witnessed it and Bill dropped her off and I will pick her up. Mom is telling the MDs who did it, so they will probably report it to APS. When I talked to her she wasn't in terrible pain so it probably was not broken. Sorry. When will God take him?

Oh, wait...so this is only intermission?
Then, minutes later...

Just got off the phone with Mom. She is fine, just sore. APS was called and police interviewed her in ER and then went to talk with Dad.

I called Gwen. "I did my best to circumvent this happening, if you'll remember."

"Sure I remember." Gwen sighed. "But at least this time she's telling the truth."

"Thank God. Um..." I hesitated. "I'm staying out of it this time."

"I don't blame you. All you got was grief."

"Plus, Jay and I are leaving in a few days on our trip."

"You are?! That's great! I'd forgotten. We leave on our trip to the lake on the sixth."

"That's right after we get back, so I won't see them for weeks. Is Mom OK?"

"Yeah, I think so."

"He could've broken her jaw, or at least shattered a tooth. I hate him."

"I know," Gwen replied. "Listen, I've got to run. Everything is fine on this end. Will you have a great trip please?"

I felt my shoulders un-hunch. "Thanks, Gwen. We will. Jay and I've been saving miles for eight years for this trip to Europe, so I'm not going to let anything mess it up."

"I'm right there with you," she said. "Love you."

"I love you too," I replied before ending the call.

*   *   *

True to my word, I didn't call my mother to ask about the incident. However, upon returning home from Europe, I stopped by Dolores Avenue to pay my folks a visit.

My father was propped up in his chair in the living room watching Fox News, so I went over and shook his hand. "Hi Dad."

"Hi." No smile.*

"I heard you socked Mom in the jaw." I held his gaze.

His eyes opened a bit more, but his expression was unchanged. "It was just a little pop."

"Enough to send her to the emergency room," I pressed. "You can't do that again."

"I know."

"Did the police come talk to you?" I asked, knowing they had.

"Yes."

"What did they tell you?"

"They said I'll go to jail if I do it again."

"Yep, off to jail," I said. "Just so you know, I didn't come visit you for the last four weeks because I was angry with you for hitting her."

He stared at me. "How much do you weigh?"

Is he trying to change the subject, or is he this demented? "My scale's broken, so I don't know."

Days later, I was throwing a tennis ball for Princeton in our backyard when my phone rang.

"Hi, Gwen. What's up?"

"Mom fired Marilu." Gwen sighed.

"*Why?* Marilu's absolutely terrific."

"She was fifteen minutes late again, so Mom refused to answer the door. It's only the third or fourth time she's been late, but she's going to nursing school and the traffic across town is unpredictable."

"Poor woman," I said. "But Marilu's so nice; she's better off not having to deal with Mom. Who's Mom going to replace her with?"

"She has *no one*. And I don't have the time to deal with this! She makes me take care of this all and then she won't listen to me and winds up doing whatever she wants. She just told me, *I'm in charge here, and I can fire whoever I want.* I can't do this anymore!"*

---

* There was never a smile—but now I know there's a name and definition for this: *hypomimia: the reduced ability to generate facial expressions,* and it's one of the symptoms of CTE.

"I know. And I'm so appreciative of everything you've done, Gwen. You've really kept the pressure off me and Miriam. What about that agency she used to use?"

"They cost too much."

"Perfect. I'll call her and tell her I'm calling the agency unless she hires Marilu back."

"Would you do that?" Gwen sang. "I'd appreciate it so much!"

"I'll call you back."

Mom answered the phone just before the machine picked up. "Hello?"

"I heard you fired Marilu. So who do you have lined up to replace her?"

"There's a woman that's contacted me."

"She'll need training. And you don't know how to administer the insulin since the doctor switched you over from the hypodermics to the pens. Right?"

"I can have Bill train them."

"Before Marilu's shift tomorrow night?"

Silence. And then, "You don't know how it feels having all of these people coming and going out of my house."

"Would you rather be back in that nursing home?"

"Of course not!"

"Because having caregivers is the only way for you and Dad to stay out of that nursing home—or an assisted living facility. You can't care for Dad anymore and you know it. You need to get Marilu back…*if she'll even come back*."

"I'm tired of her being late."

"She's going to school," I reminded her. "There's unavoidable traffic in Los Angeles."

"Plus, I had to tell Dad I fired her…and he's absolutely in love with her."

So that was it! "You fired Marilu because Dad's *in love* with her?!"

"*I'm in charge here!* And that's between your father and me."

"You'll need to get Marilu back until you can find someone else. Fire her then if you need to. Otherwise you'll need to use that agency that costs twice as much."

"There's a woman who's contacted me."

"Yes, *but...she...needs...to...be...trained*. Marilu already knows everything you need to keep Dad and yourself healthy and safe."

Silence. "I'll call her."

"Good. I call Gwen and let her know."

"I'm in charge here," Mom said again.

"You're telling me that Gwen no longer needs to be involved in this?"

"That's what I said."

"I'll let her know," I replied. "Gwen has a lot going on and doesn't need the added stress."

*   *   *

The following Saturday, while Jay and I were getting ready to head out for lunch, I received a text from Gwen: Dad tried to hit Marilu, but missed. Any chance you could talk to him and explain she could sue him? There's a fun conversation! When will God take him?

I called Gwen.

"*Hiiiiii...*" Her voice trailed exhaustedly.

"I'm calling the Glendale Police Department."

"Nooooo!" Gwen cried. "Mom will hit the roof!"

"I don't care. It's the only thing that might work; she herself said that he was genuinely shaken up when they visited before."

"Can't you just talk to Dad? Put the fear of God into him?"

"Like that'll work?" I laughed.

"Mom will know I told you. And she asked me not to tell you."

"I'm not playing her games. Make me the bad guy here: Tell her you begged me not to call. I'm...going to ask if the police will talk to him, but not arrest him or anything. Are you *sure* he didn't make contact with her?"

"That's what Mom told me, but who knows? She edits the truth."

"I'll call them and call you back."

With the GPD's number already in my phone, the task at hand only took a moment: "Yes, I've got the complaint from two months ago right here," the officer told me. "Are you certain he didn't actually strike the caregiver?"

"That's what I was told."

"I'm *sooo* sorry."

The genuine sympathy in her voice inexplicably set me on the edge of tears. I swallowed hard. "Thank you."

"Would you like the officer to call you after he pays them a visit? We're pretty quiet here today, so it probably won't be long."

"I'd appreciate it. Thank you."

Within the hour my phone rang, just as Jay and I were leaving for the gym…but it wasn't the police. "Hi, Mom."

"Two policemen were just here," she snapped.

"I know. I called them."

"You shouldn't have done that!"

"I'm only trying to protect Marilu and you and everyone else that's defenseless against him."

"Life's hard enough without policemen showing up at your door!"

"You told me that's the only thing that makes an impression on him," I reminded her. "And if he injures poor Marilu—or anyone else who doesn't have disability or workers' comp insurance—you'll need to foot the bill for her hospitalization and recovery…not to mention what'll happen if she sues you."

"You shouldn't have done that," Mom icily repeated. "Goodbye."

"You're welcome!" I shouted into the phone as the call went dead.

I turned to Jay. "Do you believe this?"

"She wanted to play victim, and you wouldn't play along."

"Look." I displayed my wrists. "My hands are shaking."

"Let it go."

"How can she just look the other way?!"

"On some level she wants this." Jay smiled kindly. "And you did the right thing. *Now, let it go.*"

"She's making excuses for him, just like she did when we were kids," I persisted. "But to actually chastise me for doing the *one thing* that might help?"

"It's maddening, isn't it?"

"Please remind me of how ripped up I feel whenever I get involved; I want to help, and I want things to change, but I feel helpless…like I'm problem solving and doing my best and being noble and hitting my head against the wall, but it's no use. It's crazy making!" I hugged my elbows. "*I wish I could walk away*, like Doc Reed said…to never see either of them again. Dealing with my mom is like dealing with an ex-wife; we're connected, but I've got nothing—*nothing!*—to gain from our contact…and I'm paying emotional alimony to her. And with my father, it's not like I have all of these warm, fuzzy memories of him to carry me through this! *Oh, thanks, Dad, for threatening to beat me up and kill me. Can I make you another sandwich?*"

Jay looked at me, his eyes moony with sympathy. "Why *don't you* walk away? Like we discussed, on some level your mom wants this."

"Because I don't want to put more stress on Gwen and Miriam."

"Hmm." Jay paused. "Maybe Terry and Carol will have some perspective on this. Isn't your interview with them sometime this week?"

"I'm taking dinner over to them tomorrow night, when you're seeing your mom."

"My guess is Terry's seen this all before," Jay said. "As has Carol; they probably have nearly a century of clinical experience between the two of them."

"You're probably right." I sighed, feeling my blood pressure deflate. "You're probably right."

CHAPTER 18

◆

Looking Under the Hood for a Certain Amount of Better Interview with Carol Cushman, LCSW, and Teresa DeCrescenzo, LCSW, LMFT

"It's Greek food from our favorite restaurant," I explained, placing the fragrant, steaming containers atop Terry's kitchen counter. "Garlic chicken and spanakopita and lemon-rice soup and hummus and fresh pita; I didn't get their baba ghanoush because I remembered you hate eggplant."

Terry snickered. "I'm probably the only Italian in the world who hates eggplant."

"The tragic equivalent of an Irishman who hates potatoes," Carol opined. "But I, for one, love both."

"Italians and Irishmen?" I asked, winking at Carol.

"If that's the case, you're in perfect company tonight," Terry deadpanned. "Shall we eat after the interview?"

We moved into their spacious living room with its floor-to-ceiling gallery of portraits and landscapes and abstracts; its deep, upholstered chairs and sectional sofa; and its gleaming black grand piano—atop which bloomed a garden of framed photos: loved ones and statesmen alike, many of whom were gone but never forgotten.

Teresa DeCrescenzo, or Terry D, as she is better known, had been my boss when I'd worked with the Gay and Lesbian Adolescent Social Services (GLASS) after graduating from college in 1992. I'd cultivated a deep friendship with Terry throughout the ensuing decades, and I think of her as the Susan B. Anthony of our times: Her steadfast support of unwanted and abused LGBT teens, her tireless work to correct social injustices, and her iron spine and unapologetic manner led Terry to make almost as many enemies as staunch supporters and fawning admirers throughout the years.

After Terry's longtime partner, noted author and psychologist Dr. Betty Berzon, lost her longtime battle with breast cancer more than a decade ago—and following a proper Jewish year of mourning—Terry met and fell in love with Carol Cushman, a Manhattan-based psychotherapist who spent her scant leisure time assisting women at a free clinic in Brooklyn. They'd been together now for more than ten years, and I'd come to love Carol as much as I loved Terry. They are a dynamic and genteel bicoastal pair, and I was fortunate to interview them both during one of Carol's social engagement–packed visits to California.

"Terry and Carol," I began, "could you please tell me about your degrees and therapeutic backgrounds?"

"I hold two licenses," Terry replied, her signature collar-length gray hair parted and gleaming under the picture-frame lighting. "An LCSW and an LMFT, and I've been practicing and licensed for almost forty years; I'm the director of social services at a large, acute-care metropolitan hospital and an adjunct professor of social work at Cal State University, Northridge."

Carol elegantly crossed her legs where she leaned back into the plump sofa cushion. "I have two degrees: a master's for my LCSW, and I went to the Psychoanalytic Training Institute in New York City, but I've never practiced Freudian psychoanalysis because, come on, *for real?*" She chuckled. "I'm influenced by the English objects relations school, the self-psychology school, and the interpersonal school—stuff that's really about people connecting. What I do is a Catskills comedian with lots of encouragement. I used to know theory, to read every book—and Terry still does—but I don't."

"Carol and Terry," I asked, "what might you tell people who're thinking about starting counseling or psychotherapy—especially those dealing with an aging parent who was WANT: wounding, absent, narcissistic, or traumatic?"

"With a new client"—Carol stopped to sip from her water glass—"if we each decide we want to work together, I say, *Here are my rules: Come on time, purely for you, but I'm always behind in something and I'll do whatever I need until you get here. Pay your bills on time, and that's purely for me—and know that I charge for missed sessions, but you get a free makeup.* But the big rule in therapy is always tell the truth.

"Now, I don't expect you to walk in here and tell me everything," Carol continued, *"because trust is built; but if you're not being truthful, your foot's gonna kick or your palms will sweat, and I want you to* know *when you're not telling the truth, because* that's where your fear is, your pain is, and your shame is. *And that's what we need to talk about."* She turned to her partner. "Terry?"

Terry faced me. "My great love is when these social workers I supervise are dealing with some crazed, coked-out, methed-out patient, and the social worker says, *I don't know what to do with him,* and I say, *Remember someone's theory about such-and-such, and do you see this behavior?* I'm fond of theory—not in a cranky academic way, but there are theories that make sense about human behavior.

"To this, I get sick of hearing so-and-so is a natural counselor," Terry continued, "and a natural therapist, because there is no such thing. Now, you might be very good at chatting and you may be very smart—all of these are fine. But if you don't have theories to hang your hat on, you'll miss something important.

"For example, think of your therapist as an old-fashioned lineman or linewoman with a blowtorch for this job or a wire splicer for that. And that's what we do: We reference Bowlby's attachment theory or the work of Harry Harlow. But I don't think getting married to one theory—Freudian, Jungian—is good practice; I mean, in some ways Freud was full of shit and Jung was kind of in la-la land."

Carol laughed, raising a hand. "When the hairs go up on your head, and it makes you think of Winnicott's objects relations theory—the drive for humans to form contacts with others—one needs to process it and have it come out of your mouth so it makes sense to the patient. And Freud said it this way, and Ainsworth said it that way, but what you're talking about is a human being and if you're mixing these theories efficiently *through who you are,* the patient stays with you; patients are smart, and they know if you're not right for them.

"So I ask myself after the first session: *Do I have enough feeling for them? Can we go through this together?* Sometimes I have a patient tell me, *I like your eyes,* or, *I like your bookshelf,* but they're really saying, *I like you and we can go through anything together.* But if you don't feel I'm right in that session, trust yourself. Your guts are telling you something."

"What about money and fees?" I asked.

"I never met a therapist who won't accommodate to your financial needs within reason and according to their time," Carol replied.

Recalling the brief exchanges my sisters and I had with social workers in the hospitals and nursing facilities where my parents had been, I turned to Terry. "If you're working in the hospital and you only have that client for a short time, and they aren't your therapy client, what might you do? And where might you steer them?"

"*Cor-rec-tion,*" Terry said, enunciating each syllable of the word. "This *is* my client. And it takes an entirely different skill set. For example, in the hospital we had a guy who was driving everyone crazy, saying, *Just get me the fuck out of here,* and I was with a student so I was showing off a little, and I said, *OK, so you're not telling me anything about your life, but I know that somewhere, someone in the United States woke up this morning and asked themselves, I wonder how Bill is doing today.* And the man started crying. So I said, *Are you really ready to have your life over with? Or maybe we can put something together.*"

Carol looked admiringly over at Terry. "She's extraordinary."

"The goals for short-term therapeutic encounters are to be *effective* and *affective,*" Terry clarified. "You have to get to the affect— the emotion. So I can say, *Yes, I have a resource, and there's a homeless shelter up the street,* but unless someone gets to the emotion, the intervention won't be effective.

"I've seen middle-aged children of elderly dying patients where there is clearly animosity. And my staff will say, *Did she* [the adult child] *just say that?* And I'll say to that person, *Are you kidding me? That's your mother!* And either they'll say, *I'm sorry,* or they'll tell me, *Until you've lived with her, don't you tell me that she's my mother, because you haven't been through what I've been through with her.* So I told myself, *Back off.* I apologized and tried a different tack. But most of the time I go for the jugular."

"So what's the different tack?" I asked. "You've got someone with a steel front, so how do you conduct emotional triage with that person?"

"It wasn't a steel front," Terry countered; "it was really an *emotional* front. And everybody basically has the same core needs—except for a true sociopath—and has the same core sensitivities, so you just have to put your finger on the pulse."

"Speaking of core sensitivities," I said, "how did the upbringings of some of your LGBT clients affect their interactions with a disapproving parent in an end-of-life situation? Are these sensitivities different from those of other populations?"

"My experience probably has to do with the era in which I grew up," Terry replied, "as well as becoming a licensed therapist in the 1970s. I'm gonna say, in oversimplified terms, that parents in those eras—the fifties through even the eighties—reflected our society and its values, which weren't accepting of LGBT people.

"On the other hand," Terry continued, "parents who love their children, love their children; even the cliché that some Christians use—*love the sinner, hate the sin*—says, *You're my child and I love you.* Having values that are anti-LGBT is no excuse for abusing your kids, because I think you'd find another reason to abuse them: *You disappointed me, you this…you that.* But lots of families have straight kids who disappoint parents: They become criminals, marry out of their kind, or whatever. Either you love your children or you don't. And sometimes I think the anti-gay stuff is a smokescreen for expressing the very bad feelings they harbor in general."

"How do you see this play out?" I asked.

"Most people come into the hospital emotionally escalated, especially people who adore their loved ones. But here's a case: We had a teenage lesbian at GLASS who had such an attitude and was driving the staff crazy, so I said, *Bring this child to me.* And when we talked, it became evident that her mother's patterns were repeating: She'd been in and out of jail, and when she'd get out, she wouldn't spend time with her daughter, and her daughter was saying, *When my mom gets out we're going to do this and that,* but I saw the unmistakable patterns.

"So I said, *Look, your mother doesn't love you. She probably wanted to, but she's incapable. And unless you accept this and move on, you're going to be forty years old and a prostitute, and drinking and doing drugs and waiting for the alcohol-induced encephalopathy to set in or your kidneys to shut down.* Because that's what I see in the hospital all the time: people in their thirties and forties and fifties with their kidneys shut down from the alcohol, all because they didn't get the things that mattered most: *love from Mom or Dad.* And they spent their lives going around about it, instead of accepting it."

Carol squared a look at me, raising a finger. "I once saw a teacher talking to a student whose parents were alcoholic, and this teacher put a pillow up in front of his face and said, *OK, now talk to your parent.* And the kid started to weep, because he realized his parent couldn't hear him through the *pillow* of alcohol. So I'll take a pillow and say to my client, *There are reasons why you won't confront your father, but mainly because he can't perceive it. So we need to deal with where your anger is, and what you're still feeling about what did or didn't happen.*"

I smiled, seeing a parallel. "That's a great metaphor for traumatic brain injury or chronic traumatic encephalopathy, and I'm guessing a similar dynamic might be there for someone with a parent who suffers from PTSD."

Carol nodded. "Then the question becomes, *What do you need?* Not *What does he need?* I treated someone who was beaten horribly by her mother, and because she needed to be seen in therapy every day, I only charged her the daily rate for the entire week. She was so ashamed by what happened that she'd only speak into a tape recorder at home and bring it in, and *I'd have to push the button*—she couldn't do it. She began to get better: better jobs, and she got married, and they lived in her apartment for ten years, and when they were ready to move, I broke a rule and gave them a down payment. And I didn't care, because *she taught me everything I needed to know about being a therapist*, and I've applied everything I learned from her to each patient I've had."

"When it comes to any sort of abuse," Terry cut in, "the question is, *How did it affect you? How is it stifling your life, and why is it the only truth?* That's what we need to work on: how to *free yourself from the encasement* of what happened. How does that keep you in a kind of prison? Somebody might need to change their name, or whatever. And as you begin to explore these questions, you start regaining territory of the world you've excluded yourself from."

"One of my clients," Carol interjected, "told me how his drunk father would pick him up from school every day. And my question was, *Could you have walked home? What were the other possibilities?* Because once you understand you're not powerless—though you may have been as a child—you have three hundred sixty degrees of choice…that is, knowing most of us won't *choose* to be an ax murderer.

"I really learned this," Carol continued, "dealing with my bulimic patients even before there was the word *bulimia*, and I asked them to be a little bird on their own shoulder, which Freud would call the *observing ego*; and when you take a laxative or throw up, I want you to pay special attention to what you're feeling. And *every one of them said they were feeling anger.* It was the first time they knew they were feeling angry.

"I began asking these people," Carol went on, "like the boy who got into the car, *Why are you turning over the power?* Most people who were abused had no choice, or *believed they had no choice at the time.* And when you can begin to conceive this, a million things come to you." Carol's eyebrows arched. "And that's what happens between you and your patient: *A certain amount of better* is going to happen. It can be *way better*, or *just a little*. But even a little better is better."

Terry turned to me. "Are you familiar with Dr. Vincent Felitti and the work he's done with adverse childhood experiences?"

My skin bloomed goose bumps. "No, but I'm a huge fan of Dr. Nadine Burke-Harris and the work she's done on ACEs. Who's Dr. Felitti?"

Terry chuckled. "Let's just say I've got something important for your book that we can discuss over that lemon-rice soup," Terry said, pushing herself up from the sofa. "Not to mention the garlic chicken that's been calling my name."

As we trailed one another back into the kitchen, Terry's and Carol's words came back to me: *How is what happened stifling your life, and why is this the only truth?* Could I *free myself* from the encasement of what happened...or is gaining freedom a lifelong process? And finally: *Once you understand you're not powerless—though you may have been as a child—you have three hundred sixty degrees of choice...*

Had I been exercising mine?

CHAPTER 19

◆

Can't Get Enough of Something That Almost Works[*]

"I might be able to get you in," Terry told me, lifting the lid on the white, disposable takeout container. "I'll email my contact there tomorrow and let you know—I'll need to pull some strings, but because I'm also presenting, it shouldn't be a problem." She sniffed the savory vapors rising from the garlic chicken. "*Oh my.*" She twitched her nose some more and then squared a look at me. "Are you sure you can make it?"

"That's my final week of break," I replied, leaning against the kitchen counter, wineglass in hand, "so I could be there Tuesday; I'm dying to learn more about adverse childhood experiences and their long-term effects."

Carol chuckled. "Now, *that's* an ironic statement if ever there were one."

Carefully, Terry scooped generous servings onto a large porcelain platter. "Consider it done."

We sat down to enjoy the meal while catching up on life and discussing ACEs and the groundbreaking work conducted by Dr. Vincent Felitti within his Kaiser Permanente longitudinal study.

I learned from Terry that Dr. Felitti's research focused on how various ACEs (abusive parents; mental illness in the home; substance abuse; physical violence; homelessness; etc.) are scored to indicate

---

* Dr. Vincent Felitti: ICAN presentation Los Angeles; 8/1/17

the extent they may affect significant, long-term, and often *life-shortening* health issues suffered by adults who experienced these stressors as children.

I'd first come upon this concept during a school faculty meeting, when one of the school district's mental health professionals shared with my colleagues and me a TED Talk by Dr. Nadine Burke-Harris. Dr. Burke-Harris, a clinician from the Bay Area and now California's first Surgeon General, worked in a public health setting with a low-income population, during which time she began noticing patterns of chronic diseases in grown adults that could be attributable to their childhood stressors.

I was transfixed by Dr. Burke-Harris's eloquent and fascinating TED presentation, as well as the wealth of information she disseminated—not only because it was applicable to my own life, but also because as a teacher, I could be on the lookout for specific red flags pertinent to my students (as Doc Reed had suggested). But what I hadn't comprehended at the time was that Dr. Burke-Harris's primary information source was Dr. Vincent Felitti, who ran a study through Kaiser Permanente that focused on nearly seventeen thousand cases over the course of more than twenty years.

And Terry had promised to squeeze me in at a forum for social workers where Dr. Felitti—along with Terry herself—would be presenting.

Which she did.

And the experience was revelatory.

The ICAN (Inter-Agency Council on Child Abuse and Neglect) symposium on the "Effects of Childhood Trauma" took place on Tuesday August 1, 2017 at The California Endowment on Alameda Street in Los Angeles, and was attended by all brands of social workers, doctors, and counselors: LCSWs, MFTs, PhDs, MSWs, EdDs, and MDs. The spacious conference room was packed, and just after finding my own seat I turned to see about a dozen clinicians standing against the back wall.

Pull strings, Terry did indeed!

Dr. Vincent J. Felitti—a tall, trim, distinguished, and well-tailored gentleman in his sixties who looked like he could walk into the starring role of any network's hospitalish soap opera—was introduced by the host and then began speaking about his study and its ramifications and implications.

(Author's Note: Unlike my interviews with the other clinicians in this book, during which I used my voice recorder, the following account is based upon the handwritten notes I scribbled during the presentation, so I've paraphrased Dr. Felitti while attempting to remain true to his words and message; I'd also condensed well over two hours of information onto a page or two, so undoubtedly I've omitted some important elements... which is why I've included hyperlinks at the end of this section. My dialogue format and quotation marks here are provided to (hopefully) assist the reader, but these are not the actual sentences spoken by Dr. Felitti; however, the statistics included are accurate.)

"Pay now or pay later," Dr. Felitti began. "There are so many abused children who wind up in the criminal courts system. ACEs are our nation's most basic public health and social problem, but there's a resistance to using the information clinically. Information on our most recent ACE Study considers information from a twenty-year follow-up, where we can state with confidence that *smoke isn't the essence; the fire is.*

"One example is a woman we treated in our weight clinic who came to us at four hundred eight pounds. After many months in the program, she reduced her weight to one hundred thirty-two pounds and then shot back up to four hundred ten.

"But she had no idea why she gained the weight back until she discovered she'd been *sleep eating*; during her waking hours she adhered to her healthy eating program, but then she'd wake up each morning and find her kitchen in shambles: There were bowls and wrappers and dirty plates and packages in the trash, which were obviously from her late-night binges...but she had no conscious recollection of having gotten out of bed in the middle of the night to prepare and eat these meals.

"After some clinical investigation, it turned out that when she had reached her weight goal, a male coworker had made a suggestive comment to her about *spending some time together*, and this comment reactivated the survival mode she'd developed to protect herself from any unwanted sexualized behavior: So she put the weight back on. Ultimately, she admitted to us that she'd been a victim of lengthy incest from the time she was eleven years old until it ended at age twenty.

"Out of two hundred eighty-six cases, fifty-five percent of overweight people were child victims of sexual abuse. So one conclusion we can draw from ACEs is that being overweight is a solution to the problem of molestation.

"This is a public health paradox: What appear to be problems are sometimes unconscious solutions to one's adverse childhood experiences. For example: Addiction correlates with characteristics intrinsic to the individual's childhood traumas, and one of the reasons addiction is so insidious is because it's hard to get enough of something that *almost* works.

"ACE scores assign a number to an adverse childhood experience: one point for violence in the home; one point for mental illness of a primary caregiver, including having chronic depression; one point for extreme poverty or homelessness, and so on. When a mother is battered, additional ACEs exist. And these factors influence the adult's health over time. How?

"Chronic, unreleased stress releases pro-inflammatory chemicals that cause the capillaries to shut down; the lining of the blood vessels attracts cholesterol and plaques and causes partial obstructions and immune system suppression.

"What underlines COPD (chronic obstructive pulmonary disease)? An underlying high ACE score. If one has an ACE score of four, that person also has a sixteen percent higher chance of alcoholism and liver disease. And a full two-thirds of alcoholics had high ACEs.

"An ACE score of four is seen in sixteen out of twenty-one autoimmune diseases, including type 1 diabetes, rheumatoid arthritis, inflammatory bowel disease, lupus, and multiple sclerosis.

"An ACE score of six results in a *forty-four thousand percent higher* chance of being an IV drug user; an ACE score of six also results in a twenty-year shorter life-span.

"Dismissing health risks as merely *bad habits* hides their functionality," Dr. Felitti continued. "In fact, what appears to be a problem, such as the woman who was *sleep eating*, may be an attempted solution, so treating the attempted solution may feel threatening to the patient and could cause flight from the program. Even suicide is sometimes a coping mechanism.

"As clinicians, how do we improve this? First, acknowledge that a problem exists. Second, seek a history from all patients. Next, ask how their ACEs affected them later in life. And finally, provide help and develop systems for early interventions.

"All of the above interventions triggered a thirty-five percent drop in doctors' visits and an eleven percent reduction in emergency room visits.

"With regard to help: Individual therapy is valuable but may not be available to all people. Small groups are valuable, and we've also discovered that hypnotherapy is useful, as is EMDR (eye movement desensitization and reprocessing). For more information, please visit *ACEsConnection.com*; *HumanExposures.com*; or email us at *info@cavalcadeproductions.com* and *AVAHealth.org*."

There was a period of questions and answers from the audience, and then after lunch the four ancillary presenters—one of whom was Terry DeCrescenzo—offered their wisdom and expertise on ACEs and their specific populations, Terry's being the LGBTQ adolescent.

As I drove home that afternoon, many of Dr. Felitti's concepts and words rang true to me, for example, high ACEs being linked to cholesterol and autoimmune diseases (I've been on statin drugs and blood pressure meds since my mid-forties, even though I don't have a familial history of high cholesterol or high blood pressure; I continue to carry an asthma inhaler, although I was supposed to *outgrow* this autoimmune disease at twelve or so; and I've suffered from irritable bowel syndrome for nearly thirty years).

And although I was reluctant, I also needed to be honest with myself: Dr. Felitti's study flayed open an uncomfortable truth about my own alcohol usage, and how I needed to focus a more watchful eye on my chardonnay consumption (and my liver values), having spent too many mornings slugging coffee and popping ibuprofen to counteract the ill effects of an excessive evening.

So I wondered: Might the people reading this book find this ACE information pertinent and helpful, especially because my target audience would be people with elderly parents who are middle-aged like me? Would they see their own behaviors on the *ACEsConnection. com* website, or their maladies on that list of autoimmune diseases? I'd come to understand that having a conclusive diagnosis—or understanding the underlying causes of a disease—is helpful or even crucial for most successful treatments. And those statistics Dr. Felitti stated in his address were astounding, that these *interventions triggered a thirty-five percent drop in doctors' visits and an eleven percent reduction in emergency room visits.*

But Felitti's three golden phrases that kept coming back to me were: *One of the reasons addiction is so insidious is because it's hard to get enough of something that almost works;* and *What appears to be a problem may be an attempted solution, so treating the attempted solution may be threatening to the patient;* and *Smoke isn't the essence; the fire is.*

Might my father's dependence on alcohol and nicotine have been his way of coping with the deterioration of his mind and personality from degenerative, probable CTE? I also recalled the abuse he suffered at the hands of his own father—those days as a child being locked in the woodshed until his dad came home to beat him.

And could this *fire versus smoke* be the reason why my mother never sought professional help or medication for her lifetime of depression and her chronic overeating? If so, what might have been the childhood fires that sparked these ongoing, decades-old *attempted solutions?*

Or perhaps, somewhere after that (presumably) happy wedding day back in 1956, did Mom learn that being a sullen victim who was both chronically depressed and perpetually overweight was the best way to gain sympathy—and some sad brand of love—from her affectionless, angry, impatient, CTE-suffering husband?

Either way, I'd wager that knowledge of her husband's probable CTE could have helped them both. *A lot.*

Finally, I wondered about the adult survivor of sexual abuse, as in the case of the patient Dr. Felitti referenced who lost and then regained more than two hundred fifty pounds as a result of surviving nearly a decade of incest? How might a therapist help that client gain healing and perspective that could help move them beyond their betrayal, especially when that offending parent—or nonprotecting LOW parent—enters an end-of-life situation?

I knew just the man to ask.

CHAPTER 20

◆

The Wounded Male (and the Cotton Ball) Interview with Allen Ruyle, LCSW

"Hey!" Allen replied, grinning. "How was your trip this time? A little easier than the last one, I hope?"

"Didn't hit the brakes once."

Allen squared a look at me. "Now or later?"

"Later will involve cocktails," I replied, "so let's do this while we're both sober."

Allen and I excused ourselves and made our way through Jay's cousin David's tastefully decorated house toward the shaded patio deck that overlooked the pool; when I'd recently shared the premise of my book with Allen in an email, we decided an in-person interview—which necessitated a weekend in San Diego—was in order, and David had generously offered Jay and me his guest room.

Luckily, the afternoon air temperature was ideal. And as Allen pulled out his chair and sat, I hurried to set up my voice recorder and check its voice levels. "Ready?"

Allen took a sip of ice water and settled back into his chair. "Anytime."

"Tell me about your qualifications and how long you've been in practice."

Allen glanced up at the pergola ceiling's heavy wooden beams. "Got my master's in social work in 2007 from San Diego State; got my LCSW license through the Board of Behavioral Sciences in 2010. I've been in practice part-time since 2011 and have been full-time since 2013. I have a private practice now where I see anywhere from twenty-five to thirty-four clients each week. I'm a member of the National Association of Social Workers, the California Society for Clinical Social Work, and *MaleSurvivor.org*."

"What're the populations that you work with?"

"The focus of my practice—more than fifty or sixty percent—is men who were sexually abused as children," Allen explained. "I also have a few male clients who were sexually assaulted as adults, but survivors of sexual abuse is the primary population I work with. The other thirty to forty percent is general practice: depression, anxiety, bipolar disorder, couples counseling—stuff like that."

"Are most of your male clients gay?" I asked.

"It's about fifty-fifty for the men I work with; right now I have two therapy groups that are evenly split: gay and straight."

"How do they find you?"

"I'm known in the local therapeutic community as the only guy in private practice that has therapy groups for male survivors of sexual abuse. There are actually three groups in San Diego County, two are mine and the other is at an agency in Mission Valley."

"Have any of your clients been sexually abused by their own parents?"

"Yes."

"As adult men, what sorts of issues do they struggle with?"

"As a group, number one would be trust and intimacy." Allen crossed his arms over his chest. "Issues around allowing people in... allowing people to get close. They have a very, very, *very* difficult time trusting and letting people in. Primarily because the relationships—"

Allen paused.

"Let me back up a little bit: When you and I were growing up, we were taught to watch out for the creepy guy in the raincoat on the playground. That's not who does this. For boys the overwhelming majority are abused by someone who's known to them; in most cases by someone in a position of authority—it generally doesn't happen inside the nuclear family—but almost always happens in the layer just beyond that. Coaches, ministers, teachers, grandparents, family friends. Someone they look up to and feel safe with."

"And this where the trust and intimacy issues come from?"

"Exactly. They have these idealized adults whom they are told are safe and will love and care for them and protect them, but then the children learn in no uncertain terms that these people are *actually harming them*. This makes it very difficult to *attach* later on, because you think *everybody* will fuck you eventually."

"Like the proverbial dog that's been kicked?" I asked. "A conditioned response?"

"That's a good way to put it."

"Have you dealt with any of these survivors when the adult abuser was in failing health?"

Allen sighed. "Not directly…again, perhaps because most childhood sexual abuse takes place from the layer just outside the nuclear family. But indirectly, yes."

"How so?"

"I've had clients who were responsible for the care of the *nonoffending but not protecting* parent…the adult who allowed it to happen. It's very conflicting."

"The Look the Other Way, or LOW, parent?" I asked. "In what ways?"

"Imagine this: You love this person, yet they allowed someone else to hurt you very deeply. You can't trust them and you're angry at them, but still you love them. As a result, many of these clients struggle to convince themselves that this parent *just didn't know*."

"How do they feel caring for and, in essence, *protecting* the aged parent *who failed to protect them?*"

"Most of the time they're very conflicted…and compartmentalized: They keep the anger at the parent over here"—Allen motioned with his hands—"off to one side, and the responsibility and nurturing of the nonprotective parent somewhere else. It's a dissociative process."

"How so?"

"Well…" Allen paused. "Have you ever seen someone telling a horrific tale of abuse or trauma, but they recount the details with a blank expression? That's a dissociative process between the cognitive aspect and the emotions: The facts of what took place and the affective—or emotive—part are completely divorced; many survivors of abuse can't allow the rage and the hurt at this nonprotecting parent into the space where they now have to care for them."

"Why can't they?" I asked.

"Because the conflict can be overwhelming. Generally, it's an anxiety about what will happen…the *fear* is that *if I let the affective part back in—to rejoin the emotions with the facts—it's going to destroy whatever functionality with caregiving is taking place and also may destroy me in the process."*

"So do you allow that fear in? Do you help them rejoin the emotions with what happened?"

"It depends on the client," Allen replied. "We try to help them map out where everything is. To gain an understanding of the *anger and hurt and sadness and grief and fear* that they've got bottled away; to help them get in touch with those emotions…to process and deal with them.

"In a way," Allen continued, "it's almost like we create a system of safe-deposit boxes in my office that we open—when it's time— and bring the contents out into the room. We deal with it. We talk about it. We use language. Because if we don't talk about it, what happened and what's happening now is this big nebulous thing that's *just too scary.* We need to organize what the client is feeling, and talking *forces* this organizational process.

Allen leaned in over the wooden patio table. "My job is to help them wrap it back up—somewhat—by the end of the session to put away. Figuratively, they leave these mental conflicts in my office; we even have a shelving unit on one wall, and we discuss finding a place where they can leave this…for now. Then we'll pull it off the shelf, so to speak, when they come back."

"Allen," I asked, "what do you see with your clients when their parent—either the abuser or the Look the Other Way parent—has been inching toward death? Were there any commonalities of feelings or breakthroughs?"

Allen tapped his fingers. "For one guy," he began, "during the therapeutic process the sexually abusive parent died, while the other parent—who also horribly abused their child in both psychological and physical ways—continues to abuse him. *So there was no nonoffending parent.* But the death of the sexually offending parent has triggered an absolute collapse."

"Why?"

"From a clinical standpoint, it's from an inability to *ever get validation* for what was done: abuse by surviving family members; inappropriate behaviors; psychological abuse; manipulation...all of the old dynamics of a *wildly* dysfunctional family revictimizing this individual again. He was already dealing with this before the offending parent died and was dealing with a basketful of diagnoses. He was barely hanging on."

"What specific diagnoses?" I asked.

"Post-traumatic stress disorder, depression, and anxiety," Allen replied. "But mostly PTSD."

"So instead of the death bringing closure and healing it was the opposite?" I asked.

"Yes—for a couple of reasons: because there had always been a desire to get some kind of concrete proof...and to be able to hold up this proof to the others and say, *Look! You didn't believe me— you never believed me!—so I have this to share with you.* And in this case the sexually offending parent's death was unexpected—it didn't come after a decline; then to make matters worse, the rest of the family began acting out, which exacerbated the unexpectedness of the death."

"How is he—how's your client—doing now?"

Allen grimaced. "Well...the effects are still unfolding, but suffice to say it's triggered an almost catastrophic failure of his internal support system."

"So would you assert that even if the toxic parent dies, there still might not be a sense of personal resolution or relief?"

"All I can say is in this case," Allen began, eyebrows arched, "because the toxic parent died before there was any degree of resolution, now there's no hope for the sort of resolution that my client desired. The game changed."

"So if you get a client with a toxic parent who's failing...or is even healthy but elderly, what advice might you suggest?"

"I wouldn't have one thing to suggest," Allen replied. "Instead, I'd say, *Let's talk about what you think you need.* Because I've had, and currently have, clients for whom the death of the toxic parent will be a relief—or a nonevent. And even if it's not a nonevent, it'll be a relief."

"Can you speak to that?"

Allen swirled the remaining ice cubes in his glass. "There's another case where the offending parent's been out of the picture for many years, but knowing that he's still out there creates anxiety. This client told me, *It'll be good for me to know when he's dead…that he can't just pop up.* I've had other clients who talk about going to the funeral and watching the casket being lowered into the ground…*Just because I wanted to make sure that motherfucker was dead and he's not coming back.* So it's an individual thing.

"But one thing's for certain: I would have to—depending on the decline of the toxic parent and the resources of the client—work as quickly as I could to find out what this person needs based upon what they should've experienced."

"What should they have experienced?"

"Someone who loved them," Allen replied. "They shouldn't have worried every time they heard footsteps coming down the hallway. They shouldn't have been so isolated. They shouldn't have felt like a freak or blamed themselves. They should never have been treated that way. They should've had someone who protected them…*and they should've been happy.*"

"And the relief knowing that the terror they survived is gone?"

"Yes! Like I said, it's knowing *for sure* that *the person who hurt me can't do it anymore.*"

"Where do you see the healing coming in?"

"It's different…for everybody. And I think the healing comes in—at least with most of my client population—the healing occurs in the beginning."

"The beginning?" I asked. "This seems counterintuitive. Why?"

"At the beginning of the work they do with me and the group— and I'm not taking credit here—it's about their being able to finally take some important steps. For instance, when I have a new group of guys sit in front of other men and say, *I was sexually abused as a child,* and most of them begin their session absolutely terrified—leaving pinch marks in the seats underneath them—and it turns to relief, *connection,* even some sense of ease within the course of two hours."

"Relief? *In two hours?*"

"Relief that *it's OK for me to speak about this...that I said it out loud...that I said it to other men and the sky didn't fall. I'm stronger than I realized, and I'm not broken.*"

"And do you see this more in group than in one-to-one therapy?" I asked.

"I'm a huge proponent of group work," Allen replied, "because my clients can sit with me for months and talk and read books and hear me tell them, *What you're experiencing is not weird or wrong or unnatural, and many other people have experienced what you have.* But to hear the same message from other survivors is so much more powerful."

"I can see why," I said. "What else helps?"

"There's a book that was written in 1988 that I give every client; they've done some updated versions since then. It's called *Victims No Longer* by Mike Lew, MEd, and it's a seminal therapeutic work while still being accessible to the lay reader. And it's not a clinical book; it's just laid out by what men experience...men telling their stories. It's similar to group work, but without having to go face-to-face with the other men, without the risk."

I checked my watch and saw we should be closing soon; the sun was fading and there were some new voices in David's house. "Do you have clients who are dealing with a parent's drawn-out demise that includes trips to the hospital or the nursing home? Anything like that?"

Allen paused. "I have a particular client who's housing the nonoffending [LOW] parent. This parent is elderly, so my client is aware that he'll be going through this extended caretaking at some point in the near future. So he's already compartmentalizing his feelings, as we talked about earlier. But there's a part we haven't discussed yet: his anger."

"Why?"

"Anger is a secondary emotion," Allen explained. "It's almost always secondary to one of two clusters: Grief, pain, and hurt is one cluster; threats and fear is the other. That's why we express anger when we're afraid…or when we're really sad. As men, anger is what we're allowed to express publically. *Boys don't cry; walk it off. Man up.* Generally speaking, boys are socialized not to show any emotion other than aggression or anger. In this case, the client's anger toward the nonprotecting [LOW] parent *must* be kept at bay, because there's this sense of obligation."

"Do you encourage him to talk about the anger when you see it, and he pushes it down?"

"Absolutely. Because any feelings or emotions that are suppressed are—in my opinion—ticking bombs…that are very likely to go off when something big happens, like when this nonprotective [LOW] parent begins to skid downward. So we *do* talk about whatever he'll allow in."

"Then would it be fair to say," I began, "that if the failing WANT parent is living with their adult child or even requires supervision and/or conservatorship—so the parent-child roles are reversed—would it be fair to assert that the child is, in essence, twice grieved?"

Allen slyly smiled, as if he already knew where I was headed. "How so?"

"Because they weren't protected as a child, and now they're protecting their parent—either the abusing parent or the LOW parent. So the individual is twice grieved, twice victimized."

"Exactly."

"So what do you see—what sort of emotions—might that person experience?"

"It's interesting," Allen said. "Oftentimes it's wrapped up and nailed down: *packaged and compartmentalized.* There's a powerlessness there—which isn't an emotion—but they think, *I have no options. I can't kick this individual to the curb because of social norms, and because of the person I see myself as. And I'll never get an apology.* So there's a sense of powerlessness."

"Is there a sense of rage?"

"Not in the cases that I'm thinking about, because again, the rage would simply be an expression of that very deep pain…*and grief.* And since the individual is often so compartmentalized, the pain and grief are not being expressed. But when the emotions start to emerge, the first thing they notice is anger."

"How might this anger manifest?"

"In a number of ways: body issues, lots of unusual chronic pain; I have many clients with fibromyalgia, and I don't say this by any means to diminish their pain, but in my opinion those somatic issues are probably related to emotions that have been repressed. *Pushed down.*"

"Psychogenic?" I asked, thinking of Dr. Felitti's work and those high ACE scores. "Meaning, having their origins in the mind?"

"Yes. I see a lot of Crohn's disease. High blood pressure. Irritable bowel syndrome. Lupus. I also hear, *I can't get my pain under control,* or, *My immune system is turning on itself.* And as clinicians, we tend to see these things together. The client rarely makes a connection until somebody starts talking to them about it; and even after they make the connection, the realization won't necessarily make it go away."

"Even after extended therapy and good medical care?"

"Let me explain it this way: It really depends on the client's coping mechanisms, and if they're working *effectively* with a clinician to explore their anger, and help them get in touch with the sadness or the fear that underlies the anger. Because you can *talk* about anger, but you really need to dig it out piece by piece. If all those pieces are in place, this gives the client their best chance to find some relief from any psychogenic and even psychosomatic issues.

"This isn't a perfect analogy," Allen continued, "but to me it makes sense: That unprocessed anger is like a big cotton ball. At first it appears *intense* and *complicated* and *so tangled* that you can't make any sense of it. But if you had the patience, and the ability, and the fine motor skills, you could take those strands and lay them side by side; and then you'd see that it's not as complicated or as big as it appears.

"This goes back to using language to take those emotional strands and break down that cotton ball so you don't have this complicated mass. Instead—even during the disassembly process—you can look down and say, *This strand hurts; I'm sad about that strand. I didn't get what I needed. I was told—or made to feel—that I was worthless. And this strand is what I deserved. It's not my fault.* Remember *Good Will Hunting*, the movie with Matt Damon?"

"Of course."

"The most clichéd line in that movie is where the therapist, played by Robin Williams, keeps saying to Matt Damon's character, *It's not your fault, it's not your fault, it's not your fault.* It's a very powerful moment…but it's oversimplified, and I've never seen anyone have a breakthrough like that. Still, it's illustrative of what therapists do: *We help you understand that it wasn't you.* And on top of this really complicated parent-child relationship, many times the child ends up taking on some of that responsibility…like they're at least somewhat to blame. They believe, *Some of this toxicity and dysfunction is my fault.*"

"Why the self-guilt when they aren't culpable?" I asked.

"That structure is underpinned by the desire to maintain the idealized caregiver: *Mom, Coach Smith, Uncle Kevin, can't be all bad…because parts of them made me feel good…parts made me feel loved; but these things they did to me are bad; therefore, part of it must be me.* Therapists help people understand it really isn't you. It wasn't you. You were a child.

"Another thing," Allen added, "is people tend to look back at their child selves with expectations they hold as adults: *Why didn't I stand up? Why did I let this happen again and again? I was an idiot. I was stupid.* So we encourage them to realize, *You weren't an idiot or stupid; you were a kid.* And kids don't have the developmental capacity to manage things like we do as adults."

"So," I asked, "what advice would you have for that adult to better manage those childhood experiences? Anything concrete?"

"Think of a child of similar age to you when *that situation* happened," Allen replied. "What responsibility would you assign to that child? Would you blame your nephew or your niece or that cute kid next door for behaving the same way you did? *Would you really hold them responsible—and if not, what is it that makes you hold yourself responsible?*

"I might also recommend *inner child work*, the sort of thing championed by author John Bradshaw in his book *Homecoming: Reclaiming and Healing Your Inner Child*. You'd visualize yourself at the age when the abuse was taking place, and you would concentrate on as many of the sensory details and experiences that you could recall. Over a period of weeks or months you'd create a relationship with that representation of yourself as a child, that inner part of yourself that didn't get what it needed. And using a lot of sensory cues—*What do you hear? See? Smell? What do you feel…what tactile sensations?*—you pull in the senses to create an integrated experience. We work toward *nurturing* that child. To imagine stepping in as my adult self to a—"

"Parental role?" I cut in.

"*Exactly.* So you can imagine *holding* yourself as a child. Pick him or her up. Hold that child on your lap. Talk to them. Tell them what *you* needed to hear…that *it's not your fault*, and that *everything will be OK; this will happen to you and this is how you'll grow.* And this is oversimplified and may sound silly, but it's reparenting yourself from the inside out—you're healing that part of yourself that didn't get what it needed…the part that was so hurt. Doing this can be extremely powerful.

"I had a client," Allen continued, "who'd see himself sitting in the corner of an attic, all curled up and scared. So he visualized himself as his adult self, pulling down those drop-down stairs. At first only his *adult* head was in the attic, but over the course of the weeks he'd get progressively closer and closer, all the while describing how the child was reacting. Finally he was able to visualize putting his arm around the child, and when he held him atop his lap, he sobbed. It was very powerful."

"Do many of your clients do this inner child work?" I asked.

"All I can say is this isn't something that works for everyone, but it can be very helpful."

"In closing, Allen, how helpful do you feel therapy is for an individual who's going through the loss of the WANT or a LOW parent?"

"Well, I'm biased"—Allen laughed—"but I believe therapy is essential. Or maybe I should stress that *dealing with it* is essential. But I don't want to suggest that people can't get through the death of their toxic parent without therapy…But when I hear many people say, *Laundry is my therapy*; *gardening is my therapy;* or whatever, I imagine these folks are actually referring to avoidance and distraction."

Allen crossed one leg over the other. "Having said this, I believe there are people who *can* process and heal without talking about it—but most of us mere mortals will need someone to push us into those corners we don't want to go into because it's *painful* work. In my opinion, the quickest and healthiest way is to work with someone—and it doesn't have to be a licensed therapist, although in most cases I think it'll be your best bet, but it could be a trusted friend.

"And this is an area, generally speaking," Allen continued, "where women have it hands down over men; even as gay men we are only a little less constrained about masculinity and vulnerability; we haven't really been socialized to talk about what we feel.

"But talking is what you need to do: You're having some intense feelings and all that baggage—and all those spiderwebbed steamer trunks from the past are getting dropped on your doorstep when the parental transitions start to happen, especially when *that parent* is starting to fail. This is when the trunks arrive, when those parents are headlong into their decline."

"Allen, do you see significant differences between the reactions of an adult who was sexually abused as a child—and either the WANT parent or the nonprotecting LOW parent is failing—and someone who was physically or emotionally abused?"

Allen cocked his head as he considered my question. "I think in broad themes it's the same. However, the sexual aspect complicates matters around physical intimacy. So…it may be at least marginally more difficult for the adult who was sexually abused, because this creates another layer of isolation that victims of physical abuse tend to not experience. But trust issues are universal across abuse survivors. Again, this is the population I work with, so I might be biased. Anyone who suffered abuse at the hands of a parent or some other supposedly *safe adult* struggles with trust. But when the sexual barrier is broken, it turns up the volume; it's a matter of degree. And regardless of whether the parent is physically, emotionally, or sexually toxic, this toxicity is going to create the same basic negative framework surrounding their decline…with differences."

"Like what?"

"Physical abuse can be interpreted by the child as linked to the parent's anger, especially when the parent perpetuates the myth of *this is for your own good.* Therefore the child thinks, *I did something wrong, so I deserved this.* Similarly, some people might imagine that the teen who's sexually abused was desired by the perpetrator. But sexual abuse is not a function of sexual desire. It's an issue of power and humiliation, just as rape isn't a crime of sex as much of one involving sex and power and aggression. It doesn't leave a survivor with the sense of being desired so much as the sense of being violated. There's no ameliorating factor."

I sighed. "So any abuse is about a differential of power: abuse is abuse, and whether emotional, physical, or sexual, there was a violation of the inherent adult/child power differential…that the child was there, basically, as a punching bag."

"Right." Allen nodded. "And in some perverted way servicing the needs of the perpetrator without regard to the needs of the child."

"Do people assume one form of abuse is worse than the other?"

"Often someone comes into a group and says, *My abuse wasn't that bad. I was fondled and molested, but I wasn't forcibly raped.* And there's also a level of trauma that goes with the physical violence, but the basic issue they're dealing with—in abuse or toxic parenting—is one of betrayal. *That child was betrayed.* There was trust…*reliance*… but they were betrayed in a way that should never have happened. Everything in the world says this person is supposed to take care of me, to provide for me…but this person is *abusing* me and *hurting me.* Even little kids understand how wrong this is!"

"So when those children become forty-, fifty-, sixty-year-old adults—"

"Which is usually when they show up at my office," Allen cut in.

"And they're going through this process, is there any overarching advice you'd give?"

"*Talk about it,*" Allen emphasized. "Please, *talk about it.* This goes back to how healing occurs…*particularly* with sexual abuse—and particularly with men. Men don't talk about it; they are so ashamed of what was done to them that they won't talk about it. And I firmly, *firmly* believe that the majority of men don't. I read recently that seventy percent of abused men *don't ever* talk about it and don't do anything about it. And we've figured out that study after study supports one out of six boys are sexually abused by the time they reach sixteen. And there are so many guys who never get help.

"But the hardest part for my clients—and the biggest relief—comes from saying it out loud. They talk about it…and the sky doesn't fall…and the world doesn't reject me…and the people around me don't blame me—well, sometimes they do and that's retraumatizing. I should add that I'm not a big advocate of having your first conversation about this with your family, especially when your family system supported that bad behavior.

"So talk about it! There are wonderful websites containing good resources where you can share with others what's happening in your life—or you can journal by yourself or discuss it with a friend you absolutely trust. And if you can find a therapist you feel comfortable with and trust, that's great too."

"That's what's saved me," I told Allen just as Jay and David appeared on the deck with cocktails for us.

"You guys finished?" Jay asked while handing me my frosted glass.

"Just now," I replied, switching off my voice recorder. "Thanks for the beverage."

David pulled out a chair and sat. "Did you uncover any great truths?"

I sipped my Cape Cod, and the vodka made a warm, happy slide down to my stomach. "Too many to say right now," I replied as one of Allen's concepts drifted to the top of my mind like an ice cube in a glass: *Unprocessed anger is like a big cotton ball: It appears so tangled that you can't make sense of it…but if you took those strands and laid them side by side, you'd see it's not as complicated or big as it appears.*

And I wondered: *Had I sufficiently unraveled my own cotton ball, or did I continue to compartmentalize my angry, scrambled strands?*

Lunch the next week with a dear friend would help me answer this.

CHAPTER 21

◆

Living with a Wounded Heart

"You're angry," Linda stated calmly while stirring a third packet of Sweet'N Low into her iced tea. "I can almost smell your rage."

While considering her accusation, I watched her rearrange the colorful assortment of vegetables she'd selected from the all-you-can-eat lunch buffet. "But I'm not angry right now," I replied indignantly, and I wasn't; in fact, I was uncharacteristically relaxed because my school day was over, and I was spending the scant remaining daylight hours with Linda-minda (as I obnoxiously called her; Linda's equally ridiculous pet name for me was Nicky-poo), an accomplished portrait painter and author who'd recently taken up residency with some generous, affluent friends—they were contemporary patrons of the arts—in another state. I leveraged a glare at her, wondering if she knew me as well as she imagined. "How do you mean?"

Linda's eyes were lasers behind her glasses. "You've got this... deep, seething anger," she announced coolly—as if reporting the time of day—and then continued stirring her milky iced tea.

"You're one of the only people besides Jay who can see that."

"I spotted it that first time we met—at the Getty." Linda lifted the straw to her lips and took a sip. "Yeah, you hide it really well."

My memory rewound to that day: I'd made Facebook pals with a group of bohemian history nuts who'd bonded over a passion for Greco-Roman antiquities and had organized a field trip to the Getty Museum to admire a traveling exhibition of ancient Olympian bronzes. I'd arrived just after noon not having actually met anyone before, so I'd selected my most benevolent social mask for the occasion. Thus, Linda's detection of sour grapes and sauerkraut beneath my ostensibly peachy persona shocked me—and tattooed her onto my heart as a lifelong friend.

Leaning back into the vinyl restaurant booth, I sighed. "I've been trying to move beyond that anger now for years."

Linda shrugged. "I think it's OK if it never goes away." She picked at the boiled egg atop her salad.

"That's good," I said, "because even though I'm eyeing retirement, my rage is just now cresting toward its professional peak."

"What's the anger about?" Linda asked, her voice lyrical.

I scanned the shopworn Italian restaurant where we'd decided to meet, and my eyes surveyed the faded, hand-painted murals of the *glories of Italy* that would've been better suited to a middle school's revival of *Tosca*: a cartoonish Colosseum; an algae-filled Venetian canal with a sinking gondola; the Leaning-too-far-over Tower of Pisa; and a rendering of Michelangelo's *David* that sported a huge fig leaf and whose face vaguely resembled Meryl Streep. "Sometimes…I kinda feel like a book on a shelf with no bookends—just sort of teetering there."

"What do you mean?"

I twirled my Diet Coke. "Parents are the first bookend to hold you up, you know?"

"If you're lucky." Linda snorted. "So what's the other bookend, Nicky-poo?"

"Being a parent."

Linda broke off a chunk of the hard-crusted bread from the napkin-swaddled basket between us. "So why didn't you have kids?" she asked, smearing margarine atop the bread from inside a wrinkle of golden foil.

"Jay didn't want any," I replied. "He was adamant. And because I loved—and still love—him, I surrendered. After all, it wouldn't have been easy raising kids, being gay and all…and none of the options for generating children are *quite as convenient or pleasurable* as straight people have—but it could've happened."

"So you became a teacher." Linda bit into the bread. "I'll bet you find that rewarding—"

"But it's also like raising seeing-eye puppies," I cut in.

"How so?" Linda mumbled.

"I get these kids for nine months, I pour my heart and soul into them, and then just as I'm beginning to see real progress, they leave for middle school and I never see them again. It's soul crushing, sometimes."

"Bet some of 'em you never want to see again."

I fiddled with my tumbler. "Of course, but some I love…like they were my own. And most are already remarkably empathic, advanced human beings. You can *see* and *feel* the potential in them, and I make them laugh and they make me laugh and we cry together sometimes, and I push them and praise them and encourage them, even though I have to scream at them sometimes."

Linda leaned her elbows atop the table. "OK, I totally get the *seeing-eye* metaphor." She paused. "But with your *no bookends* metaphor, at least you're still sitting on a shelf."

I half smiled. "Jay?"

Linda sat back in the booth and folded her arms. "Some people never even get that dream spouse, because they never recover fully enough from their shitty parenting to establish a loving, long-term relationship."

"I know. It's just that I would've loved to have watched a child grow. To have been a dad…like that V-neck-sweater-wearing, good-looking guy in *The Courtship of Eddie's Father*. Remember?"

Linda chortled. "Bill Bixby and that adorable pixie kid—and the stoic and way-too-submissive Japanese nanny." She reached in and patted my wrist. "*But*"—she stage-whispered—"*that's TV.*"

"But I actually know people who brought up their kids that way!" I protested. "You should see Jay's brothers and nephews with their sons and daughters. They're such good, loving, funny dads and husbands. And my brother-in-law, for instance; I remember seeing him at a family wedding with his wife, daughter, and son at the table, and he was actually sitting with his arm around his teenage son's shoulder! I almost bawled my eyes out."

"Your dad never did that?"

I coughed. "I've never even hugged my dad. Not once. And not that I ever got close enough to do it. A dead porcupine is more huggable."

"Did he ever tell you as a kid that he loved you?"

"Nope." I shook my head. "When I was a kid he'd say, *Your mom and I love you kids very much.* Never a personal note; I guess he was just too stunted emotionally to ever take a chance on showing emotion—other than anger—to his own son."

"Maybe it would've seemed *too gay*," Linda offered, flipping one wrist T. rex style.

"But he always told me he loved his own father; I wasn't the son he wanted—pure and simple."

"You got to wonder why someone like that becomes a parent."

"If you didn't bear offspring back then, people looked at you like you had two noses."

"True."

"So here I am now with all of this love spilling out of my heart onto the sidewalk, and no kids of my own to love; and as a gay man, I'm terrified to touch kids, to hug them even when it's what they need."

"You don't ever touch your students?" Linda asked.

"I'll tap them on the shoulder, but that's it…maybe a sideways embrace if it's graduation or their dog killed their cat—which happened this year to one poor kid." I sighed heavily. "It's just the process of learning to live with a wounded heart—not broken…just *wounded*."

Linda scrutinized me. "I know what that's like for me, but what's it like for you?"

"It's knowing…there was this great experience that you were cheated out of—like…going to see your favorite band: You've bought excellent tickets and you're wearing the band's T-shirt, but while driving there you run over a piece of scrap metal in the road and get a flat tire, so when you finally arrive at the concert it's just ended, and you're seeing everyone smiling and laughing about how *amazing* it was as they stroll to their cars, and you know you've just been screwed by something you had no control over."

"When does this sting the most?"

I glanced back at the sinking gondola and then rejoined Linda's gaze. "I…*hate* shopping for greeting cards. They infuriate me: *Mom's birthday, Dad's birthday, Mother's Day, Father's Day.* I'm telling you, my blood pressure goes up every time I'm picking through those display shelves and I read all of those gooey, effusive sentiments."

Linda cocked an eyebrow. "Because you're jealous?"

"Exactly."

"So what do you do to move beyond that jealousy?"

"In my younger days, I chased their love by being more available to them, more attentive, more loving, a better Catholic… more apologetic…more Republican, harder working; I even painted their house for free and bought them expensive gifts: a Westminster chiming wall clock, a lovely pecan coffee table, even a stupid four-hundred-dollar Electrolux vacuum that still works *forty years later.* But nothing changed, and I only got pulled deeper into their marital abyss, the Mariana Trench of Dysfunction."

"*Mariana Trench* is a great drag name, by the way."

"So like some sort of *psychic arthritis*," I continued, "I've learned to *acknowledge* the pain: *There it is again. It'll probably never go away, and that's OK.* I look beyond my sadness and disappointment and woundedness to take comfort in my blessings—and they are numerous, thank God and Jay, not necessarily in that order."

"*Woundedness.* Hmm." Linda fiddled with her butter knife and then glanced over her shoulder at the salad bar. "What's your perspective about that?"

"Would you like me to tell you now, or after you go get the slice of pizza that's been screaming your name?"

"Pizza can wait."

I had to think about this, as *woundedness* was a term Doc Reed had used in our interview. "Well…no one says someone was *injured in a battle*; soldiers are always *wounded*; instead, people get injured in car accidents."

"So wounding implies intent?" Linda asked.

"And complicity, I suppose."

"How so?"

I considered Linda's question, because I'd never thought about it. "One must *engage* in battle in order to be wounded. So the complicity would be implicit."

"Unless you're a civilian," Linda countered, "and you simply happen to be in the wrong place at the wrong time."

"A casualty of childhood," I said, smirking. "But I also think a *wounded heart* can also be thought of as a *maiming of the psyche.*"

"Yikes."

"But think about it," I went on. "That's why certain professions—teachers, doctors, nurses, for example—are mandated reporters with regard to child abuse and neglect, because we know a child's psyche can be maimed. *Stunted. Damaged. Wounded.* And it can take a lifetime to recover."

"If you're lucky." Linda chuckled. "So you think a wounded heart is on parallel with, say, being in battle and losing a leg? *Or worse?*"

"Well, let's think about it," I proposed. "You're in battle and you lose your legs to an IED, the way some of those soldiers in Iraq and Afghanistan have been wounded. So for the rest of your life, every time you see people run, or stroll along the beach, or dance, or bicycle, or—"

"Shop for roller skates?" Linda asked.

"Exactly!" I leaned in. "I'm imagining there's going to be this psychic pain. This feeling of, *Why me?* Even if you'd signed up for battle."

"So enough about woundedness. Tell me about your blessings."

"I'm healthy," I replied. "I didn't die in the AIDS plague. I made it through college on my own dime and graduate school after that. I met a wonderful, handsome, healthy, funny guy and made a wonderful life with him over the past thirty years. We have two homes, two cars—one paid for—and two dogs we adore. We still laugh together and don't run out of things to talk about. I get to work with kids and to gain their admiration, as well as that of their parents. I'll be retired in three years, and one home will be paid off. I usually have something to look forward to, and I have a small, select cluster of dear friends I adore who'll listen to me babble and complain and who laugh at my jokes…most of the time."

Linda sat back. "What's that they say about living well being the best revenge?"

I shrugged. "It's not about revenge for me," I countered. "I just don't have the stomach for revenge—especially now that I think it might've not been my father's fault, after all."

"That concussion stuff you mentioned before?" Linda asked. "I've been hearing a lot about that—all over the news, unfortunately."

"And I've got an interview at the end of this week with a top neurologist to discuss CTE, or concussion syndrome. Dr. Aaron Aronow, from Cedars-Sinai and USC."

"Oh, I can't wait to hear what he says." Linda clasped my hand. "You know, it seems to me that it hasn't been so much about *learning to live with a wounded heart* as it's been *enabling yourself to thrive with a wounded heart*. And you've done it, Nicky-poo."

I felt my eyes moisten. "Thank you," I said with a sigh. "Thank you so much for listening."

"Does it feel good to realize how far you've come?"

"Almost better than pizza," I muttered, smiling.

"Which reminds me," Linda said as she scooted out of the booth.

As I watched Linda carry her plate toward the buffet, I wondered: If I still needed to look past my compartmentalized sadness and disappointment and woundedness, then perhaps that primary emotion of balled-up anger Allen mentioned hadn't been sufficiently untangled.

Could my upcoming interview with the neurologist I mentioned to Linda possibly help me pinch and stretch some metaphorical cotton threads? I understood from Terry DeCrescenzo that Dr. Howard Aaron Aronow had years of experience with CTE and was highly, *highly* respected.

Suddenly I couldn't wait for Friday.

CHAPTER 22

◆

Gone with the Mind
Interview with Howard
Aaron Aronow, MD

As I hastily backed my SUV into the parking lot's only remaining vacancy, my head swiveled to check the restricted-parking signs for the third time.

Looks OK.

I shut off the motor, grabbed my bag, locked my car, and then hustled up the steps of the medical office building in the Boyle Heights District of downtown Los Angeles that had been built under the looming shadow of County USC Medical Center. My watch told me I only had four minutes until our designated appointment time at ten a.m. and I refused to be late: Terry DeCrescenzo had generously helped arrange this meeting today with her friend and colleague Dr. Howard Aaron Aronow—researcher for the Bronx Aging and Dementia Study, physician at Cedars-Sinai Medical Center, clinical associate professor of neurology at the USC Keck School of Medicine, and member of the world's first NeuroAIDS Study Group—and I was hoping this interview would be the pot of gold at the end of my spectral journey.

"Call me Aaron," the imposing, yet bespectacled middle-aged man with the disarmingly soft voice told me, while shaking my hand.

"It's so good to meet you," I replied, smiling into his gray-green eyes. "Thank you for spending this time with me."

"Of course! Come this way"—he extended one arm—"I think there's a place down the hall we can use."

Minutes later we were sitting opposite each other in an otherwise empty conference room, its white walls glowing under the fluorescent lighting, and three long folding tables arranged in a U surrounded by stackable chairs.

Dr. Aronow leaned forward, elbows atop the table. "According to the letter you sent me, you're interested in chronic traumatic encephalopathy, or CTE, to come to terms with why your father did what he did to you and those you love, so you can put it together and make sense of it—or at least acknowledge, and even forgive him for, things beyond his control?"

"Exactly," I replied, shifting forward in my chair to check the levels on my voice recorder. "And since CTE is only diagnosable postmortem, can you tell me what indicators might make you think this patient is dealing with an organic disorder like CTE, as opposed to something behavioral?"

"In a simple sense, cognitive experts separate forms of dementia into cortical versus subcortical," Dr. Aronow explained. "CTE is more subcortical, whereas Alzheimer's is cortical. The cortex's primary purpose is higher-level thinking, to which various areas of the brain are wired, and the subcortical tissues are the interconnections of all these areas. We like to say that cortical dementias involve language functions, but the subcortical involves speeds of processes and movements. Parkinson's disease is subcortical. HIV, which is my specialty, can trigger a subcortical dementia. I like to think of it in simple terms, that if the wheels are spinning, they're spinning slowly. For example, if a patient is asked what's two plus two, they'll say they can't do it or they'll only stare at you; but then five minutes later they'll say four. Am I making sense?"

"So one indicator of CTE is slow processing?"

"Yes, and a patient's long-term memory might be totally intact, but their short-term memory is going: They misplace things, forget where they put their keys, pens, and wallets—"

"The little things everybody does," I cut in.

"But then it'll progress to putting their phone in the fridge or leaving the gas burning on the stove," Dr. Aronow clarified. "So things get more dangerous, like getting lost while driving. Then with Alzheimer's we might see word finding we call *paraphasia*, where they say a word that's *akin* to the right word or related to it, but it's incorrect: *papple* for apple or *gingerjed* for gingerbread.

"And with CTE, due to the loss of subcortical frontal fibers, there's a lack of impulse control because of the multiple areas involved, all the way down to the limbic system; there's emotional stuff and psychiatric illnesses associated with subcortical structures, so psychotic manifestations such as hallucinations, deep depression, and irregular behaviors are more prominent in subcortical dementias.

"These are the hallmarks of CTE: this disorganized behavior where one minute your patient is making sense and the next minute they're delusional or paranoid. But the differences between pure psychosis and schizophrenia—and CTE—is that CTE usually occurs in the fourth, fifth, sixth, and seventh decades, whereas psychosis generally occurs in the second and third decades. So pure psychiatric disease is something that occurs earlier, but CTE is a later disease because it's attributable to multiple brain traumas over time."

"This makes sense," I interjected, "because my father was always terrific in math, in engineering, and he could recall on which page a passage existed from a book he'd read on Russian history. But what I'm curious about is the rage. In our house, in order to survive, we were always avoiding *anything* that might set him off; I remember this from my earliest years. So…what can you tell me about rage and the manifestation of emotions, and how CTE might affect those aspects of parenting?"

Dr. Aronow clasped his hands atop the table. "Obviously, you're not going to be able to function in terms of appropriate parenting skills. What we've seen, if you look at the prototypical football players or prizefighters—and if you've seen *Concussion*, which was a pretty good portrayal—these individuals become isolated from their families…they become homeless, in spite of the money and prestige they had when they were playing; they essentially become derelicts and display psychoses, and many take drugs and alcohol as a means of self-medicating—which may provoke *even more violence* because of their effects on the brain—because they can't control their thought processes.

"So what happens is kids such as yourself have to grow up very early, to learn how to assuage and calm down and get away…which may mean not doing *anything* that might provoke them; and because it's some crazy behaviors, the family structure *can't figure out how to behave in order to not provoke the angry man.* It's not predictable.

"So you keep trying and trying and trying, and either you become crazy yourself—along with the individual—or you have to separate yourself because *you can't protect yourself otherwise.* An entire family might say, *I can't deal with you anymore.* That's why so many individuals become isolated and homeless and divorced; their family members break off the relationship because they can't cope.

"Today it's a bit easier in terms of the medications we have to control their psychotic behavior, and those features are treated the same way schizophrenia is treated: the same meds to decrease violent behavior, and both homicidal and suicidal ideation. We've all seen violent behavior in various football players, and I wonder, *is this the function of anabolic steroids or the beginnings of CTE?* The combination of the loss of subcortical control over behavior, and the disorganization of how information is processed, makes accomplishing all that's expected very difficult to achieve. And with men from your father's generation, they were taught to be hypermasculine, and earn the money, and discipline their kids, and go fight wars, so some of this aggression was *programmed,* if you will.

"So the logical progression of somebody who's *the man of the family* and is unknowingly suffering from CTE might have resulted in violence, because they don't have the stops and breaks to manage their behavior. And if you throw in alcohol, well…"

"You're describing the house I grew up in," I quietly told him.

"There's also a high incidence of PTSD," Dr. Aronow continued, "or post-traumatic stress disorder, associated with CTE—because if you keep getting banged in the head and one blow is bad enough, it'll be strong enough to provoke PTSD."

"Really?" I asked, recalling the blow to the head my father suffered in the boxing ring that was strong enough to shatter his left eardrum. "I had no idea."

"By definition, PTSD can occur with just *one life-threatening event*, like a really bad car accident…or when a soldier has an IED blow up in their face. So the worries aren't only for sports figures, but also for those who serve multiple military deployments and experience traumas, many of which go unnoticed. Even if you are *close* to guns, there will be a mild, mild, mild, mild shaking of the brain…but over time, with enough repetitions, something bad happens. For example, you can't ever shake a baby, because that can devastate a kid for the rest of their life; they'll never be normal.

"So many small vibrations can add up to *too much*. Our soldiers are really at risk—and what we're seeing as PTSD can also be a combination of PTSD *and* CTE."

"And all of this can only be diagnosed definitively postmortem?" I asked.

"We're actually getting better at making diagnoses *pre*mortem. You've probably read that Alzheimer's is a combination of neurofibular plaques and tangles—primarily in cortical tissues—and there are proteins associated with these abnormal conditions. Tau, in particular, is associated with CTE. However, *tau is also one of the two proteins associated with Alzheimer's*. The other is beta-amyloid. Presently, we have adequate marking scans for the diagnoses of young people exhibiting early onset of Alzheimer's; we use beta-amyloid-tagging positron emission tomography to see if cortical areas are lighting up with the scan. And there are experimental studies of people with suspected CTE, where we're able to do the same thing for tau. Those subcortical structures are lighting up, including the subcortical white matter and the amygdala and other limbic structures that control behavior. So we're almost there in being able to commercially diagnosis CTE; these are in development, so maybe in another couple of years they'll be on the market.

"But we can't make the brain better once the degeneration takes place. For many years we've been trying with Alzheimer's to replace the damaged neurons, but the success has been limited.

"Instead, we need to keep looking at the realities of *what's going wrong with brain cells*, but if we can be honest about head trauma and do things to better protect kids and adults, then we wouldn't be having CTE. If I had kids, I wouldn't let them play football—touch football, yes, but *not* tackle football. I recommend against it. It's too dangerous.

"But at least when patients have PET scans that corroborate what we suspect, we can take the results seriously and *give what they're going through a name*, so they'll have a reason for why they can't remember things, and why their behavior is so erratic...*and why they hurt people when they don't mean to*. Just having this says, *I'm not crazy, and there's a reason why this is happening to me*. And finally, a diagnosis is also a reinforcement for those who're taking medications that keep the behaviors in check."

I fiddled with the pen in my hand. "So maybe if my mother had known what was going on, she would've had more self-authority to protect her kids and get us the hell out of there. But she didn't, so everyone in the house was always walking on eggshells to not upset Dad." I chuckled. "Actually, we still are."

"Remember, society told your mom, *Your marriage is forever and you do whatever it takes to keep it together*." Dr. Aronow said. "She was probably dependent on him for financial security, and she wanted to look like they were a happy couple...and she could turn to him to help raise you. Was she employed, or was she a homemaker?"

"She was a homemaker," I replied, "but she had a lifetime teaching credential, so she'd taught a couple of years before my older sister was born. She also suffered from lifelong depression, so she spent most of her life in bed; when cooking dinner she quietly sobbed at the stove...so it's like we had one monster and one victim as parents. There was nowhere to go except to my older sister, Miriam. We became very close in those dark years."

"Because Miriam became Mommy," Dr. Aronow suggested. "You had to learn to grow up really fast to protect yourself, because there was no one protecting you."

I nodded. "Right."

"Did your mother blame herself or your dad, or did she blame her kids for her plight in life?"

"Sometimes she blamed us," I said, recalling how she'd once told me, *As a child, he tried to have a relationship with you, but you rejected him; and recently, If you'd come over more, he'd be happier and wouldn't lash out at* [punch] *me.* "She still blames us."

Dr. Aronow sat back in his chair. "Did she divorce him?"

"They're still together."

"She's hung in for the entire way," Dr. Aronow murmured and then paused. "You have to bridge that gap and become even more adult. *Forgive her.*"

"Yeah," I said, not wanting to burden Dr. Aronow with my mother's twisted abuse: *You're sick; you're perverted; sometimes I think it would've been easier if you'd died of AIDS...*

"You've got to forgive him, too," Dr. Aronow added, smiling kindly. "Look, there's no excuse for violent behavior, and if they can't handle their impulses and reactions, they need to get help. This means going to professionals, getting a diagnosis, and following a course of treatment. Psychiatrists can treat people with various meds, and some of the side effects are unpleasant...but even those are better than wreaking violence on the people you care about. So what's going on with your dad at this point? Is he getting help? Does he realize CTE could be his diagnosis?"

"He wouldn't comprehend it," I told him. "Cognitively, he's about thirty percent intact; even less on a bad day. He's been in and out of nursing homes; now they have home health care attendants seven days a week."

"Has the violent behavior stopped?"

"He throws punches, and he twists arms and wrists until the person cries out. He recently sent my mom to the ER with a blow to the jaw, plus she's had mysterious black eyes *from falling into doorways*, that sort of thing. She covers for him."

"Sounds like he has subcortical dementia from the strokes, and the CTE only adds to it. It's making sense when you put it together." Dr. Aronow tapped his fingers atop the Formica table. "They haven't gotten psychiatric help for him?"

"My mother won't even try antidepressants for herself or for my father. It's stonewall denial, which she's adept at; he had the stroke nineteen years ago, but for the first fourteen years she kept saying, *He'll get better and play golf again.* And he was kind of mobile for the first ten years; he managed to get himself to the bathroom, but that ended a while ago."

"How's his language function?" Dr. Aronow asked. "And I know he won't understand current events, because he can't encode."

"But he can still recall things about growing up," I answered. "He's fuzzy on some of the details, but if I bring up *When you went to New York to spar with Rocky Marciano…*"

"So he won't go there on his own," Dr. Aronow surmised. "Can he pick you out of the room?"

"Sometimes," I replied. "One time my father said, *Where's Nicky?* And my mother pointed to me and said, *He's right there.* Then my father said, *No, the other Nicky.*"

Dr. Aronow leaned forward again. "He was probably talking about you as a boy, because for the past ten years he hasn't been encoding who you are right now. He's remembering you *before* there was more manifestation of the injury to his brain. I've heard this before: *the other child, not that person,* from so many patients when their parents have dementia. It's usually subcortical."

"What I'm curious about," I began, "is how I never felt any love from him, even as a boy." I paused, trying to conjure a pertinent example. "Like…when someone enters the room and you look at each other, and you both smile as if to say, *I'm happy to see you,* even if you aren't. But he never smiled at me, so I took it to mean that I was this unlikable child; I was the wrong son for him. So is that flat affect…that inability to generate facial expressions—except for anger—indicative of CTE?"

"Individuals with subcortical dementia have great difficulty processing emotions, because it's a cognitive process, and empathy requires cognitive ability. How can you be empathic if you can't understand cognitively what someone's going through? If you add to this the idea that some people who have subcortical dementias started out narcissistic, it's only going to get worse, because their boundaries are all about self-preservation; it really becomes *all about them.*

"They don't take in experiences the way other people are experiencing it," Dr. Aronow continued. "*They just can't do it.* So all they have is this *disjointed internal understanding* of what's going on; they aren't processing stimuli properly from the external world, because they have to concentrate on their own internal world in order to function. So your dad's been caught up in a loop with himself for many, many years. That means he can't give anybody else an appropriate prolonged emotional response that's interpersonal."

I felt my eyes welling tears upon hearing this and realizing, *I always thought it was me.*

As if reading my thoughts, Dr. Aronow said, "I know that hurts, and probably makes you feel relieved that it wasn't about you. Again, it's *always* been about him.…I'd even suspect that he comes from a family structure that encouraged his narcissism."

"He was the eldest and the favorite son," I affirmed. "The handsome athlete."

"So he was set up, in that respect." Dr. Aronow paused. And then, "Did you not even have a single experience as a kid, when he took some time with you? I don't think he's a complete monster."

I sighed. "There was a time…when he and I used to go on walks on summer evenings—just the two of us. I was always fascinated by architecture, and we lived adjacent to a really nice neighborhood from the 1920s, where we'd stroll along, and I'd point out what I liked about this big old Spanish house or that other Tudor. He also tried to show me how to throw a football and catch a baseball." I coughed a laugh.

Dr. Aronow smirked. "A failure?"

"I don't have stellar large muscle coordination," I replied. "But, he was always impressed that I was a good musician, and he told me I had talents he didn't have. But I never heard him say, *I'm proud of you.*"

"This also isn't somebody I would expect to say, *I love you,* to his children."

I smiled wistfully. "At least not to me."

"Did he ever go to bat for you?"

"He went to b-b-bat for me once," I started to say, but stopped. And then, "Sorry, my stutter comes back sometimes. But it was after I'd been bullied by some kids at school that he went around and told all their dads, *If your kid ever does this to my son again, I'll smash your face in.*"

Dr. Aronow squared a look at me. "These events took place while his brain was still organized, where he could still express caring and love. This is also a man who was probably taught not to express himself—by what you're telling me—to not be emotional. But this is also someone whom I believe had the capability of loving you and probably did, and that's still in there somewhere."

"How do you know?"

"Because he said, *the other Nicky*. He couldn't see the *you* that's here today, because that's not the *you* that's real to him; but he remembers that his son is a part of him; even in a small way, he's able to acknowledge this because he can name you, and he has an image of who you were…even if it's not you right now. I don't believe he'd do that for someone who's not part of his family. And this may be as good as it gets for you."

I tried to raise a smile but failed. "I think you're right."

"I also think you need to hold on to those things, to say, *I can't change what happened, but at least some of the time there were glimmers of love and caring.* That means he wasn't a monster—or that he never cared. And I'm not providing excuses, but he behaved in the mores of his generation and according to his family birth order. But if you can hold on to that, and realize that he really couldn't help himself…and no doctor's been caring enough to investigate CTE as a preliminary diagnosis…or to tell your mom, *Here are the actions and here's the medication or other treatments: cognitive, behavioral, and other forms of psychotherapeutic interventions.* And if someone did this she might feel better, because it's been pretty bad all these years. Then she should get into something that might give her some enjoyment."

"I'll mention this to my sister," I said. "She has contact with my mother's doctors."

"My advice to you," Dr. Aronow went on, "is to hold on to whatever good memories you have of your dad. That even if he couldn't give you what you wanted or needed, he wasn't such a bad guy—at least some of the time. Treat him with the kindness he didn't give you, and make him comfortable, knowing there's no possibility of the dad that you wanted ever coming back...even in small glimpses. Think of yourself as *the other Nicky* remembering *the other dad* who could sometimes function. And tell yourself, *I'll give myself the kindness and caring I didn't get.*"

"Compassion is *very* important to me," I told Dr. Aronow. "And I think it'll be important for people who read this book to gain your advice...to read what you just told me: that it's about giving that parent what you didn't get, and switching roles and being the bigger man...or woman. You have to be strong to be gentle. In fact, the only time in the last eighteen years I've expressed anger to him was after he'd punched my mother in the stomach. Other than that, my interactions with him are always caring and calm: I'll ask him about growing up in Connecticut, and I can make him smile with the nicknames he made up for the kids in his neighborhood, like *Stinkbomb Amenta* and *Lard Load Langdon*. He always laughs."

"Yes!" Dr. Aronow exclaimed. "But it's never easy." He paused in thought. "I'll give you some insight into this picture that you couldn't know yet: You won't feel fully like an adult until they're both gone, and until this happens you're still going to feel like you're somebody's kid. But when they're gone, it'll change. You'll assume the roles of the older generation, because you're not someone's kids anymore. Mom or Dad doesn't exist."

"I'm sure you're correct." I stood up and reached for his hand. "Dr. Aronow, I can't tell you how much this means to me. Thank you."

Dr. Aronow smiled back at me. "You're very welcome. I hope this gives you some healing."

"You've no idea."

As I drove home, Dr. Aronow's words played back in my head like scenes from a movie, especially, *You probably thought it was your* *fault...*at this, I recalled the aforementioned shoebox filled with greeting cards from me to my parents that my mother saved, and how so many of them said things like, *Thank you for putting up with me.*

The other concept that materialized was this:

If high school, college, semipro, and professional athletes—and soldiers—can acquire CTE through contact sports or battle situations, this could create a *perfect storm of aggression*, because these folks are by nature alpha males and alpha females (I don't imagine one could be a successful boxer, MMA fighter, football player, or fighting solider otherwise); and the subcortical damage caused by CTE—combined with the alpha person's inherently aggressive temperament—could synergistically *turbocharge* that individual's tendency toward violence.

No wonder I was so terrified of my father!

But the other assertion of Dr. Aronow's that kept spinning in my head was this:

"PTSD can occur with just one life-threatening event, like a really bad car accident...or when soldier has an IED blow up in their face. So the worries aren't only for sports figures, but also for those who serve multiple military deployments and experience traumas, many of which go unnoticed."

With this being the case, do children of combat veterans experience similar childhoods to mine? And how might PTSD affect marriages?

As soon as I arrived home, I sent an email to my niece's husband, Dr. Adrian Aguilera.

Because if anyone could answer my questions, Adrian could.

But first, I needed to check in with Brandy.

Because I was finally meeting with her to discuss her mother's death.

CHAPTER 23

◆

End of the Rodeo

Pressing the phone to my ear with one hand and glancing down at my wristwatch, I lifted my eyes to gaze through our sliding glass doors as the downpour inundated our backyard, the water sheeting off our roof as if underneath a fire helicopter's water drop. "If I leave now, I can get there between, maybe, eleven thirty and noon?"

"Be really careful…" Brandy's voice hesitated. "Are you sure you wanna do this? It's raining like crazy here."

"Here too, but I've got a big, all-wheel-drive SUV," I assured her. "Don't worry."

"OK," Brandy replied. "See you later? We can have lunch at the pier."

"Can't wait."

Negotiating Southern California's concrete basket weave of roadways carried risks even on sunny days. But over the past few weeks, Los Angeles had been slammed by a series of storms befitting Norse mythology, with charcoal-puff clouds, flashes of lightning, and relentless downpours that transformed our city streets into canals and our cars into rolling boats. Of course, I'd probably have been smarter to stay home cuddling our dogs, but my break was cresting to its finale, so I was running out of time to find out what had happened leading up to—and following—Brandy's mother's death only months before.

Jay had been kind enough to fill the vehicle's cavernous fuel tank, so after sipping the dregs of my coffee, I set my navigation to Brandy's address and backed out of our driveway.

And I wondered: *Would Brandy be happier? She had recently retired from teaching, so with her mother no longer an issue, how might she be filling her days? What events had transpired leading up to her mother's death?* And most important, *Was Brandy feeling relief, or was she torturing herself with regrets?*

Nearly two hours later, Brandy opened her front door and greeted me with a squeal and a grin; her head-to-toe persona now broadcasted *relaxed* in contrast to her prior demeanor of *tense, tenser, tensest.*

"You look good." I held out my arms for a hello hug. "*Really* good."

Brandy squeezed me back. "How was your drive?"

"Uneventful," I told Brandy, reaching for her hand. "Come on, I'm starving!"

We agreed to save our recorded interview for after lunch, so our meal on the Huntington Beach Pier at Rosie's Diner was casual and gave us the chance to catch up over cold, lumpy chef's salads washed down with their humble house chardonnay; I discovered Brandy's son had remarried, her father was adjusting to assisted living, Brandy had recently been to Oregon to visit her daughter, and her injurious relationship with her husband was in the early stages of recovery.

After settling the bill, we strolled umbrella-less back to my car, thankful that the rain was, apparently, also on its lunch break.

"Just look at this!" Brandy swept her arms toward the storm-churned ocean—as wrinkled and steely as a sheet of discarded aluminum foil—and Renaissance sky: cottony wisps dappled with patches of Madonna-robe blue. "How could anyone be unhappy here?"

"You've been too...*blinded* by your mom's craziness to see what was in front of you."

Brandy turned to me. "I used to bring my kids here to surf before school."

"Lucky kids, having a mom like you."

Brandy's eyes welled. "I've tried. I've really tried."

"I know you have." We resumed our stroll. "Where's a good, quiet place to record you?"

"There's a park." Brandy pointed east. "Close by."

Ten or so minutes later we'd parked and set up my voice recorder atop the SUV's dashboard. "Ready?" I asked, verifying the recording levels.

"If you are."

"When did your mom pass away?"

"Almost seven months ago.

"What happened leading up to her death?"

"It's been kind of a blur. Well…" Brandy blew out a long, exhausted sigh. "One day I got to my parents' house and there was no answer, and I thought, *What if they're dead?* So I called the police, who discovered they were actually at the hospital. But when I called the hospital, they said, *We can tell you your parents aren't dead, but we can't tell you where they are.* That began the nightmare of not having power of attorney, because my mother—who's crazy—was running the show from her hospital bed. Oh—while she was there, she hired a caregiver."

"How'd that happen?"

"They roam the halls preying on the patients like vultures. But since this company began supplying caregivers, Mom didn't need me anymore, so she started being mean to me again. I'd come over and she would say shit to the caregivers about me. And each time I showed up, she had a different caregiver doing a shitty job. Then, between January and April she was in the hospital four times, but she never told me.

"Turns out, she went in because she was dehydrated, and they said she'd be there for a month or so. But she couldn't walk or go to bathroom, so she was released into a nursing home, and my dad started living with me."

"How'd that work out?" I asked.

"I'd go to work and my dad would turn on the oven and forget to turn it off. I was scared to leave him alone, so I started trying to find him an assisted living facility. In the meantime, I'm working full-time and trying to save my marriage, and my mother's fighting me *every fucking step of the way.*

"My dad, who didn't need it, had long-term-care coverage, but my mom didn't. So she racked up five hundred thousand dollars in medical bills; *thank God for Medicare.* We moved her into my dad's assisted living: a beautiful living room with two bedrooms, because she couldn't be in the same room as my dad.

"But she started spitting at the caregivers, pulling down the curtains, and called them *putas. She's terrible,* they'd tell me. *How did you live with her? Your dad is such a sweet man.* And when the attendant would come in, my mom would say, *Oh, is that whore here to suck you off?* She used words in Romanian I didn't even know; I had to check with my cousin, who was shocked by her language.

"The caregiver said Mom was spitting food on the floor and my dad was trying to pick it up, and I'd ask, *Why did you do that?* She'd tell me, *Just to see your dad pick it up.* Super cruel. The whole time she smelled like shit, and she had this infected poo called C. diff, where they can't touch her. I had to put on coveralls to visit her.

"Later, we found out she had colon cancer, but she needed to see a heart specialist to see if she could tolerate the surgery. When we went in a taxi for her doctor visits, she'd tell the driver, *This is my daughter. She fucks her dad.* And the whole time she's barking at me in Romanian saying things only I understand."

"Like what?"

"Like everything she hates about me."

"Nice." I coughed a laugh. "So what were the events leading up to her passing?"

"They kicked her out of the assisted living, because she wouldn't let someone put in the catheter and she had five liters of urine in her bladder. *I want to die,* she'd groan. *I want to die.* I'd tell her, *Mom, you didn't let that lady put in a catheter, so they're probably going to put you back in the hospital.*

"So the next day, sure enough, she went into the hospital. And as she was getting wheeled in, she flipped off my dad and said, *Fuck you, Zoltan.* And that was my last week of school and I missed my last graduation—after thirty-three years of teaching, the last four months were spent at school on the phone with her doctors. I didn't even get the chance to say goodbye to my students, because I was taking care of my parents.

"So I went on a little end-of-the-year trip with some other teachers. We went to some casino in the desert, where I got a phone call from the doctor asking if I wanted my mother to have surgery. I told him, *I don't have power of attorney. She'll decide what she wants to do.* The next day I get a call that says, *Your mother doesn't want you to call anymore or to know what's going on, and neither is your dad welcome.* And at first I thought, *What the fuck?* Then I started relaxing.

"I didn't hear anything until the end of July—I still have her message in my voicemail if I want to torture myself—because she needed money: twenty thousand dollars, because her Medicare ran out. So that's when I got into her finances and discovered her caregiver at home had been ripping them off."

"How?"

"On Easter Sunday I called Juliann—the old caregiver I'd found for them—and said, *How did you fucking take eighty-three thousand dollars from my parents? You were sitting there watching TV with her and you got paid five hundred dollars per day? How can you sleep at night?* And Juliann tells me, *You know how hard it is to take care of her.* What a bitch.

"When I brought it up to my mom, she said, *You found her, she was your friend.* Everything was my fault. My mother even took me out of her will and went against her lawyer's wishes and gave everything to my kids. One lawyer even refused to take her case because she was being so vindictive; his letter said, *We don't believe Zoltan knows what he's signing, so any agreement is null and void.*

"The first four months of retirement were spent cleaning out my mom's house: closets packed with clothes, three dresses on one hanger, clothes deep on the floor. Every time I opened a different closet and saw all the shit she was saving, I started crying. So I paid twenty thousand bucks to empty and fix up the house so someone could live in it, but when it was finally ready to rent out, my mom said, *I want to move back in there.*"

"My head would've exploded."

"And get this: My accountant said, *You'd better not rent it out, because she has the legal right to move in.*

"So three months went by, the house was still empty, and I hadn't heard from her. Then I got this phone call that said, *Your mom needs money, whose going to pay for this?* I'd told them, *I'm not in her life anymore, so ask her how she's going to pay for it, because whatever I do will be wrong and she'll change her mind. Finally I got a call from hospice—no one had even told me she was in hospice—saying, *She's not eating, and today she's unresponsive.* I asked, *Is she ready to die?* They told me, *You should probably come and say your goodbyes.*

"My dad didn't want to go, so I went by myself, and *Oh my God, she looked like death, like a skeleton.* I told her I was sorry she was going through this, and I was sorry she's in pain, and that *it's OK to die, that I'm taking care of Daddy, that you're going to be feeling better.* I kissed her and told her I loved her and I was sorry our relationship was this way, and I forgave her. My son showed up later and was crying too, so he had his time with her.

"The next day my dad wanted to go see her. And I'm thinking, *I don't want to go back there,* but is she going to die alone? Should I stay here and hold her hand? I'd feel bad if she's by herself when she meets her maker.

"*No,* the hospice workers told me, *someone's always here, and if something happens we'll call you. Live your life, don't feel guilty…we're here.*"

"So did she die that night?" I asked.

"No! The next day we went in, and lo and behold, she's up and awake!! *She's fine,* the hospice workers tell me, *this morning, she wanted a 7Up!* And I'm thinking, *Oh fuck, here we go again!*" Brandy began sobbing. "After I walk in, she says to me, *It's so nice to see you!* Suddenly, she was the kind mother who—once in a while—kissed me and loved me and told me I was wonderful. She apologized and said, *I know it's my fault. You're a good girl.* She kept kissing my hand, saying, *You're so warm.* She told me she loved me and asked, *Is this a dream? I thought I dreamed about you last night.*

"*No, Mom,* I told her. *I was here. That was me.*" I think she finally got some good meds, because she was happy, *so happy* to see me. *And Michael,* she asked, *did he get married? Your kids, are they OK? Are the dogs OK? Your horse?* And I'm remembering that when she was in the assisted living, she had pictures of me and my son and my horse, and she tore out my face, but it didn't bug me until I saw that she tore out my son's face and my horse's face."

"Are you kidding me?!" I nearly yelled.

"But on that last day—just like the books on grieving say—she made her peace. My mom died by the book. But I wanted to stay there, because she was sweet and complimentary and—"

"Human for the first time?" I interrupted.

"Yes, human for the first time in a *very long time.* She was happy…but she looked like hell, and her breath smelled like death and she had these bruises on her hands and she was so scary-looking and her hair was up in a bun and she looked like that last scene in *Psycho* where that chair turns around. But I kissed her on the lips and on the forehead, and we were crying and saying how sorry we were. Then she'd had enough and got tired, so I left.

"So I told my son, *You should see her! She's a happy person now.* We went the next day and she was back to her old self, complaining and saying, *What do you want from me?* But I also noticed then that her hands were curling up like a baby's, like she was going back to the womb."

"You were watching death take over," I suggested.

"That's it!" Brandy exclaimed. "I was in the presence of death! But the next day when I went to visit, she was happy again and told me, *I don't want a funeral or a memorial, I want to give my body to science.* I said, *Mom, you don't just decide that right now, that's a process.* That's an impossible task! But I contacted UCLA and asked if I could do that, and they agreed!

"So the final day was Friday; she was really bad off, and she said to me, *I want to live! I want to live! I want to be selfish.* And when she was saying it, she looked like a talking skeleton, and I said, *Now you're saying you want to live? Then you gotta start eating! Here's an avocado from the backyard!*"

"Tell me about when you got the call," I suggested, feeling exhausted.

"The next morning, I saw a voicemail had come in from the care facility asking me to call them. I knew what happened, so I asked my husband to call. As he spoke to them, I was in the back saying, *Is she dead? Is she dead?* And he's going, *Hold on. Thank you, thank you, I'll call you back in a bit.* So he hung up and I said, *Is she really dead? Is she really dead? Is this for real?* I wanted to make sure this wasn't a joke, because I was living in fear that it would start all over again. And my neighbor heard me; she was in the backyard when I fell down on my knees crying and saying, *I'm so sorry;* and part of me was relieved, because I didn't want to go back there with my dad, but part of me couldn't believe it…just wouldn't allow myself to believe it. And then it dawned on me: *Insanity just ended. Now sanity can take over.* Because I was in the middle of insanity for six months—"

"Even longer," I reminded her.

"But this was worse; it ratcheted up higher—like a *hurricane* of insanity. But it didn't end," Brandy explained, "because they started calling about funeral arrangements and this and that, so it didn't end. I didn't pick up her shit from there for about a month. I couldn't do it.

"Telling my dad was hard, too. He didn't believe it. Then I called my kids, and my son was on a trip so I didn't call him until he got home; and my daughter didn't even cry when I told her."

"Did you?" I asked.

Brandy shook her head. "Not until later. Probably the most I cried was on New Year's because of certain things; remember, she liked New Year's."

I smiled. "Yeah, I remember that."

"But after her death everything was, *Oh, it's been two days, oh it's been a week. Oh, it's been two weeks.* And for the first months everything was in reference to her death. She passed away at nine fifty on a Saturday morning, so Saturday mornings were hard for me.

"Another irony is five days later when they called me from the morgue about the death certificate, the cause of death was listed as cardiac arrest with Alzheimer's. And I said, *Alzheimer's? My mother* had Alzheimer's? That's the first time *my mother* and *Alzheimer's* were in the same sentence. So I called her old facility, and sure enough, they had Alzheimer's on the chart.

"For me, that was the first beginning of relief. Like, *Wow, it's not my fault. Maybe she wasn't as wicked as she seemed.* I didn't want to think of her as this huge, wicked spirit. And now I don't think of her as an evil spirit, but as something pure; that by leaving all this shit that she hated, now she's not as angry."

"She's free?" I suggested.

"She's free—and I don't feel shackled anymore. I don't hear her critical voice in the back of my head; that stopped the day she died… her voice died in my head on that very day.

"So now when I hear my own voice imitating her in my head, I tell myself, *Why are you talking like this, Brandy? Brandy needs to be talked to nicely, like how you'd talk to a child. You got to compliment Brandy in your head, to tell her it's OK…tell her she doesn't have to be perfect.* So that self-talk changed. That self-talk changed."

"Has that been hard for you?" I asked. "How does it feel to have experienced that change?"

"I try to be kind to Brandy, to love her, to allow her some selfishness…to grab some things for herself. It started with buying my horse, which is all for me."

"In the last seven months," I asked, "what's been the progression from then to now?"

Brandy looked out the windshield of my SUV, tracking a man walking his Chihuahua. "Well, I don't have the rage anymore that you still have. *It's gone.* And I've accepted the fact that my mother was a sick, sadistic person—but maybe that wasn't all her fault. And I know now that it wasn't *my* fault. I didn't deserve her anger—and at least I had *one* parent who loved me, even if he never stood up to her for me. But he smothered me with love, so I know how it feels to be loved unconditionally.

"My therapist told me that in such a short time, I've developed a lot of compassion for this woman who was my tormentor for so long. That helps a lot, too. So those are the shackles that are gone:

knowing she was just really sick…and she was probably really sick even when I was little."

"So her death has given you some much-needed objectivity," I suggested.

"Yes—because I'm not in the mix anymore," Brandy explained. "My stomach's not tight as I drive over to see her anymore.

"But the last seven months have been hard in a different way, because I still had to get power of attorney for my dad and figure out how to get money for his care; luckily his doctor assessed him as having dementia, so his long-term care coverage kicked in to cover the assisted living. So now, everything's coming to a quiet end.

"But what makes me sad is thinking about somebody who's lost someone they *actually loved*—not that I didn't love my mom, but I was relieved to lose her. So what do people do when they lose someone they're in love with? A husband, a wife, a child? For me it was…I hate to say it, but it was a relief."

"It's OK to say that," I told her. "And it'll continue to be a relief."

"But when I want to torture myself, I listen to my mom's voice on my phone. Because I think she died alone, which was her choice."

"She made certain that would happen," I added.

"Oh, I almost forgot: One of the nurses said to me, *This is temporary. This hell that you're in is temporary. Watching your parent die. It's temporary.* So I kept saying this to myself, because she'd call in the middle of school, but it's temporary. There is another side."

"Ideally, what would you like to see happen for the rest of your life?" I asked.

Brandy sighed as she slumped into the car seat. "I'd like me and my husband to fall in love again. For him to be my partner. That's my number one longing. To love each other. I need a partner, and I don't want to go look for another one. I don't want to start over. I want him and me to joke like we used to, to not be angry and pointing fingers at each other."

"Your marriage was in the midst of a war zone," I suggested. "It's completely understandable that you took this incredible stress out on each other."

Brandy turned to me, her green eyes searching mine. "I tell him, *You gotta know I'm a different person now that my mom's gone. I hope you see that.* He acknowledges that I'm calmer and kinder, and I'm not as bold and sure. I get scared, and a couple of days after my mom passed, I told him I've just lived through what would be the scariest movie of all time.

"So my number one thing would be to reconnect with my husband. And to take care of my dad as best I can. I don't know if I want to go to Romania with him, because he's a lot of work, but if I let myself believe it, my life's pretty damn good right now. It's the way I want it to be. I like the way it is."

I smiled. "You've worked really hard for this life."

"Yeah." Brandy nodded, smiling back at me. "I have difficulty saying, *I'm happy,* because I'm afraid something's going to get fucked up. But parts of me say, *I love this.* I love taking my horse out and taking drum lessons and flying around the country, and I let myself buy this expensive saddle that's worth more than my car…and my horse loves me too. I told her we're in this together, and my grandchildren will sit on her back."

I reached out and clasped Brandy's hand. "Sounds to me like you're living a happy ending."

Brandy took a deep breath. "Not yet," she said, and then blew out a long sigh. "It's what I hope for—and that hope started when my mom passed."

"Please don't feel bad about saying that."

"Well, the insanity stopped," Brandy said. "But I wished her dead for everybody's peace. I just wished it all to stop."

"And it did."

"Yes," Brandy said, her face awash with relief. "*It was temporary,* just as the hospice people said, and it finally stopped."

"So now *you* can start," I said.

Brandy nodded. "And that's exactly what I've been doing. But it's not easy; the craziness went on for so long."

I tapped my hand on the steering wheel. "Do you think you suffer from PTSD?"

"Yep," Brandy stated. "Or at least from what I know about it."

"I've got an interview tomorrow with a therapist who specializes in PTSD," I told her. "And if I learn something that applies to you, I'll let you know."

"That's OK." Brandy snickered.

"Why?"

"My therapist told me she's already treating me for it."

CHAPTER 24

◆

Post-Traumatic Stress Disorder Interview with Adrian Aguilera, PhD

"You must be the happiest man on earth," I told Adrian via Skype; we were geographically disparate, so a face-to-face interview just wasn't in the cards. "Your kids are healthy and beautiful, your wife is smart and gorgeous, and you're traveling all over the world."

On my laptop, Adrian grinned his famous grin. "Yep, I'm a lucky guy."

Then the screen went black.

"Adrian?"

"I'm here."

"Let's try something else. Hold on…"

The screen continued to glow black. So I fiddled and tapped and moused, but nothing worked. "Do you mind if I call you via cell?"

Adrian laughed, and then recited his phone number.

Dr. Adrian Aguilera is my niece's husband, and I've known him for about ten years, having met him just before he and Lupe got married, and just after he'd finished his PhD.

Adrian worked extensively with veterans, so I figured he'd seen a lot of post-traumatic stress disorder, or PTSD—as well as more than his fair share of CTE—and could enlighten me on the tragedies of both.

The call went through. "You there?" I asked.

"All is well," Adrian replied.

"Thanks for your flexibility. Can you tell me your qualifications and education?"

"I'm a licensed clinical psychologist and a professor at UC Berkeley," Adrian explained. "I've been practicing as a licensed clinician for six years, and before that was in training for five years. So I've been doing eleven or twelve years of treatment and practice in psychology. My specialty is working with depression as well as anxiety disorders like PTSD; I do some therapy with families, and I've had experience with serious mental illnesses such as schizophrenia."

Wishing we were having this conversation in person, I glanced at my notes. "In what setting did you work with patients with PTSD?"

"The bulk of my work was at the San Francisco Veterans Administration, because with vets there's a very high rate of PTSD. Since then, I've continued my work with veterans and have extended it to folks from lower-income backgrounds who've experienced trauma."

"Trauma including PTSD, or with accidents or abuse?" I asked.

"Emotional trauma...different things that lead to trauma: military trauma in some, and in others it's related to abuse, um... sexual abuse, physical violence. Things like that."

"So PTSD in particular."

"Yes, mostly."

"Can you tell me how PTSD might affect the brain, both structurally and behaviorally?" I asked.

"Generally, it tends to heighten the parts of your brain that are vigilant."

"How?"

"Our brains are built to be sensitive to fearful memories," Dr. Aguilera began. "If you think of our early evolutionary days, if there's an animal running to kill you, your brain will encode this scenario *really* well, so you can avoid that situation and not be in danger again. Evolution does a good job of letting our brains learn what's dangerous or deadly. But then some people *overlearn* it; they encode it so well that the brain sees threats *really clearly*, but then it also generalizes this perceived danger onto other threats that aren't as dangerous. So you're attuned to the threat of a lion, but you apply this to house cats that are harmless. It becomes generalized."

"So the brain becomes hypersensitive to threats?"

"Yes, the part of the brain called the amygdala senses fear and gets triggered."

I recalled the information Dr. Aronow relayed about the brain damage CTE causes. "Would this be subcortical?"

"It's in the *limbic system*, where the subcortical structures meet up with the cerebral cortex," Dr. Aguilera clarified. "It's not part of what some think of as *the human brain*...which is the prefrontal cortex that makes humans unique; this PTSD affects part of the *earlier* brain."

"Fight or flight?" I asked.

"Yes."

"But would emotions like compassion and love also be affected?"

"Yeah, that whole area is the home of lots of these emotions," Dr. Aguilera agreed. "The limbic system also houses the hippocampus, which is implicated in memories, depression, and some of these basic emotions."

The TED talk by Dr. Nadine Burke-Harris, and the social workers' symposium with Dr. Felitti, suddenly swept back to me. "So for kids who're raised in this kind of 'threatening' environment, the lion never leaves; the lion's sitting on the couch or at the dining table or is sneaking into their bedroom at night. And these kids who weather adverse childhood experiences also suffer long-term health effects: they tend to have asthma as adults, high blood pressure, and other autoimmune issues. *So could there be long-term health effects as well as generalized emotional effects of living with a parent with PTSD, just as there are for children of parents with CTE?*"

"Yes...particularly early on, the panic areas of your brain are like an engine in a car: They are constantly revved up, so once you're set that way, you're ready to take off all the time."

"Why?"

"Because that's the part of your brain that keeps on getting exercised, so you're ready to use it. It's conditioning. But for folks who didn't have to employ this as much as kids, it's not going to be as ready...it's not as developed as an instinct as it is for other people."

"How might PTSD affect cognitive processing?" I asked. "Do you see dementia?"

"There are a variety of ways," Dr. Aguilera explained. "In the immediate realm, you're taxing your brain to be so vigilant about these threats and fears; it's using so much of its energy trying to identify threats that it's constantly overworked. So, other things that're coming into the cognitive field are harder to deal with, because you're so preoccupied with these threats that are real or perceived.

"As a result, there's this being overinvolved in emotion...*or on the flip side*, being avoidant and detached. Either way, it's dealing with these emotional and behavioral imbalances that are based upon inaccurate threat appraisal."

"This makes sense," I said, recalling how fearful I was as a child about any new experience: learning to swim; attending first grade; eating shrimp. "Regarding this detachment: Are there other sorts of emotional behaviors—or moods—that you'd typically see with PTSD?"

"One emotional manifestation that's particularly associated with PTSD is the idea of *dissociation*, which is like being *outside of oneself*...like living in the world without being an active participant."

I suddenly recalled my interview with Allen Ruyle, who also mentioned this phenomenon of dissociation with PTSD. "As these PTSD sufferers age, do you tend to see more dementia?"

"Yes. Those with PTSD tend to experience more dementia, especially if it's with *TBI. Traumatic brain injury.* The two are highly related."

"With TBI, this would include CTE, yes?" I asked.

"Yes."

"And what might be some of the more extreme behaviors you'd see with PTSD or TBI?"

"Well." Dr. Aguilera hesitated. "It's varied—but lots of aggressive behaviors, self-destructive behaviors—especially while recalling or reliving the traumatic events that sparked the PTSD or TBI. The person might also experience the *dissociation* as I mentioned, with a removal from feeling sensory stimuli; and this combination would be especially challenging, because the person is experiencing these emotions without the sense that they're living in their body; it's like acting without a sense of control while the emotions are coming out...if that makes sense."

"How might this affect parenting?" I asked.

"Oohhh," Adrian groaned. "It would certainly be impacted negatively, because that's where you see patterns of abuse...of aggression; and in particular, from a child's perspective of *Why am I in this very uncertain environment where I can't really count on anything?*

"The hallmark of a healthy development," Dr. Aguilera continued, "is a sense of structure and stability, where you know the rules of the game—and these vary by culture, of course—but one of the challenges of traumatic environments is where it's sprinkled with trauma, and there's a lot more uncertainty. The child doesn't know how that parent will react from one day to the next, so the child will be on edge, and he or she may start to take on some of these emotions as well, especially as they mature."

"That makes perfect sense," I said. "So are there successful treatments for people suffering from PTSD?"

"There's a variety of treatments that've been successful," Adrian replied. "One is *cognitive processing therapy*, where somebody's experienced a traumatic event, and you identify the initial source or stressor of the PTSD: that is, whatever it was that the person was exposed to—or perceived—that caused the actual injury, you try to get the person to face it head on. They sort of relive the actual event.

"Unfortunately, for some people there're *many* events, and PTSD makes it worse by causing people to *avoid the stressor* by shutting down emotions...by using substances...by dissociating, all kinds of ways.

"Instead, you want to *face the thing that caused so much fear...* face it *head on*, as I said, and start changing the meaning of it. Because often what happens with traumatic events is a lot of fear—even terror—gets mixed with other emotions, like guilt.

"For example, I worked with someone who was in charge of a convoy in Iraq or Afghanistan: He was driving along, and a bomb exploded a few cars back and many of the people he was in charge of died. And he talked about his sense of responsibility and *guilt*, because he was in command and it happened because of him—or at least he thought it did. His view of that situation was very much colored by his emotions...and what he thought he *should've done*, or *could've done*. He felt like he was the one that shouldn't be here, what we call *survivor's guilt*. So his way of coping was to avoid it, to never think of it, and to push it away as much as possible.

"But that process takes so much work, and it winds up having the opposite effect because it's always with you, and you can't escape it. So I tried to help him reframe the event through *cognitive processing*, and to reprocess what happened. It's an effective therapy...but as you can imagine, it can be really difficult to get people to go there.

"Another therapeutic process that's related is called *prolonged exposure*. It's similar, but frankly it's a matter of essentially rehearsing and retelling the story of the traumatic event, and hearing it and telling it to yourself. The PTSD sufferer literally voice records themselves telling about what happened, and they listen to it on a daily basis until all of the strong, scary emotions start dissipating, and it becomes not the threat it once was."

"So it's desensitizing oneself to a scary, traumatic event?" I asked, recalling Carol Cushman's client who needed to voice record the childhood trauma that her mother caused, but then Carol herself had to press *Play*.

"Exactly," Dr. Aguilera agreed. "And desensitization is a big principal in terms of anxiety in general, and PTSD is an anxiety disorder. It's similar to how you'd treat a phobia of spiders or elevators: The point would be to get slowly closer and closer until you become desensitized to the perceived trauma in it."

"What have you seen with adult children of parents who suffered from PTSD or CTE? What sorts of family dynamics play out?"

"Well..." Adrian began, "not everybody who experiences trauma reacts the same way: Some people are more—or even less—sensitive to it. But that lack of certainty, or structure, in the home environment that we discussed earlier leads many children to inherit their parents' proclivities in *responding similarly* to stress: The abused become abusers, because it's what they grew up knowing; they *assimilate* to their family dynamic.

"But some will become the opposite, which we refer to as *contrast:* The adult realizes, *I'll never do that to my child or my spouse, because I remember what that felt like and I hated it.* They develop *contrasting behaviors* instead."

"That's what I've always thought," I interjected, "because I know that neither of my sisters nor I have ever hurt kids; my sisters are both wonderful parents to their children, and I've had more than a thousand students in my care over the years as a teacher. I'd never lay a hurtful hand on a child…*or a dog* for that matter. In fact, I've always held up my father as an example of what not to be."

"*Contrast,*" Adrian emphasized.

"So when that *contrasting adult* begins dealing with that traumatizing parent who's now failing," I asked, "what are the dynamics?"

"I think it depends on *how that adult child processed those events and their accompanying emotions.* Unfortunately, we don't have a lot of vocabulary in our culture about these events; we tend to view them more as *my father is simply this way* and *my mother is simply that way,* and my sense is that it's more the exception than the norm for people to think about these problems and see how their childhood experiences continue to affect them.

"The exception might be if this behavior is transmitted in an intergenerational manner, where adult children need to get treatment for themselves, and then it becomes easier to see their counterproductive or damaging behaviors that originated with their parents. This might be their lifesaving process."

"Perhaps they'd experience anger initially and empathy later on?" I asked.

"Yes."

"Do you think forgiveness helps to facilitate the empathy?"

"Yes, definitely," Dr. Aguilera agreed. "Think about the stages of loss, death, and grief, about that continuum of process: *denial, anger, bargaining, depression,* and finally *acceptance.* I believe part of forgiveness is acceptance: Not only are you forgiving that person; you're accepting that person for who they are…and what they did… and all of their ugliness. And that's where forgiveness is. *It's accepting their failings.* But with many people, I think strong emotions come first, and then they don't always go beyond that."

"I think that's such a beautiful parallel, those stages of loss and grief from Elisabeth Kübler-Ross. Is that what you're referencing?

"Yes."

"No one's brought up that parallel until now," I said, "and I think it's very powerful."

"The stages of loss, death, and grief for one's childhood?" Adrian asked.

"And one's innocence," I added. "So when a diagnosis of PTSD or CTE or TBI is determined, is this diagnosis helpful, because there's a name for what's happened?"

"I think many times a diagnosis is helpful, because we seek meaning for our experiences; and often until a diagnosis is made, people think they're alone. Then people realize: *I'm not weird, because there are other people going through this as well.* This can be of benefit.

Again, I thought of Allen Ruyle's work.

"But with a diagnosis can also come a stigma," Adrian clarified. "*You're damaged, you're not strong enough.* It might be a catch-22."

"But if someone knows that TBI is involved," I pressed, "and there's an organic source for the rage or dementia or whatever, then it's not about someone simply being *weak of character* or someone who's choosing to be a monster. I'd think this would be helpful for people to think of their brains as damaged machines: Like a virus-infected computer, it's going to crash from time to time."

"Yes, I think anytime one can place the responsibility outside of themselves—and it's always a fuzzy gray line—it's helpful," said Dr. Aguilera. "And let's not lose sight of how the organic [what's happening inside the brain's structure] is intertwined with one's will and self-control. But if someone can frame it in a medical way, people tend to be more open. For example, if you talk about your depression as a chemical imbalance, people can think of that as less stigmatizing.

"But there are pros and cons to this, and the downside of framing something as a *medical issue* has the potential disadvantage of allowing one to feel like one doesn't have the responsibility to put effort into improving it. So it can be a double-edged sword.

"No, you can't fix the neuronal impact of CTE or TBI. However, there are usually some behaviors you can practice to manage the situation: Instead of giving up and sitting at home, if you put some efforts into engaging in life…going out for a walk and being social and other things that can at least allow the other parts of your brain to be healthy, you can make up for some of these things. And, no, it's not going to ever go back to normal, but these other behaviors can help."

"What about medications?" I asked. "Will they help?"

"They can," Dr. Aguilera replied. "And again, I think about this in a behavioral perspective, because I don't prescribe medications. But meds can be helpful when combined with behavioral changes, and this is where we tend to see the most progress. Meds often help people to engage and improve their behaviors, but taking the pills in and of themselves won't fix everything; they may help you *engage in life* and other actions that're healthy. But you can get a similar benefit by engaging in meaningful activities, which may be harder without meds, but it's possible."

"Do you see adult children abandoning those failing PTSD or CTE parents?" I asked. "Walking away and throwing up their hands with the idea: *Why should I be there for them when they weren't there for me?*"

"Definitely…but it also depends on how you perceive the situation; and it may be harder to reach that point of forgiveness. You're not seeing the problem as a result of something that happened as external factors, but instead *you're remembering what happened to you*: the rages, the anger, the dissociative personality, the substance abuse. And that type of attribution to the parent is more likely to lead to abandonment and resentment.

"But again," Dr. Aguilera continued, "you either *assimilate* the behavior or *contrast* it…and with *contrast*, you have the opposite reaction to the abusive parent: in other words, *I will never be like that* can not only extend to my spouse and kids; it can also extend to that parent I hated. But this is a conscious process, and it's often a therapeutic process, and it can involve those same stages of loss, death, and grief we talked about—with the final stage of *acceptance* walking hand in hand with *forgiveness*."

"Forgive...or regret?" I asked, pondering next week's interview with my old friend—and gifted therapist—Cissy: What might her opinions be on assimilation and contrast and forgiveness, especially considering her religious training and the tumultuous relationship she had with her own late mother?

"Acceptance *walking hand in hand* with forgiveness," Adrian emphasized. "Again: Not only are you forgiving that person, but you're also accepting that person for who they are...and what they did...and all of their ugliness. That's where healing happens."

"So one can move on," I added. "Hopefully."

"Yes, *hopefully*." Adrian laughed. "So that one can move on."

CHAPTER 25

◆

Resiliency and Parented Orphans Interviews with Jake and Natalie

Along with the vital findings illuminated by Dr. Vincent Felitti's longitudinal Kaiser Permanente study, Dr. Nadine Burke-Harris's clinical experience and book, and the Centers for Disease Control and Prevention's adverse childhood experiences (ACE) studies, researchers Mark Rains and Kate McClinn identified various and specific *childhood resilience factors* (CRFs) that help explain the offset of ACE's long-term physical and emotional damage; these resilience factors can include having felt loved as a child by at least one parent or even a nonparent (another sibling, in the manner of Miriam for me, or a grandparent), or having a neighbor—or a friend's mom or dad—who makes the child feel safe, well liked, capable, and so on. More information about these childhood resiliency factors can be found on *ACEsTooHigh.com*, a fascinating and user-friendly website that includes both the ACE and the CRF questionnaires.

I should add that Dr. Jonathan R.T. Davidson, Professor Emeritus of Psychiatry and Behavioral Sciences at Duke University School of Medicine, describes resiliency as "the ability to bounce back, pick yourself up from the ground if you've been dealt some blows, to be able to cope well or effectively with adverse conditions" (quoted in Christine Cissy White, "Putting Resilience and Resilience Surveys Under the Microscope," ACEs Too High, February 5, 2017, *ACEsTooHigh.com*).

The following two interviews perfectly illustrate childhood resilience; first up is Jake, and after Jake you'll meet Natalie, two people I think of as *parented orphans* for reasons you'll soon understand.

Jake: Parented Orphan #1

I've known Jake since 2003, when we met during a garage sale at the badly furnished fixer-upper mountain cabin Jay and I had just closed escrow on; Jake and his wife, Marie, were staying in their magnificent three-story log home (with its vast, Lake Tahoe–esque treetop view) across the street from us, and having noticed the commotion in the front yard of our dilapidated A-frame, they'd meandered over to introduce themselves.

"Hate to tell you"—Jake laughed, extending his hand—"but we're your new neighbors. And we've got an old Ping-Pong table we'd love to get rid of that's been in our garage since *we* closed escrow on *our* place. Mind if we stand it at the curb"—he hitched a thumb over his shoulder—"next to that bedroom set? We'll even split the proceeds if you help us drag it across the street; my lower back isn't what it used to be."

Jay and I glanced at each other.

"Of course we'll help," Jay replied, "but only if you keep all the profits for yourselves."

I stuck out my hand. "Deal?"

The Ping-Pong table was gone within the hour, but our friendship's been going strong for fifteen years and counting.

We still relish Jake's and Marie's jovial, genteel company—that is, when they're in town; Jake and Marie are passionate world travelers and usually take two or three extensive trips each year to somewhere they haven't yet seen: Switzerland, Vietnam, Iceland, the Galapagos Islands; China to stroll the Great Wall or Peru to scale Machu Picchu. These vacations are in addition to regular visits to Marie's close-knit family in Boston or Quebec; Jake also travels extensively as a consultant (Chicago, Minnesota, Florida, etc.), and although he's *officially retired*, his business card still carries about the same quantity of uppercase initials as Twitter allows characters.

Yes, Jake and Marie live well. *Very well.* Two beautiful homes in Southern California that Marie has remodeled to the nines (and tens) with gleaming floors, parklike grounds, and custom cabinets, furniture, and drapes (Marie is a professional interior designer, sculptor and painter, and a volunteer dog rescuer); twin luxury-brand vehicles, and so on. And it's not that they flaunt their wealth; it's just how Jake and Marie live.

Add to this Jake's magnanimous nature: He's generous to a fault, and he could teach Oprah or Jimmy Fallon a thing or two about conducting a dynamic conversation. Jake is also a self-taught scholar on just about any subject you might need information on; thus, he possesses both the medical acumen of a stoic physician and the legal expertise of a grouchy law professor. Finally, he's a meticulous gourmet cook: In addition to spontaneous Saturday night meals for hungry friends (*What are you guys up to tonight? Come on over!*), each Friday after Thanksgiving, Jake and Marie host the most sumptuous meal this side of a five-star restaurant for any family, friends, and Thanksgiving orphans who're lucky enough to sit in attendance.

Yet somehow—though Jake grew up being beaten by his father, and he left home at fifteen—Jake got even by beating the odds.

Over the years, Jake and I've traded more than a few war stories about our brutal fathers and our LOW mothers, but whereas I blathered on far too much about what I'd been through and am still experiencing (this book stands as evidence of *that*), Jake—like the expert poker player he is—always held his wretched childhood cards close to his chest. In fact, when pressed about what happened to him as a boy, he'd only say (before adroitly changing the subject), "My dad used to kick the cowboy shit out of me, and my mother never did anything to stop him. Hey, how's that new steroid doing for the dog's colitis?"

Fast-forward to this past summer, when I asked Jake—while dining, once more, at Jake and Marie's—if he'd grant me an interview for this book.

"Oh Jesus." Jake laughed, stirring a fragrant marsala sauce atop the stove. "Are you nuts?"

"I'd really appreciate it—if you wouldn't mind spilling your miserable beans into my voice recorder."

Jake shot me his *you can't be serious* look. "When?"

"My summer vacation ends this week," I told him. "How about tomorrow?"

Jake made a few more rotations with his wooden spoon. And then: "What time?"

Jake arrived at precisely ten in the morning, we stepped into Jay's office, where I'd set up my recorder and legal pad, and Jake settled back into the office chair facing me and then crossed his arms over his chest. "You sure you want to do this?"

"I was going to ask you the same."

"Shoot."

"Describe your childhood before the age of twelve."

"Fearful," Jake flatly replied, as if disclosing his least favorite color.

"What made you fearful?"

"Oh fuck." Jake rubbed his forehead and sighed. "My father was physically abusive and a narcissist. He didn't tolerate anything other than compliance. I mean, it's really funny that I hadn't thought about this in a long, long time"—Jake paused, looking up at the ceiling—"but you know how most parents worry about grades...like, those things that would've affected their kid's life later on? He just didn't care—because it was all about him."

"What's your first memory of your father?"

Jake guffawed. "Uh...wow."

"Should I get you a beer?" I deadpanned.

"Shit." Jake laughed again, shaking his head. "The first memory of my father...excuse me, but I'm operating inside a bubble of mind block. Well...if I had a first memory other than something unpleasant, I don't remember it."

"Example?"

Jakes features pinched. "Uhhhh...cowering—cowering, uh, covering up. Covering up because I was a small kid, and he was a big man. Six foot five. A gigantic guy. He imposed himself on a lot of other people."

"Like a bully from central casting?"

Jake blew a heavy sigh. "You know…it was kind of a mixed bag: He was very narcissistic, but he had a great sense of humor and liked to entertain people who provided him with a level of self-worth and gratification. I had many years to add some analysis to my recollections, but my first memories of getting swatted around are just kind of mishmashed together.

"I've got a *horrible* recollection," Jake continued, slumping back in the office chair, "of being in the bathroom, when he forced the door open and belted me with a closed fist, and I fell over backward and cracked my head onto the edge of the bathtub; and I know I lost consciousness—but I remember seeing stars. And as I'm falling backward I'm wondering, *What did I do? I didn't do anything wrong.* I just got belted."

"Christ," I said. "Where was your mother?"

"Probably hiding in the other room; we had a six-hundred-fifty-square-foot house with two tiny bedrooms and one bathroom the size of a phone booth, so it was impossible not to know what was going on."

"So you lived in fear for your life and safety every day?"

"I didn't *think* my father would kill me…but I certainly lived in fear of getting beat up. I was a little kid," Jake said, hovering his hand over the floor at the approximate height of a ten-year-old, "not even five feet tall until I got into high school—so I was a little, little kid and was fearful because of my size. I got bullied a lot—there were lots of bullies in school in the 1950s. Bullying was good sport back then."

"And no safe place to come home to," I cut in.

Jake nodded. "And living under a cloud of anxiety, because I never felt safe anywhere."

"Was becoming compliant the best way to deal with him?"

"That…and avoiding him as much as I could." Jake suddenly sat upright, leaning his elbows on his knees. "But there were those rare periods when he would show some kind of affection, and *my God* those were the best few moments of my life: I have this one recollection of my dad that's pleasant: I'm walking next to him—I'm maybe four or five—and he puts his hand on my neck, which was the father-son equivalent to putting an arm around someone, and I thought, *Oh wow.* I was glowing, I was so proud. And when he took his hand off my neck, I grabbed his wrist and put it back on my neck. I remember this like it was last week, and it happened sixty-three years ago.

"That's my only real pleasant memory—and I've always wondered why he did that, and the only thing I can come up with is he didn't want me to run into traffic and have to clean up the mess." Jake coughed a bitter chuckle. "Doesn't that blow?"

"On a scale of one to ten, with ten being happy and one being miserable, where were you?"

"A solid *ooooone*"—Jake held up his index finger—"until he died when I was twelve. Of colon cancer."

"How did you feel when your father died?"

"Confused…because I didn't feel much of anything— abandoned, probably, on some level. But I was confused, because I didn't cry. Maybe because I already knew he was going to die; he was really sick for a couple of years. The cancer ran through his entire body; it was in his liver and everywhere. It wasn't a pleasant death, he was at home, but the last few days were spent in the hospital. He'd be moaning from the pain, and my mother'd be all over him. That's why I spent so much time at my friend Abe's house."

"How did your mother act toward you during those twelve years when he was around?"

"I was good in school," Jake replied, sitting back again, "and that was important to her, so she nurtured that side of me. I skipped the second grade, and she was delighted by that. I also got picked to go on *Art Linkletter's House Party*, where Linkletter interviewed me, and she was very proud."

"So you were smart and articulate at a young age?"

Jake tracked a bird outside the window as it landed in our atrium. "Perhaps a *little too smart* for my age."

"Have you ever thought that maybe you weren't your father's son?"

"I looked just like him."

"Did your mother ever try to protect you from him?"

"No...no...no—because she was also fearful of him; I don't think he abused her physically, but emotionally he sure beat her up. There was screaming in our house, so I'd shut it out and leave—go to my friend's house."

"Was he a drinker?"

"He was simply a narcissist, so if it wasn't about him, it was secondary. His younger sister—I reconnected with her before she died—talked about him as a young boy and told me how cruel he was to her. Even she used the word *narcissist* to describe him."

"Why do you think your mother stayed with him?"

"I'm sure she loved him on some level—plus, he took her away from her family and moved to California, so she was stuck with him alone here."

"Would you describe your mother as a Look the Other Way parent?"

"Oh yeah," Jake said, cocking a half smile at me. "She was the consummate ostrich."

"Did she change after your father died?" I asked.

"She became even worse. Retreated into herself...and she was so consumed with mourning his death and feeling sorry for herself that I became even more insignificant. So when I turned fifteen I left the house."

"Where did you go?"

"I stayed with friends, then other friends; I moved to Boston and stayed with a cousin; I was in San Francisco for a while."

"Did you have contact with your mother during that time?"

Jake squared a look at me. "Sporadic."

"Did she understand why you left?"

"I never asked. She was too deep in her own...*drama.* For what it's worth, she was only in her thirties when my father died. She never went out or had a date after that. Or socialized. Ever. *Ever.* It's like she went out of her way not to. But she opened a restaurant and after that was a bookkeeper."

"Have you ever talked to your mother about why she didn't stand up for you?"

"Not until much, much, *much* later." Jake's voice trailed off.

"What did she say?"

"She said, *I have no idea what you're talking about.*"

"In a six-hundred-fifty-square-foot house?!"

"She claims to have no recollection of what he did or what happened; and the closest she's ever acknowledged it to me was to say, *If I ever did that I guess I'm really sorry; I suppose I should've left him.*"

"What about that famous maternal instinct one hears so much about?" I asked.

"She had none." Jake chuckled, shrugging his shoulders. "So maybe the title of your book should be: *Life with Stupid Parents who had No Business Having Children.*"

"How's your relationship with her now?"

"In the last few years...I've lost almost all contact with her. *By choice.*"

"What was the event that made you say, *I'm done with her and I'm not going to have any more contact?*"

Jake sucked in a deep breath. "It was very difficult doing that, and I'm still not sure why I did; I guess at one point I was still thinking I had a parent, even though we never had a mother-son relationship." Jake paused. "It's not unusual when a parent dies for a child to feel abandoned, but you can't be angry at someone who isn't there. So can you be angry with the surviving parent?"

"Probably?" I suggested, grimacing.

"In my case, I think my anger wasn't so much a function of having been abandoned by my father as it was being angry toward my mother for never defending me."

"And never admitting, even to this day, that it happened."

"She may have convinced herself that it didn't happen...I don't know."

"Where's your mother now?"

"In a nursing home; been there for twenty years, and she's ninety-seven now."

"Who arranged that?"

"I did," Jake blandly replied.

"So you did the right thing…did your duty."

"I did exactly for her what I'd do for one of my clients or for a stranger. It's a function of my humanity."

"If your father had lived, do you think your relationship might've changed once you grew up and were able to stand up to him?"

"I don't know…if I would've ever been able to," Jake stated. "It's an interesting question. My gut instinct is that I wouldn't have, but maybe I'm tougher than I think."

"Have you forgiven your mother?" I asked.

"No, no." Jake shook his head. "But I'm at peace with it."

With this, I recalled Dr. Aguilera's statement about *forgiveness* walking hand in hand with *acceptance*. "What made you move on… what gave you peace?"

Jake hesitated, deep in thought. "*Time*, I think. *Logic*. There's nothing to be done; you can't rewrite history—I couldn't transform her into the caring mother she never was."

"How do you think your upbringing affected the man you became?"

"It didn't affect me in positive ways, that's for sure—and that's a terrible thing to say. Because maybe another person would've been able to take those bad experiences and turn them into some kind of a successful endeavor."

"So you're a bully and a failure?" I asked, knowing that Jake is the 3-D, living-color antithesis of both.

"I'm not saying I turned into my father," Jake replied apologetically. "But I have some attitudes I wish I didn't have: I'm really impatient with people; I have a low tolerance for people who don't do the right things."

"It sounds like both of your parents lacked empathy. Do you?"

"Actually, I overempathize…and that's why I'm so intolerant of people with a lack of empathy. Most people are not empathic. I would've been happier if I'd been able to accept how people are."

"But what I'm floored by is your statement that your childhood experiences didn't have a positive effect on you, because I see you as this man who's…" I felt sudden tears welling as my voice caught. "Sorry, but I—"

"Stop the tape?" Jake softly suggested.

I shook my head and cleared my throat. "But you're *very* empathic, *very* successful and admirable—you're out there being everybody's buddy, all the time. Doing all these thing for everyone else."

Jake tapped the chair's arm and stared out the window. "Yeah."

"So I don't understand—"

"Thank you." Jake turned back to me with a nod. "Doing things for other people all the time probably comes from my own need to do for others what nobody did for me. Anything I could do to assuage someone else's discomfort is probably why I ended up being a professional problem solver for everybody. *My whole adult life.*"

"And that's not a positive result from all the pain you've been through?"

"It's taken its toll on me." Jake's eyes scanned the office, and it seemed as though he was looking at everything and nothing. "I'm partial to baseball as you know, and one of my ex-partners in business said, *I understand why you gravitated toward umpiring, because it's either safe or out, it's a strike or a foul, and there's no gray. No gray—that's how you are.* And at first I was insulted, and then I thought, *OK you're right.* But that's a burden. I can't let bad behavior slide or let go of personal slights; the bar is way too high."

"For yourself, *or for others?*"

Jake laughed. "For everybody."

"You mentioned to me a long time ago that you were in therapy," I said. "Did that help?"

"Oh yeah, oh yeah," Jake replied, crossing one leg over the other. "I was like eighteen…nineteen, twenty. And then I went back in my fifties for a tune-up, and it was really valuable; I got a really terrific guy." Jake paused. "I've gained a grasp on these things, and I've accepted the fact that I'll never be—nor have I ever been—truly, *truly* happy…and I know *you know* what I'm talking about: I have periods of time when I'm happy; for example, we had some really good friends over for dinner last night"—we both laughed, because he was referring to Jay and me—"and I was happy from the minute they got there until the minute they left. I mean, *I'm not unhappy*, but again it's the bar problem: I guess I perceive happiness as unattainable."

"Do you think your childhood and adolescence affected your decision to not have children?"

"Oh yeah—but not because I was afraid of having an evil kid; it's because I lived in dread of being a terrible parent."

"You?!" I asked, imagining how wonderful it might've been for any child to have this man as their dad.

"I'd have been overprotective," Jake admitted, "and I would've overtaught everything. Somewhere out there is *some unborn child* who should be very grateful." He cackled.

"Did your relationship with your mother change after your father died?"

"It was sporadic due to geography and her being so self-consumed. So, no—but we never had a substantive relationship to begin with. Then after she got sick and had her stroke, I was very attentive, and I felt sorry for her, but over the years her personality flaws and judgmental behavior overtook whatever modicum of good she once displayed—not to say she was a bad person; she was just a bad mother. *A horrible mother.* A non-mother, and an absentee mother. She gave birth to me, so she performed the initial physical function of motherhood, and that's where it ended."

"You mentioned Abe's family—"

"Abe's mother, Hazel, was the sweetest; *St. Hazel*, we used to call her. She'd feed me and allow me to sleep there, and she intuitively knew what was going on. But they had a strange family dynamic, because his father was very cold and nonemotive; he never told Abe he loved him, but his mother—"

"Made up for it?"

"She did…and she didn't have it easy: diabetic, lost one leg at a time; she wasn't well. But she was always a stabilizing emotional force for me, especially when my father was sick; I was ten and eleven."

With this I thought, *Hazel must've upped his resilience factor.* "If you were to meet a kid who was the same age going through what you went through, what advice would you give them?"

"I *have* run into that kid: my sister-in-law. She was nine years old when her father suddenly died, and she experienced many of the same things that happened to me. She's going through a rough time now, and the last time I saw her I reminded her of our conversations, and she told me, *You were like my father...you were there for me.* And she didn't always treat people well, but I understood her behavior."

"She sounds lucky to have had you," I offered. "But I'm wondering what you'd tell yourself at that young age."

"It's situational...and the fact that I had no brothers or sisters changes the dynamic. *I had nobody.* And whatever extended family I had was thirty-five hundred miles away; and since they didn't like my father, the fact that he died wasn't translatable as a trauma." Jake squared a look at me. "Can you imagine what it would've been like for you without your sisters?"

"Just picturing that makes my head want to explode," I muttered.

"I'm picturing it in my head through your eyes," Jake said, "*and my head wants to explode.*"

"I would've left at fifteen, too."

Jake laughed. "I would've taken you in."

"Thank you." I smiled wistfully. "Are there any closing thoughts that you have?"

"All of this makes me think about how it's really easy to get married but hard to get divorced, and it should be the other way around; there should be a rigorous test to get married or have kids, but a divorce should be a snap of the fingers. And just because someone has a child doesn't make them a parent; they're just someone who had a child, but hopefully they'll become a parent."

"Is there anything else you'd like to add?"

Jake began tapping invisible piano keys on the arm of the chair. "Someone once told me that everything—our successes and our failures and our shortcomings and our strengths—is a function of our experiences from cradle to grave. And the expression they used is, *You can become a prisoner of your childhood a lot easier than you can become a warden of your life.* To this I say, *Today isn't a dress rehearsal for the real life you're going to have later on.* So you can wallow in what happened—and I don't say that in a disparaging way, because God knows it's tough to shut it off—but you don't have another chance to recover the time spent, because just after this last minute is over, it's over. *It's gone.* We can never get it back.

"So the pain that somebody else inflicts," Jake continued, "shouldn't define who you are, even if you were unfortunate enough to have it be one or both of your parents. You've gotta do whatever you can *to be a warden for your own life*, whatever it is."

"Sounds like this is the advice you'd give yourself as a kid," I noted. "So where did your wisdom come from?" I asked.

"It's not wisdom."

"But some people become lifelong victims, and instead you rose above...you got yourself *off the beaten path.*"

"It's been a matter of survival," Jake stated, "because you can't put your life on rewind and get another shot at it. This isn't a rehearsal—like I said—it's the real performance. And that's why people think I'm possessed about travel and experiencing new things, because I want to see everything I can before the play ends and the curtain crashes down."

"If your father were alive today and were to witness the life you've carved for yourself, would he be proud of you?"

"He'd be too narcissistic," Jake said. "You can't be a narcissist and be proud of anyone else—not even your own child."

"Would you consider approaching your mother one final time about all of this?"

"I've just moved on," Jake stated, jingling his car keys. "And maybe I'll regret it after she dies, but I'll live with that regret because there're some acts that're unforgivable...and maybe that's part of my inability to accept people for what they are."

"Unforgivable?" I asked. "You mean like allowing your husband to *kick the cowboy shit* out of your child?"

"I know, I know—and not that I would've expected her to hold him back, but I'd expect a mother to protect her child. *No gray area.* It's either safe or out, and it's a strike or a foul. But there's no gray."

Natalie, Parented Orphan #2

"I have very mixed feelings about this," Natalie told me while I checked the levels on my voice recorder atop her glossy mahogany dining room table.

She pulled out her chair, and as she recentered the bone china plate—its cookies artfully arranged—in the center of the table, I noted her fluttering hands.

"I imagine you do," I replied.

I'd only met Natalie once before, while attending an impromptu dinner with Natalie and her husband, who were interested in discussing research we'd all been investigating separately on life-after-death phenomena we were fascinated with. During our all-too-short encounter, I was struck by Natalie's effortless international grace, her genteel manner, and her quiet elegance. Having just recently entered her sixth decade, Natalie fulfilled that well-used, but apropos, adage about how some people "ripen" the way fine spirits age: Natalie embodied a richness of character, a smooth boldness, and a relaxed poise that elevates and edifies those in her company in the same manner as *really*, really good champagne.

During dinner I happened to mention the premise for this book in progress.

Many months later, I was delighted when Natalie's husband contacted me to say Natalie might be interested in being interviewed, as she had an unusual story to tell; this surprised me, because Natalie and I didn't know each other well, and the subject matter of my interviews promised to be quite personal.

So I emailed Natalie my synopsis and then several weeks later found myself ringing her doorbell.

"I've been wondering, *What is abuse?*" Natalie proposed, pulling her chair tight into the table and straightening her posture. "It's complicated with me."

"I completely understand." I smiled in what I hoped was a comforting way while taking in my surroundings: a comfortable and graciously appointed suburban home with enough original contemporary art and carved African masks on the wall to fill a Silver Lake gallery. "Please tell me about yourself."

Natalie leaned forward. "I spent my first ten years with my grandparents; and although my mother also lived with us, she was never there: She was taking her qualifying exams to become a professor when I was born, so I lived with my grandmother and called her *Mom*, which created fury with my mother—so much so that my grandmother was forbidden to touch me."

My eyebrows arched. "Your mother forbade your grandmother to touch you?"

"She could *touch* me—but not in an affectionate way," Natalie clarified, stirring her tea. "No hugging or kissing. My grandmother told me later, *Don't think I didn't love you, I just wasn't allowed to show it,* because my mother said I'd be promiscuous if I was cuddled. So I was never, ever touched."

"How terrible for both of you!"

"Yes, my grandmother suffered," Natalie continued, "and so did I. My mother wouldn't allow me to have a doll; I was only given toy cars, so I would put a blanket over a car and hold it like a baby. Eventually, I was given a stuffed kitty, but I wore all its fur off."

"Clearly, you were starving for warmth, affection, and something to love," I said. "What about your father?"

Natalie sipped from her teacup and then nestled it back within its saucer. "He was allowed to see me once a week, and one time he gave me a doll having arms and legs attached with elastic bands. But one day I opened my toy box, and the doll was in parts because all the bands had been cut—dismembered, really—and I cried. So my grandmother quietly threw the doll away; nothing could be done. That was my mother's cruelty...and my reality."

"My other reality that I've known since childhood is that I am a very ugly woman. Growing up, my mother's favorite story was when she showed me to her girlfriends and they said, *What an ugly baby you have! She is the ugliest we ever saw!* When I grew into a teenager and was experimenting with makeup and hairstyles, my mother told me, *Don't even try, it won't help. You are an ugly creature.* Even when my husband says I'm pretty I say, *Don't be silly. We both know how ugly I am.* So after my daughter was born, I would always tell her how beautiful she is. *You are the best, you are the most beautiful.*"

This cruel revelation pushed me back in my chair while I reeled about how to respond, but my mind went blank; arguing the obvious would have seemed pandering, and I wasn't here to pander; but for her mother to have called Natalie *ugly* was the equivalent of saying the Concorde airliner had been *sluggish*; at the same time, I was happy to learn that Natalie had intuitively embraced Dr. Aguilera's concept of *contrast* versus *assimilation* regarding parenting her own daughter. Uneasily, I scanned my list of questions. "Um…what's your level of education?"

"I have the highest possible education," Natalie proudly replied. "A PhD. But because I was so ugly, I had no other choice."

Oh, there it is again. "And your profession?"

"University professor."

"What brought you to this country?"

Natalie sat back in her chair. "When I was young, going abroad was the best way to improve your finances; I wanted to earn money and then go back home. But I felt so much freedom here, like a caged animal that's been released. I remember thinking, *I can get up and do whatever I want!* After deciding I needed to give my daughter this same chance, when the university offered me a position I took it."

"How would you describe your mother's personality?"

"She is a very, *very* beautiful woman. *Truly.* I spoke with some of my old classmates recently, and they said, *We remember how beautiful your mother was, but you were so neglected: always in old clothes and leaking shoes, you looked homeless. But then your mother came, and we thought how glamorous, so well dressed, so bright. But you were the servant, you only existed to be around for what she needed.* You can't have two queens in the family"—Natalie laughed—"only one.

"If you see her," Natalie continued, leaning in, "you will like her: She has excellent manners; she is very charming and very intelligent. And the first thing she does in the morning is her makeup and hair, and then she comes out for breakfast in full glamour—a royal personality."

"A narcissist?" I asked.

Natalie smiled. "Now that I understand the term, *yes.* She likes to know that everyone says she's such a wonderful person! People ask me, *How could you have a bad relationship with her?* But only those who live with her know her tyrannical nature. She is very manipulative, and she will beg and plead and threaten and blackmail to get what she wants."

"How old is she now?"

"Eighty-seven."

"And her health?"

"Excellent—all her life. She doesn't even have osteoporosis. She keeps having physicals to find something wrong, but nothing is! Her blood pressure is one-twenty over seventy-five."

"I wish mine were one-twenty over seventy-five!" I laughed, recalling my most recent readings (and Dr. Felitti's ACEs).

"I do as well!" Natalie exclaimed. "She complains, of course… but she can hike through the mountains when she wants to."

"Is she an accomplished person?"

"Very accomplished. She is internationally known…an author of many books, and her first book was groundbreaking. Until last year, she presented at every conference in her field; if she could, she would go to another one tomorrow."

"Do you have any siblings?"

"I had a brother who died; he was less fortunate than me, because he did not have my grandparents. He was neglected severely. My brother was taken into a month-long kindergarten when he was three; he was beaten there, but she sent him there anyway. I felt so sorry for that little fellow; he was my brother from another father, but it didn't matter."

"Did your grandparents ever ask her, *How could you treat your daughter and son like this?*"

"My mother would shout at my grandmother if she tried to talk about it. So my brother and my grandmother are two subjects I can't forgive her about. My grandfather didn't talk to my mother much, and after my grandmother died he told me he couldn't live with her because of her nasty character. He died within the year after Grandmother."

"How were you affected by her treatment of you—for better or for worse?" I asked.

"I had a great youth with my grandparents, who loved me to death, and I experienced this unconditional love—the first ten years were excellent.

"My mother would show up from time to time, and she would teach me something: how to draw, for example; she also hired an English teacher for me and got me into a special school for English that was taught from the first grade.

"But my brother was like a wounded bird; he was totally broken by her. However, I became very independent: I ate at friends' houses all the time; I could be on the streets doing whatever I wished. I was fearless, and that's how I came to America not knowing anyone."

"Your upbringing made you resilient?" I asked.

"Yes, and with what my grandparents gave me, I developed strength…but my brother could never stand up to her."

"Do you stand up to her now?"

"I'm afraid to," Natalie confessed. "I'd rather go around the issues than be straightforward."

"And your husband? How does he handle her?"

"I've had two husbands," Natalie explained. "My first was a professor as well, and he opened my eyes about how worthless I felt because of her; I became a buffer between them because they hated each other. And when I came to America, I was happy because she was far away, but by that time my husband was becoming an alcoholic, so I was close to divorce.

"My husband now helps me reconcile the situation, but I still can't face her. When she's away I start loving her, but then she shows up and the wounds open again, and I wonder, *How can she do this to me?*" Natalie suddenly startled. "Oh, would you like some tea? My goodness, I did not offer you anything."

I shook my head, thinking, *Old-world manners and grace and education. No wonder her husband fell in love with her.* "I finished a huge cup of coffee on the way over, so, no, thank you. But I'd love a cookie, if you don't mind. You were saying?"

Natalie lifted the plate toward me, and I happily retrieved one. "The best she did for me was contributing to my education; but after following her lead in the university, she actually began competing with me. So I tried to build my own niche, but she would get into that niche herself and try to best me."

"Do you think you're still affected by your childhood and adolescence?" I asked.

"I think much less, because I have my husband, who tells me I'm beautiful." Natalie laughed, her sapphire eyes sparkling. "But for girls it's harmful if you're told you're ugly, because it ruins your attitude toward sex and your choice of men; girls who are told this will give themselves to anyone who pays attention, and it's easy for their husbands to put them down: *You're ugly, and you're a bad wife.* It's rich soil that allows the seeds of insults to grow and create damage. So as a young woman my mother talked me into a doctoral dissertation, because as an ugly creature, she convinced me I wasn't capable of any relationship."

Good God! How did Natalie survive this woman? "Where was your birth father during all of this?" I asked.

"He lived with us on the weekends until I was five, but no later than that. Then he moved away. Up to this day, my mother tells me how horrible my father was, and how everything bad in me comes from him. I grew up afraid of him, and the biggest threat—when I misbehaved—was her threatening me with this: *I will send you to your father.* But who knows how he was? I only heard her side."

"Did you feel loved by your mother?" I asked.

"No—because you can't be mean to your child if you love them. And I always thought it was me, that I was bad and unworthy, so I tried to show her I'm not bad. I used to fantasize that I was adopted, and there was someone, *somewhere* who loved me. But, no, I never felt loved by my mother—unless she wanted something, and then she would show all of her affection to me."

"As a manipulation?"

Sighing, Natalie leaned her elbows atop the table. "That's all it was—*a manipulation.*"

"Have you ever been in therapy?" I asked.

"Culturally, from where I come from, if you were in therapy it meant you were crazy, so why would I go to a therapist? I can cope with it myself. Besides, she was so far away."

"But when she comes back to visit for six months—" I reminded her.

"If she ever comes back again for months, I will see a therapist," Natalie declared. "Because during her last visit I started getting sick all the time; she nearly put me into the hospital: I could not do anything, and I would sit in my room and stare. I could not stand it, the endless little complaints and pressures. And all of her minor illnesses infuriated me. After all, she wouldn't take me to the doctor when I was a sick girl; I would shout and scream from the unbearable pain of my ulcers, and she would not take me to the doctor. *Just take this pain pill and shut up,* she told me. So now I have to take her to the doctor?"

"How does that make you feel?" I asked.

"Terrible!" Natalie exclaimed, her posture suddenly ironing-board straight. "Just terrible! So now I spend three of my days off in the hospital; and after they take all the cash for the exams, all she needed was moisturizing drops from the pharmacy. This, after all of the money we paid for eye exams at the hospital."

"She doesn't have medical insurance here?" I asked.

Natalie shook her head. "It's terribly expensive—and you still need to pay until you meet the deductible of ten thousand dollars."

"But overall her health is fine?"

"Yes…but she complains about everything."

"What motivated you to succeed?" I asked.

"It was natural," Natalie replied, smiling. "I think people are talented in certain areas, and I was talented in the area of arts and letters. It came naturally, so I continued until I earned my PhD."

"Did she celebrate your success?"

"Many people think the only reason I followed through with my PhD was because of her; in fact, a while later at a gathering I heard my mother say, *I helped my daughter with her PhD, otherwise she wouldn't have it, and I wrote my son-in-law's PhD as well.* To be honest, I actually wrote my first husband's PhD because he was not PhD material; but because these PhDs were in her field, it reinforced this idea that I—and my husband, of course—were worthless.

"To this, I wrote a textbook in a new area, and then she immediately began writing a book toward the same category in Canada. It was her own, but it came out two years later."

"Did you see your material in her book?"

"No, but she would tell people she had been the first—not I—but because hers was written in Canada, it was published later."

"How do you manage your feelings about her trying to steal your hard-won prestige?"

"I've lived in America for twenty years. And the further away she is, the more I love her, while the closer she is, the harder it becomes. But nobody else sees it…only the people in my family see it: My daughter and my father saw it. She treated him like dirt, she shouted at him, but never in front of anyone else. When there's an audience, she's impeccable."

"So she can control herself?"

"And she can play any role—especially the victim, she loves that. She can look very modest and very distinctive, but she can play you as you would never guess. And if I complain, I'm accused of being ungrateful for having such a wonderful mother." Natalie rolled her eyes.

"Have you considered how you might feel when she dies?"

Natalie gazed beyond my shoulder toward the sliding glass doors and the yard beyond. "About her death…I've never thought about it. I almost think I will not…"

"You will not *what?*" I asked.

"Grieve very much," Natalie muttered. "Maybe it will strike me when it happens. But as my husband says, *When she dies you won't reproach yourself, because you did everything right.* And I say, *If she dies first,* because I might die first." Natalie chuckled. "My girlfriend's mother died at ninety-five, so that made me think, *I need to survive eight more years of her? I'll die first.*"

"Does she have a caregiver at home?"

"I found a woman for her, but she doesn't want anyone living with her because she's totally capable. Of course she complains that it's hard for her to walk, but then she tells me, *Oh, I'm going to Finland.*"

"What's the interaction between your husband and her?" I asked.

"She loves him dearly…he's the best and cannot do wrong. *But I'm the worst.*"

"Is she appreciative of your time?"

Natalie's face hardened. "No, because it's expected; there's nobody else but me."

"If you could've changed anything?" I asked, thinking of Gore Vidal and his mother.

"I would've stayed with my grandparents." Natalie sighed.

"Did you see them after she took you away?"

Natalie flashed a delighted grin. "For my vacations I saw them and loved it; I'd go for Christmas, and my grandparents would buy me clothes and shoes."

"Your expression changes when you speak of them," I told her.

Natalie's smile melted. "I was in my twenties when I lost them. My grandmother had a heart attack, and then gangrene took one of her legs two years later. Instead of a wheelchair she used this rolling office chair, but she fell off that and broke her hip, and when she went to the hospital, she simply gave up." Natalie wiped away sudden tears. "I'm sorry."

"Don't be," I soothed. "I'm sorry to ask."

"I nearly had a heart attack myself," Natalie confessed. "I had such terrible chest pains when she died. Grandpa survived almost a year, but there was no reason for his death; he had nothing wrong with him. When her body was in the coffin in their house, he would sit by her and say, *You promised me I would die first.* They were my real parents, and they were very loving—maybe *too loving* and made a monster out of my mother…that's what my husband thinks, because she was the only daughter and she was smart and beautiful, and she could do no wrong.

"Do you consider yourself to be successful?" I asked.

"I don't feel I am," Natalie replied. "I'm fine, but I'm not *successful.*"

"But you have a PhD and were voted Professor of the Year by your faculty."

"That's because my department is kind to me."

"Because they feel sorry for you?" I laughed, grinning into her eyes.

Natalie dipped her head bashfully and then lifted her eyes to mine. "I work hard, and I contribute to the department...but I'm lucky to have good people around me."

"Are you a good mother and grandmother?"

"I made some mistakes in how I raised my daughter, because she deserved more love. But she grew up to be a very good person. And I'm very happy with her and my grandchildren."

"Were you channeling your grandparents when you raised her?"

"I just loved my daughter to death." Natalie beamed. "And I knew how to show that love, too. *I simply lived for her.*"

"Do you forgive your mother?" I asked.

Natalie exhaled a long, slow sigh. "I try, but I haven't succeeded so far. Perhaps when she's gone—then it will be easy to do so, because she won't be here to reopen the wounds."

"I'm sorry your mother doesn't appreciate the wonderful daughter she has," I said. "The resilience you've shown, the lives you've touched, the knowledge you've given others, the hard work you've accomplished, the books you've written, the awards you've received, and most of all the daughter and grandchildren you've loved and raised—the way you support your husband and even the people you'll be helping by sharing your story."

Natalie sighed. "I'm sorry, too."

"And in spite of her," I said, "you've found the strength to thrive and to make the world a better place."

"You're too kind," Natalie sadly replied.

"Are you all right?" I asked, worrying that I'd asked her too much.

Natalie nodded, wiped her eyes, and straightened her posture. "I'll be fine."

*   *   *

On my drive home, I considered everything Natalie had shared with me. And what struck me was not only Natalie's resiliency, but also how similar her history is to Jake's: each had a cruel parent and other guardians who looked the other way, adolescent years frequenting the homes of friends, an inherent drive to excel in spite of odds stacked against them, and ultimately successful marriages and careers.

But what also stayed with me was *how vital the adult was* who offered kindness and love to each: In Natalie's case it was her grandparents who stepped in for her mother (even though they never stood up to the woman), and in Jake's case it was his friend Abe's mother, *St. Hazel.*

These emotional guardians provided enough positive regard and love and support and safety that both Natalie and Jake were able to develop the self-confidence to weather the emotional onslaught of their WANT parents, and to live full and rich—albeit admittedly scarred—lives.

The lesson?

No one knows how powerful a kindness or a loving act toward a child can be, or how far the waves of that action will ripple.

And these two accounts demonstrate that even six decades after the songs of those kindnesses and that love were sung, the reverberations of *good* can still be heard.

And that's powerful.

In really, *really* positive ways.

CHAPTER 26

◆

Suffer the Children
Interview with Cissy Brady-Rogers, LMFT

"I'm officially done," I grumbled to Jay, after lurching through the front door and sliding my keys across the kitchen counter. "At least for this week."

"Don't know who's happier about that...me or you," Jay muttered, leaning back on the counter with a glass of mineral water fizzing in his hand. "So what've you got planned for spring break? Sorry I can't take any time off."

"It's OK. I get it." I thumbed through the day's mail. "Sleep, gym, more sleep, writing—oh, and I've got an interview that I've gotta prep for. With Cissy."

"That girl from high school?" Jay gulped a swig. "When're you meeting?"

"Tuesday."

Back when disco was thumping everywhere, Cissy and I had become great friends; we even "dated" briefly—she was blue-eyed, very pretty, and very, very bright—but without either of us understanding why, any sexual teen chemistry flat-lined. So instead of swapping kisses we swapped laughter, companionship, and empathic ears; we were both from Irish Catholic households, so we shared similar emotional wounds, well-matched senses of humor, and an inherent compulsion to help others.

I never forgot our times cackling together—or that our parents had similar narcissistic personalities. So after locating her and attending a party at the well-appointed Craftsman-style home she shared with her affable husband, Dave, I asked her to be interviewed for this book.

"Let me think about it," she told me over our long catch-up lunch one sunny afternoon. Then a week or so later the message came: I'd love to be part of helping your target population. When do you want to do the interview?

Tuesday arrived, and I drove over to Cissy and Dave's home, where we decided the living room would best serve our purposes. Then, after being sniffed and approved by their new dog, Liberty, I set up my digital voice recorder.

"I started seeing clients in 1990," Cissy stated, "when I was still in college; I graduated in '91, and I've been practicing for twenty-six years. I went to Fuller Seminary, where I earned a master's in theology, then the Fuller School of Psychology, where I got a master's in marriage and family therapy." She paused. "But I never actually planned to be a therapist.

"At first I was a religious studies and English major, and a professor from Westmont suggested I go back to Fuller for my PhD and then come teach at Westmont College. I thought, *Now, that sounds good!* But then in youth ministry I saw *good* parents, *good* kids…but lots of problems, and I started to look at my own family."

"What'd you see?"

"I saw that we were also a *good* family—but we had some problems; I was reading books about therapy and ACA—"

"Adult Children of Alcoholics?"

"Yes," Cissy continued, "ACA families, so I thought, *It would be great to help other people build emotional coping skills and to help families like mine.* That was what switched me from the academic path to the MFT program.

"But after graduating," Cissy went on, "I landed a part-time job doing family ministry at a church, I was also working my internship, and I had another part-time job in another church. Then at age thirty I was diagnosed with breast cancer, which was a real wake-up call around all the stress I was putting myself through."

I grimaced. "Thirty seems very young to handle something like breast cancer."

"Yeah."

"So what parts of your life did you change to lessen the stress?"

Cissy settled back into the sofa cushions. "The church work was *really* stressful, so I dropped that and focused on being a therapist. And my mom died six weeks before I was diagnosed with cancer—"

"How the hell did you handle that?"

"*That* was the watershed that pushed my own therapy forward," Cissy explained. "I really focused on *my* journey and came to the conclusion that it was a privilege to sit with people in pain." She paused. "My clinical specialty became eating disorders and body image, and women's health and spirituality; my practice centers on these issues packed within a Christian framework."

"What commonalities do you see in women with eating disorders, and the relationships they had or still have with their parents?" I asked.

"It's tough because eating disorders are very complex, and there's your standard emotional miscommunications that are common to many families. Typically, the eating disorder patient is a highly sensitive person—is highly intuitive; they feel things that aren't being said…and they hear the things *underneath* what *is* being said. They pick up on everything—they have really strong emotional antennae, so even in what may look like a functional, healthy family they're sensing things others aren't aware of…making *meaning* of those things. So I think there are cultural issues and many layers—but I don't think there's one specific parenting style that causes eating disorders."

"But are there commonalities?"

"There's often a temperament mismatch between the parents and the kid: the parents are very linear and logical and *things are what they are*, and the kid is asking questions that the parents never even think about. So they kind of dismiss the kid with, *Oh, you just think about things too much.* Or, *You're too emotional.* Like I said, a mismatch. It's the kid that doesn't fit in the family, so they internalize the sense that they *don't belong here*. That's something I see: *the mismatch*.

"Another is where you have a mother who has her own issues around body and diet, even if there isn't a full-blown eating disorder—or the father, if there're issues with weight, food, exercising, body image, et cetera, or there're issues in their marriage…these can be common dynamics.

"Add to this what I said about no one speaking the child's emotional language; even when the parents were doing and saying good things, but they couldn't understand their child."

I thought about Miriam and her persistent teen anorexia. "And this inability for their parents to understand them is picked up by the strong emotional antennae?"

"Yes—and there's sometimes an insecure attachment pattern from the parent; this leads to the child's insecure sense of *self* that's a product of the parental inability to meet the child emotionally, because as children we internalize the emotional stability—*or instability*—of our primary caretakers."

I tapped my pen on my clipboard, recalling the teenage lesbian Terry DeCrescenzo mentioned, and her strong advice to the poor girl who was seeking love from a mother incapable of giving it. "How does this affect our development?"

"You might spend your life looking for something, or someone, to help you feel secure. And if you don't feel that security, you might develop symptoms of anxiety, depression, addictions, something to cope with those feelings. It leads to all manner of inner dissonance.

Exactly what Terry had warned the girl about!

"I also think wounded people wound people; hurt people hurt people, and if an adult has never felt securely loved themselves, they usually can't do that for their kid. It's a cycle that goes from one generation to the next."

Immediately, I flashed upon Dr. Aguilera and his assertion of *assimilation or contrast*. "Would this be the origin of toxic parenting?" I asked.

"I don't feel *toxic parent* is a helpful term, because it creates a blaming, defensive tone."

This set me back. "Really?"

"I think the term *toxic parent* creates defensiveness in the parents; it puts too much responsibility on the parent, and once we're adults we have to *own* what's ours…and that's where the healing comes: *Who am I? What can I do to let go of this and forgive and to move forward without carrying this heavy load that my mom was a narcissistic, depressed, suicidal, alcoholic addict.*" Cissy chuckled, clearly reliving some private recollection.

"You just included the concept of *forgiveness*," I pointed out. "Were you speaking therapeutically, or spiritually, or a balance of both?"

"*Both,*" Cissy replied, "because forgiveness is certainly a big part of spirituality, but there's also psychological literature about forgiveness. And although the primary psychologist I know who's doing research on forgiveness is a faith-based person, he doesn't stress forgiveness having to do with faith; he talks about forgiveness in a human sense.

"For those of us whose parents were unable to really *parent* us," Cissy continued, "there's still a feeling of *I don't have much to give them* when they age and begin failing. However, someone whose cup was filled and had a strong sense of being loved is going to have more for that mom or dad; there will be empathy and an emotional give-and-take as the parent ages."

"How do you think caring for a failing parent is different for women?" I asked.

"Women are the caretakers; it's part of the female wiring. Dr. Helen Fisher's neuroscience research—she's a scientist who studies love and relationships—found that a female's brain at puberty gets activated in a way the male brain typically doesn't…and I don't want to be too stereotypical, but women tend to be more aware of people's suffering, so they tend to be more responsible.

"For example, Mom and Dad are sitting on the couch watching TV, and something's going on with the kids outside, and typically the mom notices and the dad's oblivious. Research says women use less brainpower to read emotions than men, and for men it's typically harder to read unspoken feelings.

"This would give women," Cissy went on, "a propensity to take on the task of caregiving, and that explains why the onus of caring for my mom fell, in my absence, on my sister-in-law instead of my brothers. But ironically, in my current status as a daughter-in-law, I'm the one going over to engage with Dave's parents more than he is." Liberty stood and went over to Cissy, so she rubbed his head. "I knew that my mom had taken care of her mother, so that became the message to me. But at some point, I decided I wouldn't be taking care of her."

"Was this because—as a child—you didn't feel that your home was a safe place to be?"

Cissy paused to consider this. "Early on…I have memories of Mom being volatile, and she would blow her top—she didn't have a mother's patience. I remember afternoons where she would go to bed; she'd started abusing prescription drugs and would knock herself out. My eldest brother was about ten, so the three of us fended for ourselves; we were instructed that if there was a problem, we should go next door, even though Mom was home in bed. Our house definitely didn't feel safe. Or secure."

"Why do you think she was like this?" I asked.

"My mom went to law school and graduated in the late 1940s; then she met my dad and six months later they were married—even though she was practicing law, which wasn't common back then. After my eldest brother was born, she gave up her professional life; Dad made the money and that was the way they lived.

"Then Dad left, and suddenly she's fifty-five and it's the 1970s, and she has to go looking for work, and she ends up getting a job making fifteen dollars per hour."

"What was life like in your house after he left?"

"There was this very caustic dynamic between us—she'd say very hurtful things, and I'd be calling her a *fucking bitch*." Cissy shook her head. "Then she'd catch me a few days later and say, *I'm sorry. Can we have a new beginning?* We had new beginnings all the time."

"So there was an effort on her part to patch things up with you?" I asked.

"Mom knew she was a mess, and she'd take responsibility; I don't think without her spiritual life this would've happened—but she knew about forgiveness, and this made a difference.

"She wrote me a letter after one of her suicide attempts, saying, *Sorry I'm crazy and I made your father leave. He's a good man and you kids are the greatest thing in my life and I want you to be happy.* So there was this part of her that was loving and wanting good for us; and it was finding those letters she wrote to me—I found them after she died—that became part of my therapeutic process, because what she wrote she never actually said to me.

"Honestly, there was a lot of goodness in her and she could be wonderful, but she could also be a pain the ass." Cissy laughed. "She hurt us, and she hurt and neglected me, but I think the redemptive thread of her faith and love made a big difference; in other words, even if the level of pathology is significant, some sort of spiritual life can be a mitigating factor." Cissy paused, her eyes staring off. "*No wonder she drank.* No wonder she knocked herself out at night. She'd given her up her profession and her soul's calling to have a family… and it all crashed down. *Dad left.* I think she lost hope.

"So when the time came when Mom's health was failing, my sister-in-law—who didn't have to grow up with my mother—was able to support her in ways I couldn't."

"So her cup was fuller going into it?" I asked.

"Probably," Cissy replied, reaching out once again to smooth Liberty's head. "But my eldest brother got the best from Mom: He was the star; he got a scholarship and lived that golden life… so I think it was easier to move in and take care of Mom…perhaps because *he'd gotten more.*"

"Did you have to balance any guilt about not taking care of her?" I asked.

Cissy sighed. "Not so much. I mean…she was a strong woman, and I needed to be equally strong to contend with her, so early on I decided I'd do whatever I wanted and not feel bad."

"But that was during your teen years."

"It went on," Cissy added, "but after college, when I found my own substance abuse issues kicking up, I thought, *Crap, what's wrong with me?*"

"What do you mean?"

"I'd come home from college on the weekends and party with my friends; then after graduating I found myself back in those entanglements…living a lifestyle I didn't want: smoking pot, snorting coke. Those weren't my values. So that's when I got into therapy and started reading about dysfunctional families, setting boundaries, and emotional coping. I was conflicted, but I fought for myself."

"Have you had clients in that position who've instead found themselves enmeshed and guilt-ridden?"

"Yep," Cissy affirmed. "People in therapy are usually conflicted about boundaries and saying *no*. So, yeah, I've worked with people who, even though they were doing their best, still felt guilty that they weren't doing enough." She paused. "And in families with religious differences, they sometimes feel responsible for their parent's lack of spiritual salvation."

This revelation floored me. "Isn't that taking guilt just a little too far?!"

"In very conservative Christian fundamentalist communities, if you haven't accepted Jesus as your savior, you'll be eternally damned to hell; and for someone who's watching their *non-saved* parent die, it can be guilt inducing and painful."

"Because they think the parent won't be with them in heaven?" I asked.

"Exactly. *Dad's not going to be waiting for me in heaven after I die*, or, *Mom will be in hell*—whatever that is. And I've found it difficult to work with that; the belief system is *so* entrenched and it's *such* a part of what they've built their life on.

"So I try to find *a little room*"—Cissy pinched two fingers together—"to explore the possibility that *maybe we don't know what happens after people die* and how can *anyone* really know who's in or who's out?"

"And if God is so forgiving," I cut in, "then who says damnation will really happen?"

"Yes! Those questions help unpack the guilt and the fears, because it's destabilizing to their very foundations…you know, because if you start messing with my theology—"

"Yikes," I said. "How would you try to steer or guide them?"

"What I'm finding most helpful is *self-compassion*, which comes from the Latin *compati*, meaning *suffer with*. There's work by a Buddhist psychologist named Kristin Neff who proposes that we need compassion for ourselves first, so we can have compassion for others. But if we haven't addressed our *own* suffering to offer *ourselves* compassion and love, we won't have compassion for the parent who's sick or dying.

"I also think accepting the parent's limitations is important; and even if I knew this all along, it wasn't until Mom died that I was *really* able to let go.…There's always this inner child who has the fantasy that the parent will come around. I was still hoping she'd give me more until the day she died."

Cissy's statement supported the information both Doc Reed and Dr. Martin had given me, that one needs to release this fantasy that the parent will eventually become the parent one deserved.

"Do you see in your practice," I asked, "where one parent is wounding and the other parent looks the other way?"

"There're certainly instances where you have what Dr. Stephen Karpman called the *drama triangle*: where within an enmeshed family no one's taking responsibility for themselves."

"What does a drama triangle look like?"

"You have the *victim*, the *persecutor*, and the *rescuer*…but those roles can change."

I held up a hand. "Can you give me an example how this might play out?"

Cissy paused. And then: "With one scenario, the rescuer parent assists the victim child from the persecutor parent because they're enmeshed and looking for someone to save; but sometimes the victim lashes out and becomes the persecutor, the one that's complaining and yelling; but ultimately the rescuer gets an ego boost for saving the victim and might unconsciously keep the victim powerless or dependent to continue receiving their ego payoff. That's called *codependency*."

I mulled this over. "OK?"

"In another scenario," Cissy continued, "you have the victim—perhaps the parent with the *poor me* problem; you have the persecutor parent, who's blaming the victim, saying, *It's all your fault,* and you have the rescuer child, who says, *Let me help you,* and feels guilty if he or she doesn't help; again, the rescuer ultimately gets an ego boost for saving the victim."

At once, I was thrown back in my chair as the realization of how this *drama triangle* applied to my parents and us, their children. "I'll…um…need to think about this later," I muttered.

Cissy stopped to appraise me. "You OK?"

I nodded, sighing. "Please, go on."

"But the rescuer never pulls themselves outside of the triangle," Cissy continued, "to say, *I'm not responsible for you; you're going to deal with your own life.* They don't set appropriate boundaries and are either overly involved or overly distant, and they don't know how to come alongside and help in a meaningful way. That's what I see in those kind of families."

"When one of those enmeshed parents dies," I asked, "what emotions and processes do you see your clients working through?"

Cissy drummed her fingers on the lamp table at her side. "Well…when my mom died, it was finally an opportunity to begin a *whole level of grieving* that was never available. A year later, there was still so much grieving to do, because I was *separating* from a lifetime of lost love and missed opportunities…and finally *making sense* of the relationship, because there was work I couldn't do when she was failing; I was just managing the reality of her physical needs.

"You're on maintenance mode, because you're *just trying to get through.*" Cissy paused, once again deep in thought. "But I don't think the real work begins until they're dead—at least this was true for me."

"Did your relationship with your mother change as she began failing?" I asked.

"Yes, because she took responsibility: She got sober; she worked the twelve steps. She got her spiritual life in order, and her last ten years were lived as a different person by the time she died; she was very different from how she was when I was in high school.

"And she did reconcile with me." Cissy smiled. "She apologized and we had some *come to Jesus* kinds of encounters, but it didn't change everything—she still wanted to be made the center of the world at times.

"So I would say my mom had deep depression and narcissistic tendencies, but she wasn't like this full-blown narcissist—which in itself can make things more complicated, because it's...*slippery*. She could sometimes be loving and I loved her, but then she'd do something crazy."

"I get it," I said, thinking of my own parents and the crumbs of support they'd scattered my way from time to time. "My last question is this: Do you think a WANT parent—one who's wounding, absent, narcissistic, or traumatic—is capable of love?"

Cissy paused while considering this. "I believe everyone is capable of love. I also believe that if a person with deep pathology can have a spiritual encounter with some source of love greater than themselves, they might love someone else."

"What overarching advice would you give someone who's going through an end-of-life situation with a parent who deeply wounded them?"

"Seek your own spiritual path," Cissy stated, "and find some meaning and purpose. *You are more than the wounding*, and choosing to not be defined by what happened is a big step."

Or as Terry had told me, *How is the abuse stifling your life, and why is it the only truth? That's what we need to work on: how to free yourself from the encasement of what happened.*

"What about for people who are religion-phobic, like me?"

Cissy sat back, smiling. "For some, therapy is a spiritual path; in fact, the Jungian path is *very* spiritual: It's about the transpersonal experience of yourself as God itself. Also, a big part of healing is to find some sort of *meaning in suffering.*"

"How perfectly Catholic." I laughed.

"But it's important to *find the gifts of suffering*," Cissy explained. "I wouldn't have signed up for suffering and neither would you, but it's made us who we are: your compassion, your kindness, your empathy...you probably wouldn't have had those qualities without the parents you had because you wouldn't have suffered so much; and because you knew what it was like to be treated horribly, it became critical for you to treat people right. Those experiences *form* us, for better or for worse."

"And whether it's *for better or for worse* is up to us?"

"Yeah." Cissy grinned at me. "It's *all* up to us: getting help, finding a therapist, seeking spiritual guidance, whatever it takes. It's up to us."

*   *   *

After arriving home, I emptied my messenger bag of its interview contents: my yellow legal pad with its scribbled questions; my crappy laptop; and my RadioShack voice recorder, which I rewound to recheck what I thought I'd heard Cissy say.

After a few minutes I found the clip of Cissy's voice pressing into my heart perhaps the most important interlocking piece—with its do-it-or-else loops and sad, empty sockets—of the Nolan jigsaw puzzle I'd ever been given:

"You have the victim...the parent with the poor me *problem; you have the persecutor parent, who's blaming the victim, saying,* It's all your fault, *and you have the rescuer child, who says,* Let me help you, *and feels guilty if he or she doesn't help...the rescuer ultimately gets an ego boost for saving the victim."*

And there it was: Dad the persecutor with his authoritarian, hair-trigger rages; Mom the victim with her clinical depression and eating disorder; and three compliant, patient, hardworking, studious, selfless, supportive, and generous rescuer kids.

Only we weren't rescuing for an ego payoff.

We were rescuing for Mom's love.

Much like Brandy had been the rescuer for her Dad's affections.

It was all beginning to make sense.

CHAPTER 27

◆

Freedom from WANT

Just a few weeks after my interview with Dr. Aronow, I felt a lightness in my being, and the top number on my blood pressure actually dropped ten points. The cherry on the sundae was that I no longer dreaded speaking on the phone—or in person—with my mother or father, and I didn't find myself hamster-wheeling those same exhausting grudges through my head.

I'd finally moved on.

But why? *How?*

I fathomed that the four streams of therapy (at nineteen, twenty-five, thirty-eight, and fifty-two) helped. *A lot.* I believe the sessions interacting on a deeply interpersonal level with those kind, skilled clinicians laid the foundation—and built the metaphorical framing, plumbing, and electrical conduits—for the continued growth and evolution of my psyche. In therapy I learned about asserting myself, about taking measured risks, and about extricating myself from the chaotic emotional triangle that was—and still is—my birth family's dysfunctional system.

Therapy also equipped me with strategies for handling the stress of birthdays and holidays when—instead of feeling like I'd stepped into Norman Rockwell's iconic ode to Thanksgiving, ironically entitled *Freedom from Want*—my reality was akin to Edvard Munch's *The Scream.*

But what Dr. Aronow's imparted knowledge granted me was *a reason to forgive.* Like the parent who discovers that his bratty, impulsive, can't-sit-still child has been diagnosed with ADHD, from the confluence of Dr. Aronow's practiced opinion with my own suspicions that my father suffers from CTE I received the peace of knowing *there's a name for this based upon an individual's history and observable behaviors, I'm not alone, and it's not anyone's fault.* Henceforth, I could sail away from what happened because there's an organic reason for my father's anger and lack of affect; and I thank God we each somehow managed to navigate our interpersonal ships amidst those rocky shoals between the living room sofa, the dining table, and our bedrooms.

We all survived…but not without repeatedly scraping our keels (though my mother's metaphorical ship often flounders while my father continues to storm).

"I've come to forgive him instead of being angry with him," Mom told me recently.

So there it is. *Again.*

Why is forgiveness so difficult? Is it a survival mechanism to believe by allowing forgiveness we are somehow losing our power? Or if we forgive, we might be permitting the same abuses to be done to us again?

In some cases of domestic abuse, this would appear to be the case: look at Nicole Brown Simpson, what she experienced, and what she returned to. How could she or her family ever forgive OJ Simpson (another former professional athlete / alpha male, by the way) for the many times he pummeled her before ostensibly taking her life?

And consider the cases of molestations and rape, or even murder. How does one forgive the individual who perpetrated those crimes?

I don't pretend to know. But I've heard of it happening: the Charleston church victims' families as they confronted mass murderer Dylann Roof; the family of the infamous Facebook Live murder victim; and the family of Dr. Martin Luther King and their forgiveness of James Earl Ray, based upon the convicted murderer's assertion that Ray did not, in fact, kill the civil rights leader.

But perhaps some of the most powerful examples of forgiveness were reported by Naveena Kottoor of *BBC News Magazine*, on August 20, 2013, in a piece she wrote called "How Do People Forgive a Crime Like Murder?" (*https://www.bbc.com/news/magazine-23716713*)

where family members of victims of murder and other brutal, violent crimes have each come to the same anguishing conclusion: either forgive the culprit and move on with one's life, or remain mired in anger and resentment.

The one instance that touched me most in Kottoor's revelatory article was the account by Linda White (whose pregnant daughter was abducted, raped, and murdered by two teenage boys), where White reported what happened in the victims' support group and her thoughts on healing: "'...Nobody moved, everyone stayed the same...People stayed angry. I didn't want to be five years down the road and be the way they were—full of bitterness...If you let grief take over your life, it's as if the offence continues over and over again. It turns you angry and bitter...'"

Forgive...or regret?

CHAPTER 28

◆

Forgive or Regret

"He's suffered enough," I told Gwen over the phone. "He's done his penance."

"I'm so glad to hear you say that." Gwen gasped, her voice suddenly hoarse.

"Has…has she signed the do-not-resuscitate order?"

"I'll check and get back to you."

It'd been a tumultuous week at my parents' home. My father was suffering from brutal, cavernous bedsores, and I recently learned that my mother's way of dealing with my father's striking her was to hit him back. Gwen had reported these findings to their doctor, their doctor involved a social worker and prescribed medications, then our mother did, in fact, sign the DNR.

Mom also got into her first car accident since learning to drive in 1950. Not a bad one, but enough to ensure that her Buick would be out of commission for a couple of weeks.

In the meantime, I had some quiet time to allow Dr. Aronow's perspective to grow some synaptic roots, so I shared my germinations with Jay.

"It mostly wasn't his fault," I told Jay, as we sat down to what turned into a bedtime dinner; we'd assembled another Blue Apron meal—spicy Korean chicken with red cabbage slaw—that took far longer to prepare than the instructions or the lovely photos had suggested.

Jay had been ready to take a sip of sauvignon blanc, but paused mid–glass lift. "Does that change anything for you?"

"Well…" I sighed while poking at the magenta tangle of shredded cabbage atop my plate. "It makes me think that the hero my mother fell in love with in 1952 is still lurking around inside my dad's brain, in an *amygdala in the haystack* kind of way. But it also makes me realize that if things'd been different—if he hadn't had all of that head trauma—that he'd actually have been the father I needed…and that it would've been so much easier to bridge our differences, and to express affection toward each other. That maybe—" I suddenly couldn't talk, as if the years of sorrow began rising inside me like dirty dishwater in a clogged drain.

Jay's eyes shined. "Tell me."

I cleared my throat. "It seems like without the CTE, there could've been more of those scant gentle moments, like the time I told him I might be gay, or when we took those summer evening walks together. We could've laughed easily together and I might've been able to joke with him and have some *real* heart-to-hearts instead of lectures about everything I did wrong; that maybe he'd've been able to explain to me, in a fatherly way, how my body worked when puberty hit, even if it was only handing me a book…or a *Playboy* and some lube; that he could've smiled when I came into a room. That he might've even been able to help make my mother be a better mom, and to have loved her the way she deserved, so she didn't become the miserable victim she's been most of her life.

"That man—that phantom Dad of my imagination—I can see his grinning face now, and I've never been able to imagine him until now! Because now I suspect, thanks to Dr. Aronow, that this was what his soul had been capable of, and this was the man my mother had chosen to help raise her kids. It's like his brain's been a lab rat during his adult life, and it was only allowed to roam freely once in a great while.

"I guess that's why I hated him so much, because occasionally a jovial laugh would escape him—or he'd coo and caw over a baby in a restaurant—and I could see what he *could* be like, and it tore me up inside that he withheld that love and good humor from his one and only son. And of course, I thought it was my fault."

"What else?"

"That instead of him being a 'recovering' alcoholic who secretly got smashed at his desk every day at lunch so he could be sober for his drive home, that I…could've had a Coors with him like he always had with his own father; I don't even know what it feels like to not feel on edge with my stomach in knots every moment in his presence…that I could've had a hug just once, or even a comforting arm around my shoulder when I was devastated—like at seventeen when Marco wouldn't talk to me after we slept together and I told him I loved him; I walked down that gangplank all on my own, because I knew that if my father found out I was in love with another boy he'd have sent me to the hospital—or morgue—with God knows how many broken bones."

"We all went through that on our own," Jay reminded me softly.

"I know. And that makes me sad for you, too."

"But we survived. And thrived."

"We continue to do both, don't we?" I smiled. "Thank you for listening to all of this for the past thirty years."

Jay lifted his eyes to mine. "Is it getting better?"

I stabbed the cabbage with my fork. "I'm finally gaining some real peace on this. *Because now I understand. It wasn't him, and it wasn't me. It was the CTE.* And because the one word I keep hearing from these clinicians is *forgive*, suddenly this seems like the only thing to do."

"Well then, as we used to say in church"—Jay chuckled—"*Peace be with you.*"

"And also with you." I lifted my wineglass in a salute. "By the way, I'm going over to see them tomorrow."

"Think it'll be different?"

I shrugged. "I'm different, so it's gotta be."

*   *   *

"I'm running late because I had a stop to make," I yammered into my phone. "I'll be there closer to twelve."

"We might be eating lunch," Mom replied. "But we'll see you when you get here."

I ended the call and marched across the parking lot—with *The Ring* magazine in my hand—to where my car was parked; I'm not sure what possessed me to search out a boxing magazine for my father, but somehow it was important enough for me to scour the magazine shelves of two markets until I located one.

*   *   *

I rolled to a stop in front of their house just shy of noon.

My parents were in the dining room with Matthew, their caregiver, hovering close by.

Since this would be my first visit to see my father since my enlightening interview with Dr. Aronow, I was armed with a mental checklist of behaviors: slowed mental processing; short-term memory in absentia; long-term memory still functioning; flat affect; et cetera.

My father met each of the criteria.

He asked me how old I was and if I was still with Jay. Then he asked to see my watch, because he loved watches.

During my time with him, I found myself more relaxed. I was smiling, and I asked him about *Stink Bomb Amenta* and *Madge Bigasahouseski*. I also asked about his cousin Jack, who'd passed away recently.

I even got him to laugh.

Then just as Matthew was rolling my father up to the table for his meal, my mother—eyes imploring—asked, "Could you go to lunch with me? There's this new place that I like down on San Fernando and Irving."

"Sure." I smiled, recalling Dr. Aronow's recommendation to forgive her as well. "Sounds good."

*   *   *

Half an hour later, my mother scooted her walker—with me trailing close behind—inside what had once been the very same Bob's Big Boy in Glendale our family frequented *after payday*, where once upon a time we were waited upon by a flock of perky, skilled, pretty women with pressed uniforms and their hair pinned up and lacquered into identical loaves.

The coffee shop's Googie-style roofline and walls of glass were still intact, but the Formica tables, comfy booths, and Sputnik light fixtures had long been supplanted by cheap tables and chairs and nondescript ceiling fixtures. Nonetheless, it was comforting to be under the same roof that had seen so many Big Boy combos and silver goblet milk shakes savored.

After ordering our salads, my mother and I exchanged pleasantries.

Then I briefly explained to her what I'd learned from Dr. Aronow. "It's really helped me to reframe how I think of him and my childhood."

"Has it changed how you feel about him?" Mom asked.

I nodded, my eyes suddenly brimming. "It wasn't my fault. It wasn't your fault. And to a large extent, it wasn't even his."

"How can you say that?"

"He's brain damaged, and he's been that way all along," I told her, surprised that she was listening without arguing. "Hoping he'd be able to emote or show empathy or hold his temper is like hoping someone with cerebral palsy could become an Olympic figure skater."

Mom squinted at me. "Why don't more people know about this? Why didn't his doctors ever say anything? And why don't those big football teams do something?"

"The big teams just settled a lawsuit for *three-quarters of a billion dollars* with their former players," I told her. "As for his doctors, this CTE information has only recently come to light…maybe in the last ten years or so. And by that time, Dad was already incapacitated by the stroke, so everyone believed this was his primary problem— besides the diabetes." I paused. "I remember you being so distraught over his rages. How long ago did they start?"

She sagged more in her chair. "I don't remember."

"I can still see myself as a little boy holding out my arms and yelling, *Don't hit her! Don't hit her!* So they must've started pretty early on in your marriage."

"You were afraid he was going to kill me."

"So either I'd seen him hit you or he was mad enough that I thought he would."

She stared at me, but I didn't have the courage to ask if I'd witnessed what I thought I had. It didn't matter. "If he knocked out Miriam's teeth when she was six, the rages must've started in his thirties."

"That sounds about right. But—" She stopped.

"What?"

She shook her head. "He was so handsome and strong…and I was so in love with him. I was going to have the perfect marriage."

"Did you ever think of divorcing him?"

"No." She paused. And then: "But I probably should have. Even Grandad knew Dad treated me badly, but he never said a word."

"I remember Dad twisting Grandad's arm behind him, *just for fun*," I reminded her. "But it was really more like *gorilla warfare*, just to show every male in attendance who was in charge. So you didn't see any rages when you were first married?"

Mom fiddled nervously with her napkin. "He…he told me once about getting into an argument with a man on the road, and Dad signaled him to pull over. And when the man got out of the car, Dad decked him. Punched him so hard he knocked him out. Then Dad got in his car and took off; left the man lying unconscious by the side of the road."

"What?! I remember him coming home with a black eye once, from a road-rage situation."

"That must've been another time. But I remember him telling his friends Bart and Harry about it once—Dad was laughing about it—and Bart and Harry just stared at him and then at each other. They didn't laugh. In fact, they didn't say a word." She drew in a quick breath. "And he threw someone off a bridge once."

"He what?! Where!?"

"Back in Connecticut. I think he was still a teenager. Someone had treated his little brother Jimmy badly, so Dad threw him off a bridge." She lowered her voice, and her eyes were glossy with sadness—and perhaps shame—for having kept this secret for so long.

"He told me later that he felt bad afterward, because it was mostly rocks down below."

Suddenly I felt nauseous, thinking of my father physically picking up some mischievous teenager and then hurling him through the air; then I imagined the still, broken body bleeding underneath the bridge. *Why hadn't he been arrested?* I wondered. And then two answers came to me: *The young man must've died, so there was nobody to bear witness against him—or—he was a teenager himself, so nobody pursued charges because the fall wasn't that high and the kid was OK: Boys will be boys.*

"How do you explain that?" Mom asked. "He'd have been too young to have this thing you're describing."

"Dr. Aronow told me they've seen this concussion syndrome in kids as young as fourteen—and remember, his father used to train him in the ring as a boy; Dad always told me the happiest day of his life was knocking out his own father when he was just fourteen, so he had to have been boxing since he was probably eight or nine years old."

"I remember that," Mom said. "It's all just devastating… especially when I think of how different our lives could've been. I see families out in public and they actually look happy. The fathers are smiling."

"And that's what's changed for me, Mom. I've finally been able to imagine what Dad would've been like if he hadn't had this unknown brain damage for so long—that he might've been gentle. And kind. And had empathy. And have found a way to talk to me."

Mom's face brightened. "Can they treat it?"

I shook my head. "The neurologist explained that once the brain is damaged, there's nothing yet they can do. The only treatment is similar to how they deal with schizophrenia and other psychoses: They can medicate in order to diminish their homicidal and suicidal tendencies."

Her smile faded. "He doesn't do well on medications. In fact, we just tried out that new antidepressant, but it made him wail like a banshee after only two days on it."

"But at least now we have a name for what he has," I reminded her, "and that helps."

"I suppose it does."

*　*　*

We arrived home in time to see the caregiver trying to get my father situated in his hospital bed; Dad was moaning and groaning and yelling out in pain as Matthew lifted and adjusted and turned and pillowed underneath him.

"Why's Dad groaning so much?" I asked.

"Bedsores on his backside," Mom answered. "But he'll settle down."

Still, the yelling continued even after the caregiver left; it was clear that my father was in a continuing state of misery. "Shouldn't he be taking something for pain management?"

"I can give him a Tylenol," Mom replied, pushing herself up from the chair.

Dad began making garbling noises in his throat.

I went in to check on him. "Dad?"

"My foot," he cawed. "My left…foot. It…feels like…hitting…end…of the bed."

I lifted the sheets and saw that my father's feet had been wrapped in sponge protectors that looked like oversize hotdog buns joined with Velcro fasteners. "Your feet aren't near the end, Dad. You've got about six inches of space there."

Silence. "Do they have the sponges on them?"

"Yep…Maybe the position is bad. I'm going to move them, OK?"

A moment later. "OK."

Carefully and slowly, I adjusted his feet as well as the Velcro straps, which I loosened and then gently reattached. "How's that?"

"Better."

Just then, my mother arrived with a pill and a cup of water, which she administered.

"OK then, Dad. I've gotta run."

"I know you hate me," Dad said all of a sudden, "but…I'm more…concerned about…you leaving…the church."

He'd been asking me repeatedly over the past year if I was still a Catholic, and each time I told him no; deeply spiritual I am, but I couldn't explain my beliefs in terms I thought he might understand. "That's an individual decision, Dad. You know other people who've left the church." *I sure wasn't expecting this! Where is this sudden honesty coming from?!* I took a breath. "And I don't hate you, Dad. Would I be here fixing your feet trying to help you feel better if I hated you?"

He fixed a look at me. "No."

My mind zigzagged for what to say. "What would…make you think I hate you?"

He paused for some time, which I recognized as the slow cognitive processing Dr. Aronow referenced. "Because I…didn't like…your choice…to become…homosexual."

I sighed, wondering how to proceed; clearly he still held to his 1940s understanding of human sexuality. And then Dr. Lawrence Martin's words came to mind about Dr. Ira Byock's book, *Dying Well*, which had arrived just last week and was on my nightstand—albeit unread—at that very moment. "I stayed away from you because you scared me. Your violent temper."

Dad blinked at me.

"But I think some of that you couldn't help," I continued, "and I understand this now."

He gave me a short nod.

Then suddenly, unexpected words flew out of my mouth: "I love you, Dad."

My father stared at me. "Thank you."

Thank you?

"I've got to run," I told him as tears began clouding my vision. *Thank you? I've been a thousand times better son to you than you ever were a father to me.* In spite of my hurt, I reached down and smoothed a hand on his shoulder, the closest we'd ever get to a hug. "I hope you feel better."

Fully and silently choking down a sob, I pushed past his bedroom doorway and found my mother standing in the kitchen. Had Mom heard our exchange? She didn't give me a clue. And her hearing was pretty faint these days, in spite of the game-show-announcer voice I utilized when visiting them.

Wait: She had to hear—she was standing in the doorway and then walked off after I said I love you.

Mom's head was down, and I figured she couldn't or wouldn't look me in the eye; after all, this failed father-son relationship was nearly as much her doing as Dad's. "Bye, Mom." I kissed her cheek.

"Goodbye."

I began the drive home with Terry D's sage advice to that teenage girl reverberating in my head, old movie style: *So I said, Look, your mother doesn't love you. She probably wanted to, but she's incapable... incapable...incapable...incapable...*

CHAPTER 29

◆

Past, Present, and Future Imperfect

Upon arriving home after that emotional drive from Dolores Avenue, I mulled over this revelation of knowing—at last—what we'd all been dealing with as a family, especially with Mom's confession to me of my father committing what must have been at least two very serious physical assaults resulting in bodily injury.

At the same time it hit me that if Dad was so concerned about my leaving the church, did his trepidation about the fate of my soul signal the fact that he actually worried about where his son would spend eternity?

Regarding this, I have no fear: I've been in the service of humanity as a social worker and a public schoolteacher for nearly thirty years; Jay and I've rescued seven dogs and counting; I donate to five nonprofits each month, and so on. Hence, in spite of my not having partaken in Sunday Communion or even Saturday confession like the rest of the world's good Catholics, I'm still looking forward to brushing my heavenly teeth with something akin to marzipan like the other "saved" souls, angels, and saints.

So I wondered: If my mother were experiencing today what she'd endured fifty years ago—and we kids were young and she and my father were in their thirties, what might this information about CTE have changed for us? And more important, what could someone do today who's dealing with a loved one suffering from probable CTE?

First of all consult a doctor, preferably a neurologist. Investigate medications, therapies, and behavioral strategies that could help the CTE sufferer deal more effectively with the physical and emotional ramifications of such a profound—and tragically progressive—disease.

Additionally, get the kids and yourself into therapy—if at all possible; I can't imagine how transformative it might've been as a child and/or a teenager to have heard Dr. Aronow's recent words to me: *You probably always thought it was your fault,* or for my mother to have told my father, *We're getting out of here for a while; the kids and I need a break from your anger.* Perhaps by the time this book is published, there will be thriving therapy groups for children and spouses who've survived the unpredictability and violence of living with someone who suffers from probable CTE.

And finally, I believe everyone should have an exit plan if things get too tough and every intervention has been attempted. After all, look what happened most notably to NFL player Jovan Belcher (Belcher killed himself and his girlfriend and was later conclusively diagnosed with CTE); Aaron Hernandez (the NFL player who murdered Odin Lloyd and then committed suicide in jail; he was later conclusively diagnosed with CTE); and WWE wrestler Chris Benoit (Benoit killed his wife and son before hanging himself; he was also conclusively diagnosed with CTE).

Because no dining room, living room, or bedroom should be a place where the innocent show up for love, support, and companionship and are slaughtered instead.

This maxim also applies to each of the scenarios presented within these pages, CTE or not: the one commonality shared by every LOW parent was that they *stood by and failed to protect*: Jake's mother denied that her son was getting slammed around. Natalie's grandparents and absent father allowed her to be visibly neglected and emotionally ravaged. Brandy's father never stood up for his daughter. Even Cissy's father simply packed up and left. And it's not that they did nothing, it's that *they didn't do enough.* They didn't protect their children from a known abuser.

Why?

My guess is there are secondary gains for the ostensibly *good, loving parent*: first and foremost, the LOW parent gains the love, gratitude, and adoration of their emotionally and/or physically battered child in a similar way to how the so-called *Disneyland Dad* gets to play good cop in the dysfunctional family drama. Additionally,

LOW parents married to WANT partners gain sympathy from others: "He's a saint! I don't know how he puts up with her!" or, "Thank God she's in that house, because without her those kids would be *fill in the blank.*" It's as Cissy Brady-Rogers explained to me about Karpman's drama triangle: *The rescuer ultimately gets an ego boost for saving the victim...but never really comes alongside to help in a productive way.* And finally, LOW parents can delude themselves into thinking *they're actually good parents,* all the while avoiding their own lack of courage and authenticity as well as their poisoned marriage.

To address this child abuse, our country has laws, statutes, and regulations about various professions and mandated reporting: If a nurse or police officer or teacher or fireman or doctor sees or hears something indicating an endangered child, that professional *is required to report the abuse,* or they will be disciplined and even fired and/or may lose their license.

So if we hold our professionals to this rigorous standard, why do we allow child endangerment to be perpetuated under our own roofs?

* * *

I now think of emotional woundedness as a dragon, and when we're at our most vulnerable, this winged beast—with its plated scales of defensiveness—can eviscerate our well-being with its fangs of self-loathing and flaming exhalations of guilt.

But if we're brave—and if we utilize the cognitive lances, rational armor, and emotional shields we've acquired through wisdom, therapy, and love from others—I believe we can drive our dragons back to their caves, where, even if they never die, they'll live out their days huffing and snorting and stomping within their caverns instead of devouring our psyches.

For example: Today I did my best trying to teach thirty-one boisterous eleven-year-olds long division, characterization in novels, paragraph structure, the water cycle, and being fair while playing on the yard.

After work I came home and napped, and I almost made it to the gym, but my persistent cough and lingering depression won out over my self-loathing, which is fueled by the twenty pounds that are determined to *stick by me* through thick and thin. But mostly thick.

Then I watered some plants and skimmed lots of crud from our swimming pool; this time of year the Santa Ana winds are as persistent as they are inexhaustible. Naturally, a cable on our automatic pool cover snapped just in time for our region's unrelenting leaf shower, and money's too tight this month to call the repairman.

Finally, I forgot Jay was having dinner with his nephew in Studio City…so the chicken Parmesan I was looking forward to assembling will languish in the fridge for another day.

So I feel alone tonight but for the (thank God!) napping dogs by my side. And although I know this situation with my parents will someday pass, it stuns me that for fifty-seven years—from before middle school to well into middle age—I've managed this mental discomfort and these feelings that *whatever efforts I make it'll never be enough…but if I don't go ahead and perform those tasks anyway, I won't be able to live with myself.*

Will this ever go away?

Probably? But I still need to prepare myself for the possibility it won't.

Maybe I'll die before my parents; after all, I'm the one with the 4-plus ACE score.

And I wonder: Does my father remember throwing that guy off the bridge, or leaving the man he right-hooked unconscious by the side of the road? Does he recall knocking out his daughter's front teeth? Does he recollect the terror on his son's face as he was chased through the house so Dad could *teach him a lesson for his own good?* Does Dad realize that no one in his immediate family wants to touch him, and that we avoid his physical presence like junkyard dogs who've known only kicks and insults?

However, Dad's most recent caregiver recently let me know that my father enjoys watching *The Golden Girls*. This made me smile.

Does this mean I've forgiven him?

As the scales tip, *yes*; there's simply too much evidence to support the notion that my father's anger and rages—and his emotional hollowness—were not fully his fault, due to the strong probability of CTE coupled with his inherent narcissistic tendencies and inborn alpha qualities. I'd even wager that if he'd been of sounder mind, he would've evolved into a better dad to his children and a more loving husband to his wife, not to mention being able to better handle the stressors of the business world—especially sales and management— that fueled both the alcohol dependence and addiction to cigarettes that contributed to his strokes.

Therefore, it's profound to *imagine what might have been*—and what might've *not* been—had we possessed knowledge of this CTE condition decades ago, when a doctor might've provided our mother with a quiet diagnosis to let her know what's probably happening (as well as what we might be in for), so she could've made an informed decision about treatments and—if necessary—when to get out.

That didn't happen. But today it can for someone else.

*   *   *

Recently, a good friend's dad passed away, and Jay and I attended his funeral. Dave's father, Bud, was a kind man, a funny man, a good man, and a man who was loved by everyone; he was the archetypal dad/grandpa (imagine equal parts Brian Keith from *Family Affair* and Andy Griffith) whom everyone looked up to; and at the memorial, everyone ate and drank and toasted Bud and listened to the family's warm, poignant anecdotes, and by the end there were three hundred people grinning through tears.

Later that night, while perched upon a barstool at our kitchen counter—nursing a glass of chardonnay—I suddenly looked up at Jay, who was readying the dogs' dinner bowls. "You know what slayed me at Bud's service?"

Jay paused at the pantry door, a brimming cup of kibble in his hand. "What?"

"When Dave said, *My dad told me once that if I could do it all over, I'd want to come back and be you.* Can you imagine any finer words for a young man to hear from his father? My father's never even told me he was proud of me."

Jay put down the kibble and draped his arm around my shoulders, and I snuffled and sobbed for a few minutes…not only because the memorial (and the wine) had transformed me into a porcupine of emotions, but also because Jay's simple gesture was so very comforting and so absolutely dadlike. And I realized—as if I hadn't already known this my entire life—that this is what everyone sometimes needs: a kind smile offered with a warm, reassuring arm around the shoulders that says, *I'm here to help, I'm protecting you, we're connected through love and laughter and respect, and everything's going to be all right.*

In fifty-seven years I've never felt loved by my father, and I never will. And I grieve for this…but not as much as I used to.

Because I've found some substitutes for the loss. Including my role as a teacher.

And I guess, largely due to the early love and laughter and support from my sisters, Miriam and Gwen, I'm resilient—just like Jake and Natalie and Brandy.

So what's next for me?

I'm caught up in the final three years of teaching before I can throw in the whiteboard eraser, Jay is deftly scaling the rungs on his corporate ladder, our dogs—one even in spite of his tenacious colitis—are providing more than excellent companionship, and like everyone else's, our lives list from the shifting of our circumstantial ballast: waiting for the doctor or vet to call with test results; being on call for jury duty, encroaching report cards and parent conferences, harried trips to Costco, barely affordable property taxes, the necessity for a crown atop a throbbing molar, broken yard sprinklers, and soaring prices on new car tires.

But it's all good: Jay and I continue to cherish each other's company after three decades together. And hopefully, we'll have another two decades or so before our bodies begin betraying us, so we're attempting to muster the cash for more travel while we're able; at fifty-seven I've never seen Paris or London, and we're both so enamored with sailing the Mediterranean that the subject of this or that discounted cruise is a matter of weekly discussion.

In sum, things aren't perfect…but they're pretty damn good.

And that's all anyone can sanely wish for.

*   *   *

In closing: There are some relationships I simply can't change, and that's why I keep my *chosen family* close: monthly dinners with Margo. Twice-a-year dinners with Judie. Laughing on the phone with Miriam. Checking in with Gwen. Occasional lunches with Doc Reed and dinners with Terry and Carol or Jake and Marie. Bohemian opera nights with old friends John and Greg, or a weekend getaway with Jay's cousin David and his partner, Bruce. And those funny catch-up chats with Cathryn before and after school.

And upon awakening every blessed dawn, where—instead of squeezing my eyes shut in my squeaking Murphy bed, watching the darkness thawing under the sun's unwelcome heat lamp—it's Jay by my side, with Romeo and Princeton impatiently nosing us for their breakfasts.

CHAPTER 30

◆

The End

My phone rang: Gwen.

"Hey, Gwen."

"Is this a bad time?"

"Not at all," I replied. "What's up?"

"The mortuary called," Gwen began. "There's a late arrival of flowers that just came in."

"Two days after the funeral?"

"Yeah, well, it looks like these actually came *for you*."

"But the last time I checked, I was alive."

"They're *addressed* to you," Gwen clarified. "From a *Carol* and someone else?"

I paused, rolling the three Carols I knew through my head. And then: "Carol...*and Terry?*"

"Yes!" Gwen exclaimed. "The mortuary director said they're really beautiful and quite lavish...like nothing they'd seen before."

Knowing Terry and Carol, I pictured a small Rose Parade float. "I can pick up the arrangement tomorrow after school and then take them to Mom's on Friday; I told her I'd visit her after work."

"That's so nice of you."

"Not a problem." I hesitated. "How are you?"

"Just...tired."

"Like, jet-lagged-from-Europe tired?"

"Exactly. And you?"

"Glad the funeral's over."

Gwen and I then spent the better part of an hour discussing the details of my father's memorial and reception: the gracious guests, Gwen's clever eulogy, the array of Costco food (lasagna, salads, garlic toast, gargantuan cake) at the reception, Miriam's kind and handsome sons, Gwen's daughter's stirring rendition of "Ave Maria," and so on. Finally, we got around to Dad's burial. "I only wish I'd been able to nail down Mom a year ago about having Dad's brain examined for CTE," I said, "but when the time came last week I couldn't bring it up, because urging her in the midst of her grief would've been pushing my own agenda, and that wouldn't have been right."

"Even if you had gotten her to agree to it a year ago, she'd have probably changed her mind," Gwen suggested.

"I hadn't thought of that—and you're probably right...but when Mom and I discussed it back then, she seemed really interested in how Dad's hits to the head from all of the boxing and playing football might've affected his behavior, but—"

"No one thought he'd die. And when he did, it was unexpected—as silly as it sounds now with him turning eighty-eight. He'd bounced back so many times!"

"I guess that's why she seemed so grief-stricken when you told her he was gone," I said, "so there was no way I was gonna mention removing her husband's brain. Especially after—"

"After she wanted Miriam to drive her over to the mortuary *a week after he'd died to see if he was still breathing?*"

"Exactly!" I paused. "And when she wouldn't even consider cremation, that sealed the deal; I didn't want her to think of me forever as the unfeeling son who suggested slicing open his father's head."

"You know," Gwen began, "when you brought up CTE years ago and sent us those articles about it, I figured it was a sure thing. So why would we need a test to tell us something we already knew? Especially after you interviewed that neurologist."

"To conclude—once and for all—why he was the way he was." I paused. "But it's too late now."

"It's too late for *so* many things." Gwen sighed. "I'm just hoping Mom might be different now with Dad gone."

"Me, too—and seeing as we're in uncharted territory now, who knows what'll happen?"

*   *   *

Two weeks before, my father's bedsores had necessitated a short stint in the hospital followed up by his transfer to the skilled nursing facility where he'd been admitted multiple times throughout the years. To make his stay there more enjoyable, Gwen had somehow managed to have Dad's brother Richard transferred from *his* nursing home across town into Dad's, so they were able to share the same room—just as they had as boys.

A week later—during Labor Day weekend—I'd left my phone on the kitchen counter as Jay and I spent our Saturday evening watching *I, Tonya* on Netflix, so I hadn't read Miriam's text until just after the dogs had been fed at seven in the morning. In fact, I'd been stirring creamer into my second mug of coffee when I retrieved my phone and scanned Miriam's message: Can you please go over with Gwen to tell Mom about Dad?

I dropped my spoon into the kitchen sink. *Huh?*

It was only after rereading the message that I also noticed Miriam had left me a voicemail at 5:22 a.m. (which as of this writing I still have not listened to).

And it hit me: *He's finally gone.*

Jay was languishing in bed playing Words with Friends on his iPad while Romeo lounged contentedly atop Jay's splayed-out legs.

"I gotta call Miriam," I told Jay as I made my way toward the sliding glass doors that led onto our back patio.

Jay put down his iPad, eyebrows knitted. "What's going on?"

"I think my father just died."

"*What?!*"

After throwing Jay a *just hold on* hand gesture, I made my way across the yard to our set of Target outdoor lounge chairs; this was my favorite place to have a phone chat with my sisters when I didn't want to burden my partner with yet another episode of my family's melodrama.

Miriam's phone rang twice. "Hi."

"You OK?" I asked.

"Yeah." Miriam sighed, sounding tired. "You?"

"I'm fine. What happened?"

"The nurse checked on him at three in the morning," Miriam began, "and he seemed all right; she asked if he was OK and he nodded. Then the next nurse checked him an hour or so later and saw he'd stopped breathing. They called me right after that."

"Mom actually had a do-not-resuscitate order in place?" I asked.

"No, they went ahead and called the paramedics, but for once they couldn't revive him. Time of death was around four thirty or five in the morning."

"Jesus. How's Gwen?"

"She's nervous about telling Mom, and we're out of town for Labor Day. Is there any way you could go over with Gwen? I'm so sorry."

"Of course I'll go. I'll give Gwen a call right now."

After arranging a rendezvous with Gwen—eight thirty—I went back inside to let Jay know what happened. Then I showered, dressed, and grabbed a cheese stick along with my phone and car keys.

"Do you have any idea when you'll be back?" Jay asked, scratching Romeo's ears.

I blew a sigh from Louis Armstrong cheeks, shaking my head. "I'll text you with updates."

"Don't worry about us."

I turned and made for the door. "I love you."

"I love you, too."

*   *   *

The next morning was Labor Day, so after being aroused by the snoring of our coffee machine, I left Jay dreaming upon his pillow and padded outside with the dogs, where I sipped my Yuban and contemplated the distant San Fernando Valley hillsides, their teddy-bear-hued slopes pockmarked with clusters of bottle-green oaks.

About an hour into my zombielike meditation, Jay appeared over my shoulder clutching a steaming white mug. "You OK?"

"My mind…is a washing machine on spin-dry; it's whirling like crazy and it won't stop."

Jay pulled out a metal chair and sat. "Tell me."

I put down my now frigid coffee cup, folded my arms over my chest, and met Jay's imploring gaze. "I'm still amazed that my mother was so shocked, like it'd never occurred to her that he'd die; her grief was so profound…like the young wife of a cop who's just been killed in the line of duty; I guess she loved him after all."

"How does his death feel to you?"

"Not real…like my father's just been transferred to yet another hospital. I was thinking about heading over there on Saturday, the day before he died, but knowing that this coming Thursday's his birthday, I figured I'd see him then."

"I can't believe he died just four days before his eighty-eighth."

"Maybe he admired how John McCain died four days before his eighty-second."

"Just last week," Jay added. "So what else is on your mind—besides feeling guilty?"

I scanned the foothills once again. "Who said I'm feeling guilty?"

"I've been here for *thirty-one years*, so I know when you're second-guessing yourself." Jay shot me a kind smile. "Nick, you were there for him so many times. Hundreds and hundreds of times."

"But not lately," I cut in. "Because I'd given up. *I was done.* I couldn't bring myself to participate in the charade anymore, especially after telling him I loved him, and he couldn't say it back to me." I sighed. "It's like he'd finally lost his filters enough to be truthful: *You're my offspring, but I never loved you.* And that made me see a truth that's been staring me in the face all of my life: I was the son he didn't like and was embarrassed by, just as he was the dad I was terrified of. Remember his fatherly wisdom: *If I didn't know your mother better, I'd swear you were someone else's son?*"

"Of course."

"Then after I figured out that his asking me if you and I were *still together* was his way of asking if we'd broken up yet so I could go back to dating women—at age fifty-seven, and with us having been together for over three decades!—I couldn't act like I cared anymore." I stood up and made my way over to the edge of our yard, where I was suddenly, for the first time since learning of my father's death, overcome.

Moments later, I felt Jay's hands smoothing my shoulders.

"I'm not crying because he's gone," I muttered. "I'm crying because he was never there."

"But you were," Jay told me. "All of those hospital visits. Those years when you visited your parents once a week...the trips to the nursing homes after working all day; taking them both out to lunch, out to dinner. The Father's Days and the anniversaries and the Thanksgivings when you fed everyone and on and on."

Wiping my tears, I turned and faced Jay. "But not two days ago, when I should've been."

"*You tried for nineteen years,*" Jay reminded me. "And even before that, before his stroke. Even though he hit you and threatened you and ignored you and rejected you, *you always tried your best.*"

"And it's only now sinking in that I don't need to try anymore." I sighed. "It's over."

"So what're you going to do now?"

I coughed a laugh. "I guess I'll...help with the planning, the funeral, and the reception, which will probably be here at our house. Do you mind?"

Jay smiled, shaking his head. "Of course not."

"So I'll soldier on and get it done."

"Like you always have."

"Like we always have."

*   *   *

It's been three weeks now since my father was alive, two weeks since we buried him, and a few days since I threw out the remaining flowers from the funeral.

Terry and Carol's arrangement was the last to go, and from it I saved the handmade willow basket.

I also salvaged one vivid white carnation from another arrangement, which I pressed between the pages of *My Cavafy*, a thick coffee table book filled with breathtaking black-and-white photos and aching homoerotic poetry.

My mother is now officially a widow, living alone in the home where her children played—or sought refuge—in the backyard, and her husband once glowered and growled from the head of the dining table. The house, always too small for five, is suddenly too large for one, with its sad overgrown bushes, eggshelled driveway, chaotic closets, and precarious piles of papers and forgotten mementos. There's always something broken begging for repair, and Mom carries a list of chores in her head with no one handy who's handy enough to accomplish them.

She left me a panicked message last night about things around her house that need fixing...all the tasks she's unable to do for herself anymore. And she's preoccupied with grieving for her husband while imagining that surely there was something she could've done differently to have prevented what she will forever consider an untimely death.

We speak daily now—something we haven't done in almost forty years; yesterday's phone conversation went something like this: "Were you with him in the nursing home?" Mom asked me. "Were you by his side?"

"Not this time I wasn't," I replied, feeling my defensive sap rising. "Other times I was, but not this time."

"I should've been there," Mom said.

"You saw him that day, on Saturday. And he died—passed away—in his sleep that night, with his brother in the bed next to him. He didn't die alone, Mom."

"It hurts so much thinking of Dad down there under all of that dirt," Mom said, "that it makes me want to go over there and dig him up and see what I can do for him."

Yikes.

"It's...a...*huge adjustment*, Mom. It'll just take time."

Over this last week, I've found myself (inexplicably?) praying for my father's soul.

But I'm neither Catholic nor Christian.

So, why?

I suppose because I'd like to do anything I could for him to finally be happy, and because I believe Dad made efforts to be a good father and husband—in spite of the probable CTE that vandalized his emotional capabilities. He tried to set a good example, and he attempted to make me into a respectable man. And I think in some way he was proud of me, even though he never had the emotional capacity to let me know.

Which brings me to a funny thing that happened yesterday at school:

Just after recess, Carlos, a bright-minded eleven-year-old with an affable character, presented me with a drawing he'd made for me: It was a blue fighter jet with dandelion-yellow stripes on its wings soaring amid a cloud-dappled sky.

Just like that old postcard! How the devil?!

Then I recalled the lie I'd told my kindergarten class: My unemployed ball-bearing salesman father was in fact a Blue Angels pilot.

"Carlos," I said, beaming. "Is this plane a Blue Angels fighter jet?"

Carlos's dark eyes sparkled. "Yeah!"

I examined the drawing's careful details. "You did a great job! But why a Blue Angel? We've never talked about them—or any other airplanes, for that matter."

The boy shrugged.

"I haven't thought about the Blue Angels in fifty years!" I furrowed my bow and stared at him. "How...did you know I loved these airplanes as a boy?"

"I don't know," Carlos replied, smiling. "I just figured you'd like it."

In an instant, I pictured my father—safely ensconced wherever souls go when the body dies—being shown the stories of his children's' lives with the intent of gaining empathy and perspective. And the Blue Angels lie I'd so enthusiastically relayed to my kindergarten classmates had touched him, so he wanted to let me know he knew.

He finally knew.

I held Carlos's drawing in my hands with my heart warming to the idea that perhaps my father was now an "angel" of a different sort...and he'd just *buzzed the tower* of his son's fifth-grade classroom.

Forgive, or regret.

EPILOGUE

◆

Favorite Statements

The following is a summary of many of my favorite statements made by the clinicians in this book; yours will probably be different from mine. Again, thank you for taking a chance on my work.

—Nick

Edward F. Reed, EdD

"I think if a child doesn't have a safe environment, or if the environment isn't made to feel safe, that's bad parenting."

"*Toxic* means *crippling*…it's going to do something bad to you. And it does. *Toxic*…[kills] the *emotional you*."

"[An adult child's] natural instinct is to avoid because they know the zingers won't stop. The adult child suspects that their biggest hope is going to be smashed once more."

"[Their dying can be] a truth-telling moment. [This should be the time when the kid says,] *You know, Mom or Dad*—or whoever it is—*you really harmed me when you did this*…this *honesty* heals…*truth* heals…*transparency* heals."

"Most children *don't* leave; they're still emotionally attached. But there's nothing wrong with finally saying, *Fuck you, I'm outta here*. Because you know that anything further will continue to damage you."

"They might need to tell themselves, *I'll learn to live with a wounded heart, because I'll never have the mother or father I deserved.*

And this makes that person more inclined to be a better parent with their own children by cutting it off."

"Take some time to process what you need to do for yourself to let that parent die—but don't focus on what's best for them; focus on what's in *your* best interest. You're going to still be around."

"I think a child can be affected so badly, so early in his life, that his spirit is killed. His soul. We see this in sociopaths, where they weren't developed at all or their development was arrested"

"That *need to be needed* compulsion originates in a toxic upbringing, and it can be manifested in many different ways. That's why adult children of toxic parents blend so well into society."

Cissy Brady-Rogers, LMFT

"Typically, the eating disorder patient is a highly sensitive person—is highly intuitive; they feel things that aren't being said… and they hear the things *underneath* what *is* being said.…I think… there's often a temperament mismatch between the parents and the kid: the parents are very linear and logical and *things are what they are*, and the kid is asking questions that the parents never even think about."

"I also think wounded people wound people; hurt people hurt people, and if an adult has never felt securely loved themselves, they can't do that for their kid. It's a cycle that goes from one generation to the next."

"I think the term *toxic parent* creates defensiveness in the parents; it puts too much responsibility on the parent, and once we're adults we have to own what's ours…and that's where the healing comes: *Who am I? What can I do to let go of this and forgive and to move forward without carrying this heavy load that my mom was a narcissistic, depressed, suicidal, alcoholic addict.*"

"You have the victim—perhaps the parent with the *poor me* problem; you have the persecutor parent, who's blaming the victim, saying, *It's all your fault,* and you have the rescuer child, who says, *Let me help you,* and feels guilty if he or she doesn't help…[and] the rescuer ultimately gets an ego boost for saving the victim."

"I don't think the real work begins until they're dead—at least this was true for me."

"Seek your own spiritual path...find some meaning and purpose. You are more than the wounding, and choosing not to be defined by what happened is a big step."

"But it's important to *find the gifts of suffering*. I wouldn't have signed up for suffering...but it's made us who we are: [For example,] your compassion, your kindness, your empathy...it became critical for you to treat people right."

"It's *all* up to us: getting help, finding a therapist, seeking spiritual guidance, whatever it takes."

Allen Ruyle, LCSW

"Imagine this: You love this person, yet they allowed someone else to hurt you very deeply. You can't trust them and you're angry at them, but still you love them. As a result, many of these clients struggle to convince themselves that this parent *just didn't know.*"

"I wouldn't have one thing to suggest. Instead, I'd say, *Let's talk about what you think you need.* Because I've had, and currently have, clients for whom the death of the toxic parent will be a relief—or a nonevent. And even if it's not a nonevent, it'll be a relief."

"They shouldn't have worried every time they heard footsteps coming down the hallway. They shouldn't have been so isolated. They shouldn't have felt like a freak or blamed themselves. They should never have been treated that way. They should've had someone who protected them...*and they should've been happy.*"

"Relief that *it's OK for me to speak about this...that I said it out loud...that I said it to other men and the sky didn't fall. I'm stronger than I realized, and I'm not broken.*"

"I'm a huge proponent of group work because my clients can sit with me for months and talk and read books and hear me tell them, *What you're experiencing is not weird or wrong or unnatural, and many other people have experienced what you have.* But to hear the same message from other survivors is so much more powerful."

"Anger is a secondary emotion. It's almost always secondary to one of two clusters: Grief, pain, and hurt is one cluster; threats and fear is the other. That's why we express anger when we're afraid…or when we are really sad. As men, anger is what we're allowed to express publically. *Boys don't cry; walk it off. Man up…*Boys are socialized not to show any emotion other than aggression or anger. In this case, the client's anger toward the nonprotecting [LOW] parent *must* be kept at bay, because there's this sense of obligation."

"Any feelings or emotions that are suppressed are—in my opinion—ticking bombs…that are very likely to go off when something big happens, like when this nonprotective [LOW] parent begins to skid downward."

"*I can't kick this individual to the curb because of social norms, and because of the person I see myself as. And I'll never get an apology.* So there is a sense of powerlessness."

"I see a lot of Crohn's disease. High blood pressure. Irritable bowel syndrome. Lupus. I also hear, *I can't get my pain under control,* or, *My immune system is turning on itself.* And as clinicians, we tend to see these things together. The client rarely makes a connection until somebody starts talking to them about it; and even after they make the connection, the realization won't necessarily make it go away."

"That unprocessed anger is like a big cotton ball: At first it appears *intense* and *complicated* and *so tangled* that you can't make any sense of it. But if you had the patience, and the ability, and the fine motor skills, you could take those strands and lay them side by side; and then you'd see that it's not as complicated or as big as it appears…Instead—even during the disassembly process—you can look down and say, *This strand hurts; I'm sad about that strand. I didn't get what I needed. I was told—or made to feel—that I was worthless. And this strand is what I deserved. It's not my fault.*"

"People tend to look back at their child selves with expectations they hold as adults: *Why didn't I stand up? Why did I let this happen again and again? I was an idiot. I was stupid.* So we encourage them to realize, *You weren't an idiot or stupid; you were a kid.* And kids don't have the developmental capacity to manage things we do as adults."

"So you can imagine *holding* yourself as a child. Pick him or her up. Hold that child on your lap. Talk to them. Tell them what *you* needed to hear…that *it's not your fault*, that *everything will be OK; this will happen to you and this is how you'll grow*. And this is oversimplified and may sound silly, but it's reparenting yourself from the inside out—you're healing that part of yourself that didn't get what it needed…the part that was so hurt."

"Anyone who suffered abuse at the hands of a parent or some other supposedly *safe adult* struggles with trust. But when the sexual barrier is broken, it turns up the volume; it's a matter of degree."

"Please, *talk about it*. This goes back to how healing occurs… *particularly* with sexual abuse—and particularly with men. Men don't talk about it; they are so ashamed of what was done to them that they won't talk about it."

Howard Aaron Aronow, MD

"Obviously, you're not going to be able to function in terms of appropriate parenting skills. What we've seen, if you look at the prototypical football players or prizefighters—and if you've seen *Concussion*, which was a pretty good portrayal—these individuals become isolated from their families…and many take drugs and alcohol as a means of self-medicating—which may provoke *even more violence* because of their effects on the brain—because they can't control their thought processes."

"Kids such as yourself have to grow up very early, to learn how to assuage and calm down and get away…which may mean not doing *anything* that might provoke them; and because it's some crazy behaviors, the family structure *can't figure out how to behave in order to not provoke the angry man*. It's not predictable."

"You keep trying and trying and trying, and you either become crazy yourself—along with the individual—or you have to separate yourself because *you can't protect yourself otherwise*. An entire family might say, *I can't deal with you anymore*."

"The logical progression of somebody who's *the man of the family* and is unknowingly suffering from CTE might have resulted in violence, because they don't have the stops and breaks to manage their behavior. And if you throw in alcohol, well…"

"But if we can be honest about head trauma and do things to better protect kids and adults, then we wouldn't be having CTE. If I had kids, I wouldn't let them play football—touch football, yes, but *not* tackle football. I recommend against it. It's too dangerous."

"He's remembering you *before* there was more manifestation of the injury to his brain. I've heard this before: *the other child, not that person*, from so many patients when their parents have dementia. It's usually subcortical."

"Individuals with subcortical dementia have great difficulty processing emotions, because it's a cognitive process, and empathy requires cognitive ability. How can you be empathic if you can't understand cognitively what someone's going through? If you add to this the idea that some people who have subcortical dementias started out narcissistic, it's only going to get worse, because their boundaries are all about self-preservation; it really becomes *all about them*…So your dad's been caught up in a loop with himself for many, many years. That means he can't give anybody else an appropriate prolonged emotional response that's interpersonal."

"I also think you need to hold on to those things, to say, *I can't change what happened, but at least some of the time there were glimmers of love and caring*. That means he wasn't a monster—or that he never cared…and no doctor's been caring enough to investigate CTE as a preliminary diagnosis…or to tell your mom, *Here are the actions and here's the medication or other treatments: cognitive, behavioral, and other forms of psychotherapeutic interventions*. And…she might feel better, because it's been pretty bad all these years. Then she should get into something that might give her some enjoyment."

"My advice to you is to hold on to whatever good memories you have of your dad. That even if he couldn't give you what you wanted or needed, he wasn't such a bad guy—at least some of the time. Treat him with the kindness he didn't give you, and make him comfortable, knowing there's no possibility of the dad that you wanted ever coming back…even in small glimpses. Think of yourself as *the other Nicky* remembering *the other dad* who could sometimes function. And tell yourself, *I'll give myself the kindness and caring I didn't get*."

Adrian Aguilera, PhD

"Our brains are built to be sensitive to fearful memories…But then some people overlearn it; they encode it so well that the brain sees threats *really clearly*, but then it also generalizes this perceived danger onto other threats that aren't as dangerous. So you're attuned to the threat of a lion, but you apply this to house cats that are harmless. It becomes generalized."

"One emotional manifestation that's particularly associated with PTSD is the idea of *dissociation*, which is like being *outside of oneself*…like living in the world without being an active participant."

"The hallmark of a healthy development is a sense of structure and stability, where you know the rules of the game—and these vary by culture, of course—but one of the challenges of traumatic environments is where it's sprinkled with trauma, and there's a lot more uncertainty. The child doesn't don't' know how that [PTSD-suffering] parent will react from one day to the next, so the child will be on edge, and he or she may start to take on some of these emotions as well, especially as they mature."

"Instead, you want to *face that thing that caused so much fear*…face it *head on*…and start changing the meaning of it. Because often what happens with traumatic events is a lot of fear…mixed with other emotions, like guilt."

"But that lack of certainty, or structure, in the home environment that we discussed earlier leads many children to inherit their parents' proclivities in *responding similarly* to stress: The abused become abusers, because it's what they grew up knowing; they *assimilate* to their family dynamic. But some will become the opposite, which we refer to as *contrast*: The adult realizes, *I'll never do that to my child or my spouse, because I remember exactly what that felt like and I hated it*. They develop *contrasting behaviors* instead."

"Think about the stages of loss, death, and grief, about that continuum of process: *denial, anger, bargaining, depression,* and finally *acceptance.* I believe part of forgiveness is acceptance: Not only are you forgiving that person; you're accepting that person for who they are…and what they did…and all of their ugliness. And that's where forgiveness is. *It's accepting their failings.*"

Lawrence J. Martin, PsyD

"Bad parenting happens, of course, in all cultures. But even when I'm working with my own folk, I never forget that we're a diverse group—just as white people are also…diverse."

"With many people of color…the family is…of critical importance; and there've been situations where a family member can't be present—not because of abuse or neglect, but maybe they're working a lot; and now decades later, when the child's grown up but still feels the old absence, the lack of parenting…they may have built up resentment, so it's important to recognize the pain and the loss."

"Sometimes that person is in a wheelchair and they can still be abusive—to the end. So that's a situation where the adult child needs to find a way to take care of themselves; my training says: *You've got to protect yourself and make sure you're whole.* When you're a productive adult—especially with a family—your life can't stop."

"It's critical to take care of oneself. Sometimes people overlook their needs when they're working with others…We're all really adult toddlers, and when a toddler misses a snack or a nap, it's not pretty."

"What I've been finding is that many children who're raised by a narcissistic parent always learned when they were coming up to put their own needs as secondary. So now, as adults, when they're running off to the hospital or nursing home, they may have difficulty paying attention to what's going on internally; this can impair their functioning and result in an increase in anxiety and other mental health symptoms. And then their lives start falling apart and they *really start to become unglued*: anxiety attacks, things like that."

"Your parent may be one hundred and ten, and even if you're ninety, you still may feel seven; you might be the CEO of the company, but you're still the youngest of your sibling and your parents or siblings will enforce those old roles."

"I'm not trying to be overly specific and I may be missing clarity, but if you have a parent who's not there…who's addicted… or absent, or is intermittently present—which is not uncommon—it could have been hard to hold their feet to the fire, because everyone could see the other pressures on them from that bad job situation, where they were mistreated or underpaid or outright abused. They'd come home and were unavailable, and—if we use the stereotype— Mom might say, *You need to cut your dad some slack.* But [that] doesn't erase the child's need for that parent."

"When it comes to caring for one's family member who has a history of being abusive but is now elderly, disabled, or dependent, there is a significant change in the power dynamic, and that family member who was the victim—who is now the caretaker—needs to be cognizant. In some important ways the roles have switched, and if they haven't adequately addressed their own history of victimization, they risk being abusive themselves: physically, emotionally, sexually, or financially. *Dad owes me a thousand dollars,* or *Grandma was really a fill in the blank to me.* And these are actually crimes, but one can easily slip into that position."

"Like with Alzheimer's or CTE…[or] if you're dealing with a severely narcissistic person, there's some sort of barrier that'll prevent them from understanding…no capacity for empathy."

"When we look back on all of the cases of football players and boxers…we say, *Holy cow!* That man lost his mind at forty-two, someone else at forty-five. But they don't come to you crying, saying, *I'm really sad and really hurt.* [No, they become monsters that don't] have the qualities they had before; the brain no longer access [those] emotions…You could've been the best kid in the world bringing home A-plus-pluses and scouring the house with your toothbrush; but it wouldn't have made a difference, because it wasn't you."

"Dr. Ira Byock wrote a book called *Dying Well*…And every time I say it, it hits me here [Dr. Martin patted his heart]…the first point is, *Forgive me,* and it could be something minor, like I wasn't the son or grandson or husband I should've been. Next is, *I forgive you*—and this is optional, because if they don't deserve it, don't say it. Third is, *I thank you,* for whatever you were thankful for, and, *I love you,* and the last is, *Goodbye.*"

Carol Cushman, MSW and Teresa DeCrescenzo, LCSW, LMFT

"Parents who love their children, love their children; even the cliché that some Christians use—*love the sinner, hate the sin*—says, *You're my child and I love you.* Having values that are anti-LGBT is no excuse for abusing your kids, because I think you'd find another reason to abuse them: *You disappointed me, you this...you that.* But lots of families have straight kids who disappoint parents: They become criminals, marry out of their kind, or whatever. Either you love your children or you don't. And sometimes I think the anti-gay stuff is a smokescreen for expressing the very bad feelings they [have]."

"Because once you understand you're not powerless—though you may have been as a child—you have three hundred sixty degrees of choice."

"I've seen middle-aged children of elderly dying patients where there is clearly animosity. And my staff will say, *Did she* [the adult child] *just say that?* And I'll say to that person, *Are you kidding me? That's your mother!* And either they'll say, *I'm sorry,* or they'll tell me, *Until you've lived with her, don't you tell me that she's my mother, because you haven't been through what I've been through with her.* So I told myself, *Back off.* I apologized and tried a different tack. But most of the time I go for the jugular."

"Because that's what I see in the hospital all the time: people in their thirties and forties and fifties with their kidneys shut down from the alcohol, all because they didn't get the things that mattered the most: *love from Mom or Dad.* And they spent their lives going around and around about it, instead of accepting it."

"*There are reasons why you won't confront your father, but mainly because he can't perceive it...We need to deal with where your anger is, and what you're still feeling about what did or didn't happen.*"

"And that's what happens between you and your patient: *A certain amount of better* is going to happen. It can be *way better,* or *just a little.* But even a little better is better."

About the Author

◆

A native of Los Angeles who grew up mowing lawns, practicing the clarinet, and dreaming of the '69 Corvette he'd someday own, Nick Nolan's bestselling trilogy *Tales from Ballena Beach (Strings Attached; Double Bound; Wide Asleep)* garnered five Book of the Year* awards, while Nolan's Black as Snow became the #1 Contemporary Fiction Amazon Best Seller in the United Kingdom and #12 in the USA following its release. Nick's latest work **No Place Like Home** breaks new ground in the self-help genre by weaving clinical perspectives inside a heart-rending, yet ultimately uplifting, memoir.

After taking fourteen years to put himself through college, Mr. Nolan worked for four years in social services and then for more than two decades as a public schoolteacher in Los Angeles, California. Today, Nick shares a home in the San Fernando Valley and a cabin in the mountains with his husband, creative director Jaime Flores, and their two retrievers Princeton and Romeo. Nick still dreams about owning that Corvette.

*Book of the Year Awards:

ForeWord Magazine, 2006 Gay/Lesbian Fiction, First Place: **Strings Attached**

ForeWord Magazine, 2008 Gay/Lesbian Fiction, First Place: **Double Bound**

ReaderViews, 2008 Reader's Choice Award, Gay/Lesbian Fiction, Gold: **Double Bound**

International Book Awards, 2014 Gay/Lesbian Fiction, First Place, **Wide Asleep**

Rainbow Awards, 2014 Best Paranormal Fiction, First Place, **Wide Asleep**